Dickens and the Short Story

DICKENS

AND THE

SHORT STORY

DEBORAH A. THOMAS

UNIVERSITY OF PENNSYLVANIA PRESS

PHILADELPHIA

1982

THIS WORK WAS PUBLISHED
WITH THE SUPPORT OF THE HANEY FOUNDATION.

Library of Congress Cataloging in Publication Data

Thomas, Deborah A.
  Dickens and the short story.

  Bibliography: p.
  Includes index.
  1. Dickens, Charles, 1812-1870--Criticism and
interpretation.   2. Dickens, Charles, 1812-1870--
Technique.   3. Short story.   I. Title.
PR4591.T5   1982   823'.8   81-43523
ISBN O-8122-7828-3   AACR2

Printed in the United States of America

[*Doctor Marigold's Prescriptions*] expressed, as perfectly as anything he has ever done, that which constitutes in itself very much of the genius of all his writing, the wonderful neighbourhood in this life of ours, of serious and humorous things; the laughter close to the pathos, but never touching it with ridicule.

FORSTER, *The Life of Charles Dickens*

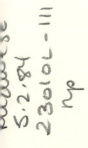

CONTENTS

ACKNOWLEDGMENTS

Much of the research for this book was done at the New York Public Library. I am enormously appreciative of the resources offered to me by this institution, particularly by the Henry W. and Albert A. Berg Collection. I would also like to thank the staffs of the libraries at Drew, Harvard, Princeton, Rochester, Rutgers, and Villanova Universities for allowing me to use their collections.

Portions of chapters 4 and 6 and a version of Appendix A were respectively published in the *Dickens Studies Newsletter,* the *Dickens Studies Annual,* and the *Dickensian.* My gratitude is due to the editors of these journals, as well as to the Dickens Society in the case of the *Dickens Studies Newsletter,* for allowing me to include this material here. I am also grateful to Penguin Books for its willingness to let me incorporate occasional passages from the introduction and notes to my edition of Dickens' *Selected Short Fiction* in my present study.

On a personal note, I would like to thank Donald Fanger who introduced Dickens to me as an undergraduate many years ago in a comparative literature course on "Romantic Realism." I am indebted to Mark Spilka who supervised my undergraduate honors thesis on Dickens' comic villains almost as many years ago, and the late Lionel Stevenson who further helped me to understand the nature of "loose baggy monsters" in a graduate course in Victorian fiction. I am especially grateful to George H. Ford for doctoral training and, more recently, for postdoctoral advice. I am also indebted for counsel of various types to J. Hillis Miller, Robert L. Patten, Elaine Showalter, Michael Slater, and Harry Stone. I owe special thanks to the late Leslie C. Staples for kindly given information about the contributors to Dickens' Christmas numbers.

I am appreciative of the conscientious work of my typist, Carol Criss. Finally, I would like to thank my husband, who insists that he desires no acknowledgment.

ABBREVIATIONS

Unless otherwise indicated, citations from Dickens' works in my text are to the Oxford Illustrated edition, 21 vols. (London: Oxford University Press, 1947–58). In most instances, particular volumes in this edition are given in context; however, I have occasionally used the following abbreviations:

Christmas Books	*CB*
Christmas Stories	*CS*
Master Humphrey's Clock and A Child's History of England	*MHC*
The Old Curiosity Shop	*OCS*
The Posthumous Papers of the Pickwick Club	*PP*
Sketches by Boz: Illustrative of Every-Day Life and Every-Day People	*SB*
The Uncommercial Traveller and Reprinted Pieces Etc.	*UT & RP*

My remarks about Dickens' Christmas numbers are based on a study of the versions of these works as they appeared in *Household Words* and *All the Year Round.* The titles which I have used for these numbers and the various contributions to them are the ones with which they were originally published. Nevertheless, as a convenience for the reader, my citations from Dickens' contributions to the Christmas numbers are generally to the Oxford Illustrated edition of *Christmas Stories.* Additional or alternative references to Dickens' works are explained by notes.

Among the notes, I have referred in shortened form to the editions of Dickens' letters specified below:

The Letters of Charles Dickens, ed. Walter Dexter, Nonesuch edition, 3 vols. (Bloomsbury: Nonesuch Press, 1938).	*NL*

The Letters of Charles Dickens,
  Pilgrim edition (Oxford:
  Clarendon Press, 1965–). The
  following volumes, covering the
  years 1820–49, have thus far been
  published: I, II (ed. Madeline
  House and Graham Storey, 1965,
  1969); III (ed. Madeline House,
  Graham Storey, and Kathleen
  Tillotson, 1974); IV (ed. Kathleen
  Tillotson, 1977); V (ed. Graham
  Storey and K. J. Fielding, 1981).   *PL*

Dates of letters in brackets are those supplied by the editors of these editions.

CHAPTER I

Imaginative License

> [The Smallweed family] discountenanced all
> story-books, fairy tales, fictions, and fables, and
> banished all levities whatsoever. Hence the
> gratifying fact, that it has had no child born to it,
> and that the complete little men and women
> whom it has produced, have been observed to
> bear a likeness to old monkeys with something
> depressing on their minds.
>
> *Bleak House*

Like undesired heirlooms acquired with a rich estate, Dickens' short stories have often been ignored by twentieth-century critics of his novels.[1] Those who do turn their attention to this neglected area of his writing frequently find it baffling, largely because of the manner in which much of it is republished in editions of his collected works. With the exception of *A Christmas Carol,* the samples of Dickens' short work that the modern reader often encounters—the pieces collected in *Sketches by Boz* and the tales introduced into *Pickwick Papers*—are among his earliest compositions, and they inevitably reflect the occasionally unsteady hand of the developing artist. Thus it is not surprising that, faced with the infinite variety of Dickens' better-known writings from *Pickwick Papers* to *The Mystery of Edwin Drood,* few people have explored these unfamiliar pieces in any depth. Sylvère Monod's passing comment that "his shorter stories . . . however intrinsically interesting, seemed to me to belong to another literary genre [than his novels] and to deserve a separate study"[2] is an unusual tribute to the value of this material in its own right. Nevertheless, Dickens' stories are sometimes very lively, as well as artistically experimental. In terms of such subjects as the supernatural, psychological abnormality, public entertainment, the idea of joint authorship, and the whole issue of the role of "fancy" in a pervasively factual age, these stories occupied an important position in Dickens' thoughts.

1

According to Percy Fitzgerald, one of his young associates, Dickens "always seemed to hanker after the short story."[3] However, just as personal hankerings sometimes defy conventional explanation, so Dickens' short fiction often resists ordinary labels. Edgar Allan Poe's celebrated dictum that in a well-constructed tale "there should be no word written, of which the tendency, direct or indirect, is not to the one pre-established design" (*Graham's Magazine,* May 1842) is seldom an adequate explanation of these brief excursions of a novelist whose "outstanding, unmistakable mark," according to George Orwell, "is the *unnecessary detail.*"[4] Indeed, in the case of many of Dickens' sketches, even the seemingly simple distinction between realistic reporting and artistic creation becomes an extremely complex issue. Some of Dickens' fictionalized "impressionistic sketches," such as "A Flight" (*Household Words,* 30 August 1851) or "The Calais Night-Mail" (*All the Year Round,* 2 May 1863, in the "Uncommercial Traveller" series), are, in fact, more polished than many of his "stories," and more attention should be given to Dickens' handling of the genre of the familiar essay from *Sketches by Boz* to *The Uncommercial Traveller.*[5] In his own thinking, however, Dickens differentiated, at least loosely, between "stories" and "sketches,"[6] and the present study, in order to limit the subject to dimensions that may be managed within a single volume, will make the same distinction. Thus Dickens' sketches will be discussed here only to the extent that they evolve into stories or, as in the case of "Nurse's Stories" (another "Uncommercial Traveller" piece, *All the Year Round,* 8 September 1860), contain stories encapsulated within them.

Similarly, the analysis here is intended to be restrictive rather than exhaustive. Of the approximately seventy-five distinct pieces written wholly by Dickens (not counting embryonic stories such as those in "Nurse's Stories") which fall into the category of short story as Dickens conceived it, I shall discuss some only briefly and others not at all. A number of articles could and should be written on stories that I have omitted. The purpose of this study is not to attempt to offer definitive commentaries on all of Dickens' short stories, but rather to focus on a limited number of notable examples while dealing with the more general question of the reason for the recurring presence of such stories in the larger context of Dickens' art.

A major obstacle confronting such an analysis is the problem of definition, for Dickens' stories have little in common with more modern concepts of the term "short story" with its connotations, many derived from Poe, of rigidly plotted tightness and compression. Dickens might have responded to this discrepancy in the manner of Humpty Dumpty in *Through the Looking-Glass:* "When *I* use a word . . . it means just what I choose it to mean—neither more nor less. . . . The question is

... which is to be master—that's all." However, like the Jamesian critics of the novel earlier in this century who dismissed the "loose baggy monsters" of the great Victorian novelists because they failed to conform to the kind of novel adumbrated by James,[7] historians of the short story have tended to be intolerant of the difference between Dickens' view of the short story and their own. H. E. Bates remarks tersely in *The Modern Short Story*, "Dickens wrote short stories, but as far as the present survey goes he could well have saved his ink."[8] T. O. Beachcroft has declared that Dickens "is essentially a flamboyant, dashing personality, and it is not at all in his character to confine himself to woodwind effects, or to spend time polishing up a modest art."[9] More recently, Wendell V. Harris has argued that "unfortunately, the closer the tale approached the novel, the further it was forced to move from the essentially ahistorical, sonnet-like, and highly focused vision which is characteristic of the true short story. That is why the bulk of the short fiction of writers like Dickens, Trollope, or Hardy seems so uninspired —it tried to translate a vision for which the short fiction piece simply could not be appropriate."[10] Some of Dickens' stories, especially some of the early tales in *Sketches by Boz* and *Pickwick Papers,* are indeed awkwardly constructed, although that fact does not lessen their significance for a complete understanding of his work. At the same time, viewed in Dickens' own terms, some of his later stories are quite sophisticated, and their place, against the background of Dickens' other writings, warrants more detailed consideration than it has thus far received.

Any analysis of these pieces in Dickens' terms must be largely inductive, however, for in keeping with his conviction that "a man makes a weak case when he writes to explain his writing,"[11] Dickens rarely articulated the assumptions behind his work whether short or long. Nevertheless, his editorial practice in the latter part of his career illustrates the idea of the short story that he had in mind. For example, in October 1852, as editor of *Household Words,* Dickens wrote enthusiastically to the Reverend James White:

> We are now getting our Christmas extra number together, and I think you are the boy to do, if you will, one of the stories.
> I propose to give the number some fireside name, and to make it consist entirely of short stories supposed to be told by a family sitting round the fire.[12]

The contents of the resulting Christmas number (further discussed in Appendix A) are illuminating. The title of this Christmas number is the matter-of-factly vague one of *A Round of Stories by the Christmas Fire.* The stories (including "The Poor Relation's Story" and "The Child's Story" by Dickens, "The Old Nurse's Story" by Mrs. Gaskell, "The

Grandfather's Story" by White, and other narratives in prose and verse by various hands) adhere to no set form. Indeed, as Dickens' remark to White that the "short stories" are "supposed to be told by a family sitting round the fire" demonstrates, the only recurring feature in Dickens' thinking about the form of the short story on this and most other occasions appears to be the concept of oral narration. For Dickens, a story is fundamentally a story told by someone, and throughout this study, unless otherwise indicated, the word *story* refers to a piece with characters, setting, plot, and conscious narrative design, told directly by a storyteller or placed within a framework which suggests the idea of oral narration. In practice, following Dickens' own practice of viewing his short stories in contrast to his "long" ones,[13] the term *short story* will be used in this discussion to describe a piece which meets these criteria and which, although in rare cases it might have been briefly serialized, was too short to warrant publication in more than four installments.[14] Dickens would have scorned such definitions as meaningless pedantry of the M'Choakumchild variety, however, for in Dickens' thinking, the primary significance of his short stories lay not in their measurements but in their imaginative value.

As readers have occasionally noticed, there is an intensity to these pieces. Jack Lindsay has remarked that Dickens' "dream-transmutation of actuality . . . . which lies at the root of all his creative writing, is most easily detected in the stories, where the compression brings out the lines of force in the fantasy and prevents it from much pretence of being assimilated in normal event."[15] Likewise, much earlier, Forster called attention to the comic exaggeration present in what he considered Dickens' minor work: "In this . . . humour was not his servant but his master: because it reproduced too readily, and carried too far, the grotesque imaginings to which great humourists are prone . . . . But Dickens was too conscious of these excesses from time to time, not zealously to endeavour to keep the leading characters in his more important stories under some strictness of discipline."[16] In the context of Forster's discussion, the less "important stories" are short ones. He clearly disapproved of Dickens' readiness to let his imagination run wild within them. Nevertheless, despite his disapproval, Forster seems to have discerned Dickens' attitude on these brief occasions: in his short stories, Dickens willingly exaggerated qualities implicit in his longer work.

If Dickens' short stories simply exaggerated the worst aspects of his novels, they would deserve the neglect into which they have fallen. However, Forster's remaining comments on this point indicate that the element Dickens emphasized in his brief writing was the one that he felt gave all of his work its peculiar strength. As Forster conscientiously pointed out, Dickens often indulged in such imaginative freedom: "In regard to mere description, it is true, he let himself loose more frequently...."[17] The ambiguous expression "mere description" broadens the discussion from that of only humorous episodes, and one of Dickens' rare defenses of his art, which Forster then repeats, applies to all of Dickens' work:

> It does not seem to me to be enough to say of any description that it is the exact truth. The exact truth must be there; but the merit or art in the narrator, is the manner of stating the truth. As to which thing in literature, it always seems to me that there is a world to be done. And in these times, when the tendency is to be frightfully literal and catalogue-like—to make the thing, in short, a sort of sum in reduction that any miserable creature can do in that way—I have an idea (really founded on the love of what I profess), that the very holding of popular literature through a kind of popular dark age, may depend on such fanciful treatment.[18]

The phrase "fanciful treatment" is a crucial one. It suggests that the element Dickens felt free to express in his short stories was fancy—the vague but vital quality that triumphs over utilitarian practicality in *Hard Times.* The term appears repeatedly in his writing, not as a clearly defined critical concept as Wordsworth and Coleridge used it but rather as an infallible panacea for a debilitating overdose of fact.[19] Fancy, for Dickens, was roughly synonymous with imagination. However, the meanings which he attached to this protean word range (among a host of others) from temporarily escaping the workaday world, to softening it with feeling, to transforming it into something strange and new through the power of a contemplative, creative eye. As Dickens openly acknowledged, fancy was fundamental to his concept of literature, and it appears in one or more of these senses in his novels as well as in his stories. Nonetheless, as Forster's remarks suggest, Dickens seems to have valued his short stories precisely because they provided special opportunities to express fancy in concentration.

Not all of the results, at least to modern palates, are felicitous. A few of Dickens' short pieces contain an even higher proportion of pathos to lines of print than his description of the demise of the unfortunate Little Nell. In other short pieces, however, Dickens' penetration of the secrets of the human psyche surpasses anything in his longer works, and the stories formally and informally set within his novels allow him to move beyond the confines of their framing narratives. As Barbara Hardy has contended, "Dickens's novels are full of travellers' tales, confessions, lies, reports, warnings, autobiographies, tall stories, anecdotes, narrative jokes, books, readings and fairy tales,"[20] and "Dickens's story-tellers allow him to produce effects and to move into reaches where his own narrative, unaided, dare not go."[21] The present study will focus primarily on Dickens' work with short stories extrinsic to his novels, although it will also examine the interpolated tales in *Pickwick Papers, Nicholas Nickleby,* and *Little Dorrit,* and it will deal primarily with two evolving types of stories, termed in my edition of his *Selected Short Fiction* "Tales of the Supernatural" and "Dramatic Monologues." The analysis here will trace the development in Dickens' awareness of the imaginative potential of such stories and will concentrate on three stages in this development. In the first stage (1833–1840), discussed in chapter 2, Dickens was actively writing stories until his experience with *Master Humphrey's Clock* taught him that his readers wanted novels rather than shorter fiction from his hands. In the second stage (the 1840s), examined in chapter 3, Dickens wrote virtually no short stories with the exception of the Christmas Books but refined his theories about the value of such stories in the context of his work. In the final stage (1850–1868), explored in chapters 4 through 6, Dickens again turned to the writing of short stories, many of them the "Christmas Stories" which appeared in the Christmas numbers of *Household Words* and its successor *All the Year Round,* the weekly periodicals that Dickens edited respectively from 1850 to 1859 and from 1859 to his death in 1870. Some of the pieces that he produced even in this last phase, from 1850 to 1868, are by no means masterpieces, but others are astounding, and they all warrant consideration. For Dickens, by the 1850s, the creation of short stories provided a welcome opportunity to "let himself loose" imaginatively from everyday constraints. As Sissy Jupe explained to Louisa in *Hard Times* about her father's fondness for the tales of Scheherazade (p. 59), "They kept him, many times, from what did him real harm. And often and often of a night, he used to forget all his troubles in wondering whether the Sultan would let the lady go on with the story, or would have her head cut off before it was finished."

CHAPTER 2

Imaginative Overindulgence

... God knows he has succeeded in selecting a
truly novel method of introducing his tales to the
readers: whether it will prove a useful one we
cannot as yet say.

Review of the initial numbers of
Master Humphrey's Clock,
Monthly Review, May 1840[1]

I

An important clue to Dickens' concept of the short story in the early
years of his career lies in *Master Humphrey's Clock.* As Angus Wilson
has noted, the original scheme for this fondly conceived work represents the most striking effort in Dickens' fiction to depict "the Scheherazade narrator"—the kind of storyteller with an immediate, personal
relationship with attentive listeners evident in *The Arabian Nights.*[2]
The short writings that were to have been supplied by this latter-day
Scheherazade proved unpopular with their audience, however, and
despite his creator's affection for him, Master Humphrey met a version
of the fate that the original Scheherazade avoided. At its inauguration
on 4 April 1840, the *Clock* was designed as a periodical miscellany, to
be filled each week with a variety of short pieces, supposedly stored in
an ancient clock, by Master Humphrey, an elderly cripple, who would
remove these writings from the clock and read them to his group of
friends. Not surprisingly, readers who had relished *Pickwick Papers,*
Oliver Twist, and *Nicholas Nickleby* discerned this scheme with disappointment. As F. B. Perkins remarked in 1870, "To be put off with a
'miscellany,' here and there beset with fragments of a story, the reading
public would not consent. They very quickly showed their impatience
for another whole work. They experienced a dissatisfaction, almost as
distinct, though not as intense, as that of the Highland chieftain in
'Glenfinlas,' whose companion had gone out from the solitary hut in bad

7

company, and, instead of coming back whole, was flung down the chimney, one bleeding limb at a time."[3] When the journal suffered a marked drop in sales after the opening number, Dickens jettisoned his original plan and transformed a "little child-story"—which had begun to exert a growing power over his thinking—into his fourth full-length novel, *The Old Curiosity Shop,*[4] succeeded in the following year, in the same weekly format, by *Barnaby Rudge.* Eventually, Dickens omitted the *Clock* material when he published *The Old Curiosity Shop* and *Barnaby Rudge* as separate works. As he explained wistfully in the 1848 preface to *The Old Curiosity Shop:* "MASTER HUMPHREY'S CLOCK, as originally constructed, became one of the lost books of the earth— which, we all know, are far more precious than any that can be read for love or money" (p. xi).

Critics have generally not dealt kindly with this cancelled *Clock* machinery,[5] and their strictures to a large extent are justified. Two of the three tales that survive from Dickens' original design seem uninspired. The predominant tone of the framing material is sentimentally elegiac. In light of his subsequent, more successful stories, Dickens' experiment with *Master Humphrey's Clock* appears misguided. However, failed experiments are often well worth study, and in the context of Dickens' earlier and later work with the short story, the *Clock* remains hauntingly significant. As G. K. Chesterton remarked about its disregarded writings, "Though not very important in literature they are somehow quite important in criticism. They show us better than anything else the whole unconscious trend of Dickens, the stuff of which his very dreams were made."[6] In a sense, *Master Humphrey's Clock* does indeed provide a glimpse of "the stuff of" Dickens' dreams. It offers a sustained plunge into what Dickens viewed as the world of fancy, and it indicates the affinity, in Dickens' thinking, of short stories with this world. At the same time, it demonstrates what Dickens appears to have recognized as the perils of a permanent self-indulgent immersion in this kind of imaginative never-never land. Stages in the development that culminated—so disastrously but so revealingly—in *Master Humphrey's Clock* are apparent in the earlier interpolated tales in *Nicholas Nickleby* and *Pickwick Papers* as well as in some of the pieces in *Sketches by Boz,* but its basis lies even deeper in the literature that Dickens absorbed so eagerly as a child.

II

The crucial role played by Dickens' youthful reading in his subsequent imaginative development has frequently been noticed. Duane DeVries' recent study of *Dickens's Apprentice Years* provides an outstanding survey of the literary influences on Dickens as a child and as a young man.[7] Nevertheless, it is worth emphasizing that the books which appear to have exerted the strongest influence upon Dickens' thinking are those he encountered in his happy years in Chatham before his family moved to London, where financial improvidence brought his father temporarily to a debtors' prison and forced Dickens at the age of twelve to work for a few indelibly unhappy months in a blacking warehouse—an experience that terminated forever his childhood sense of security and freedom from care. In later life (like Wordsworth's account of the restorative power of recollections of nature—amidst "the din / Of towns and cities"), Dickens considered this early reading particularly crucial. He viewed it as the manna that had preserved his own imagination in the desert of the blacking warehouse. He repeatedly insisted that similar literature could provide essential nourishment in an age which he portrayed in *Hard Times* as one of frigid fact. As George Gissing has remarked, "Those which he read first were practically the only books which influenced Dickens as an author."[8] As Kathleen Tillotson has observed, "He is perhaps chiefly a re-reader—going back and back to that shelf of boyhood favourites lovingly enumerated in *David Copperfield.*"[9]

Significantly, David's collection contained not only novels but also two volumes of short stories, *The Arabian Nights* and *The Tales of the Genii.* In addition, other forms of short writing went into Dickens' imaginative diet as a child. He was familiar with the *Tatler* and the *Spectator,* Johnson's *Idler,* and Goldsmith's *Citizen of the World.* As a parting gift, when Dickens left Chatham for London, his first schoolmaster, William Giles, presented him with a copy of Goldsmith's *Bee.* Not all of the brief writing that Dickens encountered was so reputable. For example, he delightedly devoured chapbooks—miniature books sold by chapmen (peddlers)—which commonly contained accounts of folktales and sometimes retellings of well-known works by noted writers and that, in Walter Allen's words, "were not unlike the comic-book versions of classical novels now put out for children."[10] Moreover, many of Dickens' early literary experiences were not even confined to the pages of books. His nurse, Mary Weller—who worked for the Dickens family from 1817 to 1822—terrified him with the dreadful apparitions remembered and re-created in "Nurse's Stories," like the figure of Captain Murderer who makes his successive wives into meat pies and greedily consumes them. As the narrator recalls in this sketch,

> Hundreds of times did I hear this legend of Captain Murderer, in my early youth, and added hundreds of times was there a mental compulsion upon me in bed, to peep in at his window . . . and to revisit his horrible house, and look at him in his blue and spotty

and screaming stage, as he reached from floor to ceiling and from wall to wall. The young woman who brought me acquainted with Captain Murderer had a fiendish enjoyment of my terrors, and used to begin, I remember—as a sort of introductory overture— by clawing the air with both hands, and uttering a long low hollow groan. So acutely did I suffer from this ceremony in combination with this infernal Captain, that I sometimes used to plead I thought I was hardly strong enough and old enough to hear the story again just yet. But, she never spared me one word of it, and indeed commended the awful chalice to my lips as the only preservative known to science against "The Black Cat"—a weird and glaring-eyed supernatural Tom, who was reputed to prowl about the world by night, sucking the breath of infancy, and who was endowed with a special thirst (as I was given to understand) for mine. (*UT & RP,* p. 153)

Such stories, along with the other heterogeneous material that Dickens absorbed in childhood, contributed to his distinctive imaginative vision. More particularly, from this eclectic assortment of brief literature, two varieties of short writing emerge.

The first of these varieties evident in the literary hodgepodge of Dickens' childhood is the descriptive sketch, a kind of writing that, in itself, lies outside the confines of this study but that gave an impetus to Dickens' fondness for short "papers" of all types. Although he apparently read selectively—he remarked in later years to Forster that he found "the serious papers in The Spectator . . . as indifferent as the humour of The Spectator is delightful"[11]—he read much of the periodical writing of Addison, Steele, Goldsmith, and Johnson with enthusiasm. This enthusiasm carried over into some of the major decisions of his adult career, including his eventual editorship of *Household Words* and *All the Year Round.* His early proposal for *Master Humphrey's Clock* (in an 1839 letter to Forster) underscores the importance of this aspect of his childhood reading:

> The best general idea of the plan of the work might be given perhaps by reference to *The Tatler, The Spectator,* and Goldsmith's *Bee;* but it would be far more popular both in the subjects of which it treats and its mode of treating them.
>
> I should propose to start, as *The Spectator* does, with some pleasant fiction relative to the origin of the publication; to introduce a little club or knot of characters and to carry their personal histories and proceedings through the work; to introduce fresh characters constantly; to reintroduce Mr. Pickwick and Sam Weller, the latter of whom might furnish an occasional communication with great effect; to write amusing essays on the various foibles of the day as they arise; to take advantage of all passing

events; and to vary the form of the papers by throwing them into sketches, essays, tales, adventures, letters from imaginary correspondents and so forth, so as to diversify the contents as much as possible.

. . . .

I would also commence, and continue from time to time, a series of satirical papers purporting to be translated from some Savage Chronicles, and to describe the administration of justice in some country that never existed, and record the proceedings of its wise men. The object of this series (which if I can compare it with anything would be something between *Gulliver's Travels* and the *Citizen of the World*) would be to keep a special look-out upon the magistrates in town and country, and never to leave those worthies alone.[12]

As Malcolm Andrews has noted, a marked change in Dickens' view of the *Clock* evidently occurred between this letter of 14 July 1839, outlining a scheme for a periodical miscellany that would emphasize topical writing of various types, tempered by occasional pieces in a different mode for the sake of variety, and the not so miscellaneous miscellany that ultimately emerged which, in Andrews' words, gives "no sign of topical writing" and whose "dominant tone . . . right from the start, hardly promises accommodation for 'satirical papers'."[13] The reason for this change remains ambiguous. However, it may suggest the growing power in Dickens' thinking, at this stage in his career, of a second variety of short work.

In any case, in this 14 July 1839 outline, an indication of Dickens' thinking in this second direction appears in his remark about "the *Arabian Nights*":

. . . under particular heads I should strive to establish certain features in the work, which should be so many veins of interest and amusement running through the whole. Thus the Chapters on Chambers which I have long thought and spoken of, might be very well incorporated with it; and a series of papers has occurred to me containing stories and descriptions of London as it was many years ago, as it is now, and as it will be many years hence, to which I would give some such title as The Relaxations of Gog and Magog, dividing them into portions like the *Arabian Nights,* and supposing Gog and Magog to entertain each other with such narrations in Guildhall all night long, and to break off every morning at daylight. An almost inexhaustible field of fun, raillery, and interest, would be laid upon by pursuing this idea.[14]

In addition, Dickens alludes in this outline to Washington Irving's *Alhambra* (a collection of sketches and stories based on Spanish legends, first published in 1832 and evocative of the world of *The Arabian Nights*):

> In order to give fresh novelty and interest to this undertaking, I should be ready to contract to go at any specified time (say in the midsummer or autumn of the year, when a sufficient quantity of matter in advance should have been prepared, or earlier if it were thought fit) either to Ireland or to America, and to write from thence a series of papers descriptive of the places and people I see, introducing local tales, traditions, and legends, something after the plan of Washington Irving's *Alhambra.*[15]

Further evidence of Dickens' musing in this out-of-the-ordinary direction can be seen in his comment in this proposal about "Chapters on Chambers" (an apparent reference to the chambers in the London Inns of Court and Chancery that the narrator of "The Old Man's Tale about the Queer Client" in *Pickwick* describes as "no ordinary houses, those. There is not a panel in the old wainscotting, but what, if it were endowed with the powers of speech and memory, could start from the wall, and tell its tale of horror—the romance of life, sir, the romance of life!" [p. 279]). As DeVries has argued, Dickens' early "apprentice" work with the descriptive sketches of "every-day life and every-day people" which he produced so successfully between 1833 and 1836, and eventually collected in *Sketches by Boz,* led gradually to his novels.[16] In terms of his career as a novelist, Dickens' childhood affection for the essays of Addison and Steele and their successors is clearly important. However, in terms of his lifelong fascination with short stories—as well as his general awareness of what he described in his 1853 preface to *Bleak House* as "the romantic side of familiar things" (p. xiv)—a second type of brief literature, suggested by his proposal for *Master Humphrey's Clock* and apparent in his early literary experiences, is especially significant.

This latter variety is the extraordinary tale. For Dickens in his happy childhood at Chatham, a tale might be simply an account of an unusual experience of the kind interpolated in the novels with which he was familiar, such as the "Story of One Who Was Too Curious for His Own Good" in *Don Quixote* or the self-history told by the Man of the Hill in *Tom Jones.* On the basis of the short fiction to which he was most addicted, however, a tale was far more likely to be sensational, exotic, or preternatural. Many of the stories in *The Arabian Nights* combine all three elements, and the importance of this collection on Dickens' concept of the short story cannot be underestimated. Gissing observed that "Dickens seems to make more allusions throughout his work to the *Arabian Nights* than to any other book or author."[17] All the books in his small library, David Copperfield tells us, "kept alive my fancy" (p. 55), but the fact that Sissy Jupe, one of the strongest advocates for this vital quality in *Hard Times,* singles out *The Arabian Nights* as the work that she remembers reading to her father indicates Dickens' belief in its exceptionally fanciful value. Moreover, along with *The Tales of the Genii* (a collection of pseudo-oriental adventure stories by James Ridley, first published in 1764 in the wake of *The Arabian Nights*),[18] Dickens placed this work in the category of the fairy tale.

The world of witches, fairy godmothers, sultans, and genii is a fermentative ingredient in all of Dickens' writing, although Dickens' terminology in this context, as in his remarks about fancy, is somewhat more enthusiastic than precise. As Harry Stone has argued, Dickens employed the designation "fairy tale" as simply "a convenient label . . . [for] his special blend of fairy story, fantasy, myth, magic, and folklore,"[19] but in Dickens' thought, this combination was vitally important. Fairy-tale motifs appear again and again in his novels,[20] and his admission in "Frauds on the Fairies" (*Household Words,* 1 October 1853) that he had always entertained "a very great tenderness for the fairy literature of . . . childhood" is not surprising. The reason for this affection lies in Dickens' faith in fancy. As he explained in the same article, fairy tales are "nurseries of fancy," and "in a utilitarian age, of all other times, it is a matter of grave importance that Fairy tales should be respected." In "the fairy literature of . . . childhood," according to Dickens, fancy flourished beneficently and freely.

Not all of the stories that Dickens remembered from his own childhood are pleasant. His nurse's tales of terror undoubtedly contributed to the strain of the horrific that runs throughout his writing and surfaces in many of his own short tales.[21] Once again, however, Dickens' interest in such terrifying material was focused primarily on its ability to disturb the familiar assumptions of its listeners or readers. The significant element in avowedly haunting stories was the all-important quality of fancy, as the full title of his 1848 Christmas Book indicates: "The Haunted Man and the Ghost's Bargain: A Fancy for Christmas Time."

With tales of the uncanny like that of Captain Murderer, as with fairy tales like "Little Red Riding Hood," the kind of fancy present in Dickens' thinking appears to be fundamentally an imaginative escape from actuality. In fairy tales, the kind of escapism involved is obviously make-believe. With such tales, as Freud has observed, "the world of reality is left behind from the very start."[22] In keeping with this assumption, Dickens not only exploded in outrage in "Frauds on the Fairies" when the noted illustrator and fanatic teetotaller George Cruikshank altered the story of "Hop o' My Thumb" to show the evils of inebriation, but Dickens also rewrote the tale of "Cinderella" as it might have been told by someone with a "mission" (like Mrs. Jellyby in his recently concluded novel *Bleak House*), presenting it as a parody of attempts to pin "the harmless little books" of "fairy text" to contemporary life. In contrast, tales of the uncanny, while still remote from everyday experience, derive their effect from a degree of plausibility. As Freud has noted, in a useful distinction between stories of this type and fairy tales, the sensation of the uncanny occurs in the presence of "a conflict of judgement whether things which have been 'surmounted' and are regarded as incredible are not, after all, possible."[23] Moreover, Dickens' sense of the link between tales of the uncanny and what he described in "Nurse's Stories" as mental "dark corners" (*UT & RP*, p. 150) gradually became explicit in his thinking. As he wrote in 1851 to Mrs. Gaskell, a contributor to *Household Words* and later to *All the Year Round* whom he admired for her talented writing of such tales, "Ghost-stories, illustrating particular states of mind and processes of the imagination, are common-property, I always think—except in the manner of relating them, and O who can rob some people of *that!*"[24] As Forster observed about Dickens, "Among his good things should not be omitted his telling of a ghost story."[25] Significantly, the stories that Dickens produced in the first seven years of his career (culminating eventually in those intended to be told by Master Humphrey's circle of reclusive friends) reflect his growing awareness of the way in which preternaturally fanciful—in essence supernatural—tales can remove their audience from actuality. These early stories also show Dickens' growing awareness of the manner in which uncanny tales, specifically, can evoke "particular" —generally abnormal—"states of mind."

III

At first glance, the pieces that Dickens eventually grouped under the heading of "Tales" in *Sketches by Boz,* including some of his earliest fictional experiments, offer little evidence of his fascination with uncanny and fairy-tale material. Along with five of the pieces placed by Dickens under the heading of "Characters," which DeVries has argued belong stylistically in the category of "Tales," they are largely satiric treatments of human folly and absurdity, strongly influenced by the short farces popular on the contemporary stage.[26] Nonetheless, as DeVries has demonstrated, when these seventeen tales are examined in the order of their composition, certain distinctions become apparent. Dickens' first eight tales, published from 1833 to 1835, are clearly "exercises in the craft of fiction"[27] that sometimes end on what readers of Dickens' subsequent works may view as an uncharacteristically bitter note.[28] The next five tales, published in autumn 1835 after an interval of sketches and eventually placed by Dickens in the ambiguous category of "Characters," are more sophisticated in their construction and more sympathetic in their tone.[29] Finally, the remaining four tales—two farcical pieces entitled "The Great Winglebury Duel" and "The Tuggses at Ramsgate" and two melodramatic pieces entitled "The Black Veil" and "The Drunkard's Death" (all published in 1836)—reveal Dickens' growing control of the elements of fiction in the final stage of his "apprentice years."[30]

At the same time, however, the last four tales seem indicative of more than simply their author's growing fictional expertise. In each of these last pieces, the subject of some form of mental disorder recurs. The presence of this motif is made all the more remarkable by its absence, in large part, from the earlier tales. In "The Great Winglebury Duel" and "The Tuggses at Ramsgate," the respective topics of madness and extreme nervous excitability are treated farcically. The plot of the former tale deals with a case of mistaken identity in which a cowardly young man, attempting to escape from a duel, is assumed to be a young nobleman whose middle-aged fiancée has instructed him to feign madness so that they may elope without detection. As an illustration by Cruikshank emphasizes, the high point of the story is an episode at the inn at Winglebury in which the supposed "wretched loo-nattic" is guarded by a one-eyed boots, brandishing a large stick, whose behavior seems so erratic to "the victim of mistakes" that the latter assumes that the boots, in turn, is mad (p. 416). Somewhat more heavy-handedly, "The Tuggses at Ramsgate" pokes fun at the abnormal sensitivity of the nerves of the young man who forms one of its central characters. When his shopkeeping father unexpectedly inherits twenty thousand pounds, this young man faints twice from excitement; then, once recovered, he changes his name from "Simon" to "Cymon" and departs with his parents and sister for a vacation at Ramsgate, where he is duped into a platonic flirtation with a married woman, Mrs. Captain Waters, who describes her husband as "a maniac in his jealousy" (p. 352). At the climax of this story, Captain Waters discovers the unfortunate young man behind a curtain in the Waterses' residence, where he has been concealed by Mrs. Waters, a discovery that throws the innocent Cymon into a "nervous disorder" (p. 354) and costs his family fifteen hundred pounds. In these two instances, the subject of mental instability is treated humorously, but in the two other concluding tales, this topic assumes a more disturbing form.

Of these two pieces, "The Black Veil" deals directly with the idea of insanity. As indicated by the title, reminiscent of the famous black veil in Ann Radcliffe's *The Mysteries of Udolpho*,[31] this story is clearly linked with the line of Gothic terror, although, as Harvey Peter Sucksmith has observed, Dickens seems more immediately influenced in this piece by the tales of terror published in *Blackwood's Edinburgh Magazine* in the 1820s and 1830s, which evoked a sense of fear through specific, realistic details in contrast to the more vaguely suggested fears aroused by earlier, traditional Gothic works like those of Mrs. Radcliffe.[32] More precisely, as Sucksmith has noted, sections of "The Black Veil" are strikingly similar to parts of Samuel Warren's *Passages from the Diary of a Late Physician,* published in installments in *Blackwood's* between 1830 and 1837; a number of episodes in Warren's *Passages* deal specifically with the subject of madness.[33] Whatever its immediate antecedents, as the first of Dickens' pieces to give serious emphasis to the topic of mental abnormality that recurs repeatedly in a large proportion of his subsequent short stories, "The Black Veil" deserves particular attention.

The plot of the tale is melodramatic. A young physician, recently begun in practice, receives his first request for help on a dismal winter night. His visitor, "a singularly tall woman, dressed in deep mourning" with a face "shrouded by a thick black veil" (p. 372) is a mysterious individual who implores the young doctor's assistance for a patient who cannot be seen immediately "though he is in deadly peril" and can only be seen on the following morning when he will be "beyond the reach of human aid" (p. 374). The true explanation of the woman's errand is the subject of suspense throughout the tale, although, at the end, the mystery is resolved when the physician conquers his misgivings, keeps his appointment at an isolated address with the man whom he has been summoned to assist, and discovers that the latter is a criminal who has been hanged that morning and whose distraught mother has summoned medical aid in the vain hope that her son's corpse might thus be restored to life.

Viewed in the context of Dickens' other tales, however, the striking feature of "The Black Veil" is not its plot but the stress that it places on the subject of mental aberration. At the end of the story, overwhelmed by grief, the hanged man's mother collapses into madness. As even the narrator observes, the events—reminiscent of those in the progress of Hogarth's Idle 'Prentice and some of the vignettes in Bunyan's *Pilgrim's Progress*—are trite: "The history was an every-day one. The mother was a widow without friends or money, and had denied herself necessaries to bestow them on her orphan boy. That boy, unmindful of her prayers, and forgetful of the sufferings she had endured for him—incessant anxiety of mind, and voluntary starvation of body— had plunged into a career of dissipation and crime. And this was the result; his own death by the hangman's hands, and his mother's shame, and incurable insanity" (p. 381). Nonetheless, long before this conclusion, it is evident that the imaginations of both the young doctor and the woman who seeks his aid are feverishly overwrought. As the story opens, the doctor drowses before his fire, "revolving a thousand matters in his wandering imagination" (p. 371). His opening conversation with the mysterious veiled visitor also strikes this note of imaginative disorder:

> "You are very wet," he said.
> "I am," said the stranger, in a low deep voice.
> "And you are ill?" added the surgeon, compassionately, for the tone was that of a person in pain.
> "I am," was the reply—"very ill; not bodily, but mentally . . . ." (P. 373)

Similarly, as the young physician struggles with insomnia on the night before his mysterious appointment, his frame of mind approximates that which he attributes to the woman who has sought his help: "his original impression that the woman's intellects were disordered, recurred; and, as it was the only mode of solving the difficulty with any degree of satisfaction, he obstinately made up his mind to believe that she was mad. Certain misgivings upon this point, however, stole upon his thoughts at the time, and presented themselves again and again through the long dull course of a sleepless night; during which, in spite of all his efforts to the contrary, he was unable to banish the black veil from his disturbed imagination" (p. 376). As DeVries has noted, the gloomy details of the setting through which the doctor passes as he walks the next morning to meet his unknown patient skillfully serve as an objective correlative of his mental state.[34] Dickens' primary preoccupation in "The Black Veil" appears to be not so much the story's suspenseful plot as its careful cultivation of the motif of the "disturbed imagination," a motif that is even more obviously present in the last piece written among the tales in *Sketches by Boz*, "The Drunkard's Death."

Here, even more melodramatically than in "The Black Veil," Dickens deliberately evokes the theme of madness. Once again, as the narrator of "The Drunkard's Death" declares, the events of the plot that lead to the climax at the end of the story are familiar ones, "of too frequent occurrence to be rare items in any man's experience" (p. 484). In this case, an alcoholic father neglects his saintly wife who eventually dies of a broken heart, drives his sons away from home, and exploits his daughter. The latter, in turn, eventually leaves him when one of her brothers, now a murderer who has returned to their slum apartment for refuge, is drunkenly betrayed by the father "into the hangman's hands" (p. 491). Once again, the primary purpose of this piece appears to be not its deliberately conventional account of the road to ruin—in this instance along the route later depicted in Cruikshank's *The Bottle*—but rather its presentation of an irrational state of mind. In particular, this irrational mental state is that of the reprobate father whose drunkenness is equated with madness. As the narrator observes, when the drunkard accepts the offers of liquor that cause him to betray his son, "He *did* drink; and his reason left him" (p. 490). In the opening paragraph, alcoholism is described as "that fierce rage for the slow, sure poison, that . . . hurries its victims madly on to degradation and death" (p. 484), and the father's eventual suicide, with which the story ends, is presented as the result of madness induced not only by his thirst for alcohol but also by the absolute isolation to which his drunkenness has led.

Thus, in varying ways, the last four of the tales in *Sketches by Boz* reveal Dickens' fascination with the subject of abnormal mental states. In comparison with the writings of Dickens' maturity, these pieces are still clearly "apprentice" productions, but the presence in "The Drunkard's Death" of an artistically extraneous paragraph about the potentially delirious ravings of a dying person and their potentially maddening effect on a listener only corroborates Dickens' preoccupation in this story with the topic of mental aberration. Near the beginning of "The Drunkard's Death," the narrator describes the deathbed of the drunkard's long-suffering wife and then digresses to explain:

> It is a dreadful thing to wait and watch for the approach of death; to know that hope is gone, and recovery impossible; and to sit and count the dreary hours through long, long nights—such nights as only watchers by the bed of sickness know. It chills the blood to hear the dearest secrets of the heart—the pent-up, hidden secrets of many years—poured forth by the unconscious helpless being before you; and to think how little the reserve and cunning of a whole life will avail, when fever and delirium tear off the mask at last. Strange tales have been told in the wanderings of dying men; tales so full of guilt and crime, that those who stood by the sick person's couch have fled in horror and affright, lest they should be scared to madness by what they heard and saw; and many a wretch has died alone, raving of deeds the very name of which has driven the boldest man away. (P. 485)

However, as the narrator observes at the opening of the following paragraph, "no such ravings were to be heard at the bedside by which the children knelt" (p. 486). Indeed, "no such ravings" are appropriate at the bedside of this woman whom the plot of the story presents as a pallid angel who needs only to die to ascend to her rightful sphere. Viewed out of context, against the background of Dickens' later writings and the fiction that has been published in the more than one hundred years since Dickens' death, pieces such as "The Great Winglebury Duel," "The Tuggses at Ramsgate," "The Black Veil," and "The Drunkard's Death" can seem trivial. The last story, in particular, appears artistically unbalanced. In later years, Dickens himself was critical of *Sketches by Boz,* and in his 1850 preface, he attempted to devalue the entire work: "I am conscious of their often being extremely crude and ill-considered, and bearing obvious marks of haste and inexperience; particularly in that section of the present volume which is comprised under the general head of Tales" (p. xiii). Not all of Dickens' devaluation is justified, as a number of critics have demonstrated.[35] Nevertheless, the fact that Dickens singled out the "Tales" for particular debasement —combined with his practice in his later stories—suggests not only his clear mastery by 1850 of fictional techniques and his sensitivity to the way in which readers' expectations had changed since the 1830s. It also suggests his possible awareness that a kind of short story had evolved in his writing that differed significantly from the farcical treatments of human foolishness that predominate in the twelve pieces labeled "Tales" in *Sketches by Boz* as well as in the five analogous "Characters" grouped by DeVries with the "Tales." Furthermore, Dickens' somewhat awkwardly handled interest in abnormal states of mind in the last four of these tales indicates his effort, even in 1836, to go beyond the farcical pieces that DeVries contends Dickens felt were expected by popular taste at the outset of his career.[36] Comically, in "The Great Winglebury Duel" and "The Tuggses at Ramsgate," and melodramatically, in "The Black Veil" and "The Drunkard's Death," Dickens seems to be attempting to explore the link—suggested by the uncanny tales to which he was addicted as a child—between short stories and a realm of experience remote from "every-day life and every-day people." The tales introduced into *Pickwick Papers* also reveal his increasingly confident use of the short story to probe this irrational realm.

IV

Most critics who have given any notice to the nine tales in *Pickwick* have found little good to say. For example, Edmund Wilson declares categorically that "these stories are mostly pretty bad and deserve from the literary point of view no more attention than they usually get...."[37] Similarly, Edgar Johnson dwells upon, in his words, the "artistic badness" of these pieces, which he contends not even the picaresque example of setting stories within the larger framework of a novel can justify.[38] In view of the widely accepted opinion of the "badness" of these stories, excuses for their apparent intrusion in *Pickwick Papers* abound. For instance, John Butt and Kathleen Tillotson theorize that Dickens included the tales in the novel, when searching for material to fill out his numbers, simply because he happened to have them on hand.[39] In contrast, both Wilson and Johnson, among others, explain the appearance of these pieces largely on biographical and psychological grounds. Thus Wilson discusses the way in which certain of the tales reveal Dickens' obsessions with criminals and prisons,[40] while Johnson observes that "their presence betrays a vein of morbid horror in Dickens deeply significant of his submerged griefs and fears."[41] However, the fact remains that Dickens placed these tales in the novel, and evidence indicates that he admired the results.

As Dickens explained in a letter to Robert Seymour, the original illustrator of *Pickwick Papers,* "I am extremely anxious about 'The Stroller's Tale'—the more especially as many literary friends, on whose judgment I place great reliance, think it will create considerable sensation."[42] As Heinz Reinhold has noted, the response of contemporary readers seems to have proved Dickens' friends correct.[43] In addition, Robert L. Patten has presented evidence indicating "that all of *Pickwick*'s tales were probably written at the time the novel was composed, for the places in which they originally appeared."[44] Like other recent critics including Reinhold, Patten has consequently focused upon previously ignored relationships between the inset tales and the fabric of the novel.[45] Moreover, although the tales in *Pickwick* seem indubitably linked with the overall framework of the novel, when they are temporarily examined apart from that framework—in their own terms as a group—significant characteristics become apparent.

Fundamentally, the tales in *Pickwick Papers* reflect Dickens' concentrated experimentation with the link between short stories and the realm of the imagination, leading to gentle parody of this mode of writing. As Garrett Stewart has observed about these inset pieces, "It is not darkness but imagination itself which seems to be the common denominator."[46] In eight of the nine tales in *Pickwick,* as in "The Black Veil" and "The Drunkard's Death"—as well as, to a lesser degree, in "The Great Winglebury Duel" and "The Tuggses at Ramsgate"—Dickens appears to be deliberately working with the subject of some kind of imaginative deviation from everyday thinking. Four of the tales, which seem designed to evoke a sensation of the uncanny, deal with abnormally intense emotions. "The Stroller's Tale" is a grim description of the ravings of an alcoholic clown, who dies in the midst of financial, physical, and marital ruin. In "The Convict's Return," a former convict comes back to his native village after seventeen years only to find that his mother, who loved him tenderly as a child, has died in his absence; his father, who previously abused him, bursts a blood vessel and dies at the sight of his return. "A Madman's Manuscript" is a horrifying, largely first-person account of a dangerous lunatic who temporarily conceals his insanity, destroys his wife, and finally runs amok until he is captured and confined. "The Old Man's Tale about the Queer Client" describes a wronged man's relentless determination to do as he has been done by —to take revenge upon his father-in-law, who has put him into a debtors' prison and caused the death of his wife and child. Four of the other stories, like fairy tales, flagrantly defy credibility. The two tales told by the bagman deal with the supernatural animation of lifeless objects, while the very title of "The Story of the Goblins who stole a Sexton" suggests the nature of the activity involved. The whimsical "True Legend of Prince Bladud," in which the "heathen deities" (p. 511) grant Bladud's wish—as a disappointed lover—to mourn forever on the site of the present city of Bath, ends in a similarly preternatural vein. Stewart's contention that these interpolated stories provide a kind of "quarantine of imagination"[47] in the larger context of the novel seems perceptive, although Dickens would probably have described the element in which he appears to be indulging so uninhibitedly in these tales as that of fancy, analogous to the remote-from-actuality quality that he believed flourished so freely in the fairy tales and tales of the uncanny familiar to him as a child. Moreover, Stewart's remark that Dickens' stylistic experimentation with rendering imaginative frenzy in "The Stroller's Tale" "takes up quite literally where *Sketches by Boz* left off" is misleading.[48]

Stewart illustrates his point with an allusion to "The Drunkard's Death." In actuality, however, "The Drunkard's Death" was published in December 1836 in the Second Series of *Sketches by Boz,* seven months after "The Stroller's Tale" appeared in the May 1836 issue of *Pickwick Papers.* In addition, of the eight other tales in *Pickwick,* five pieces—"The Convict's Return," "A Madman's Manuscript," "The Bagman's Story," "The Parish Clerk: A Tale of True Love," and "The Old Man's Tale about the Queer Client" (published respectively in the June, July, August, September, and November 1836 issues of *Pickwick*)—also preceded "The Drunkard's Death." Throughout much of 1836, beginning in February with the appearance of "The Black Veil" and "The Great Winglebury Duel" in the First Series of *Sketches by Boz,* Dickens seems to have been fascinated with the idea of using short stories to examine the mentally abnormal and, in the case of "The Bagman's Story," the obviously fantastic aspects of imagination. By the fall of 1836, his handling of this type of short story was clearly conscious, as his parody of such stories in "The Parish Clerk" confirms.

As readers have occasionally noted, "The Parish Clerk: A Tale of True Love" stands apart from the other tales in *Pickwick.* In Stewart's words, "It is the only interpolation of the nine which is not weird or demented in some way, which does not dip into fantasy or dive into some psychic abyss."[49] However, the manner in which this atypical tale functions as a kind of gentle critique of the others has generally been ignored. Appropriately, the source of this story is Mr. Pickwick's down-to-earth servant Sam, who knows a tall tale when he hears one. Near the end of the novel, in a passage that prepares for the introduction of the last interpolated tale ("[T]he Story of the Bagman's Uncle"), Sam remarks about the one-eyed bagman whom he has observed upon entering an inn: " 'He's a queer customer, the vun-eyed vun, sir,' . . . 'He's a gammonin' that 'ere landlord, he is, sir, till he don't rightly know wether he's a standing on the soles of his boots or the crown of his hat' " (p. 679). The omniscient narrator provides further explanation:

> The individual to whom this observation referred, was sitting at the upper end of the room when Mr. Pickwick entered, and was smoking a large Dutch pipe, with his eye intently fixed on the round face of the landlord: a jolly looking old personage, to whom he had recently been relating some tale of wonder, as was testified by sundry disjointed exclamations of, "Well, I wouldn't have believed it! The strangest thing I ever heard! Couldn't have supposed it possible!" and other expressions of astonishment which burst spontaneously from his lips, as he returned the fixed gaze of the one-eyed man. (P. 679)

Although the "tale of wonder" with which the wily bagman "gammons" the landlord is not related, it is followed, as soon as Sam and Mr. Pickwick join the scene, by an equally far-fetched (and to the gullible landlord, equally credible) description. In Dickens' thinking, the element of wonder was closely linked with that of fancy (as indicated by his later emphasis in *Hard Times* on the phrase "never wonder" as the "keynote" of the hard-facts philosophy refuted by that novel). Moreover, as manifested by the content of the interpolated pieces in *Pickwick Papers* prior to Sam Weller's observation, the term "tale of wonder" is an appropriate label for all of the tales in *Pickwick* except "The Parish Clerk."

While the other stories in *Pickwick* deal with extremely diverse situations, each situation is an unusual one and remote from everyday life. Also, each of these eight far-fetched tales of wonder is in some way suggested or asserted to be truth—in manners ranging from the simple implication of veracity conveyed by the fact that the narrator of "The Convict's Return" is a clergyman to the sweeping preamble of "The Old Man's Tale about the Queer Client." As Jack Bamber declares at the outset of the latter story, "It is enough for me to say that some of its circumstances passed before my own eyes. For the remainder I know them to have happened, and there are some persons yet living, who will remember them but too well" (p. 284). In contrast, although "The

Parish Clerk: A Tale of True Love" also bears an assertion of authenticity in its title, this "tale of true love" does indeed seem genuine, in an ironic, worldly sense: the impoverished and insignificant country schoolmaster Nathaniel Pipkin accepts the marriage of the girl whom he loves to another man and decides to cultivate the friendship of her rich father. In a similarly down-to-earth vein, the tale is present in the novel solely because Mr. Pickwick has been afflicted with a bout of rheumatism after his disastrous attempt to prevent a feigned elopement between Jingle and a rich heiress from a boarding school. The piece is introduced "as having been 'edited' by . . . [Pickwick] . . . from his notes of Mr. Weller's unsophisticated recital" (p. 227). Like some of the farcical stories of human folly and absurdity in *Sketches by Boz*, such as "The Misplaced Attachment of Mr. John Dounce" or "The Election for Beadle"—a sketch which evolves into a farcical story in the "Our Parish" series—it appears more closely tied to actual human behavior than the other tales in *Pickwick*. In the context of the novel, it perhaps functions as a gentle reminder to Mr. Pickwick of the foolishness of romantic efforts to rescue damsels from distress. As the narrator (presumably Mr. Pickwick under Sam's guidance) observes about Nathaniel Pipkin's staring at the girl to whom he is attracted and his subsequent punishment of one of his students when the girl retreats, "All this was very natural, and there's nothing at all to wonder at about it" (p. 228). Indeed, the only "matter of wonder," as the narrator continues, is the fact "that any one of Mr. Nathaniel Pipkin's retiring disposition, nervous temperament, and most particularly diminutive income, should from this day forth, have dared to aspire to the hand and heart of the only daughter of the fiery old Lobbs" (p. 228). Eventually, sensibly, Nathaniel Pipkin recognizes his mistake. In this fashion, Sam Weller's apparent conscious mockery of the kind of "tale of wonder" exemplified by the other stories in *Pickwick Papers* illustrates his practical wisdom at the same time that it demonstrates Dickens' awareness, by September 1836, of the distinctive nature of this kind of tale.

Thus, the eight stories in *Pickwick* whose genre "The Parish Clerk" quietly parodies should not be dismissed, as critics following the lead of Edmund Wilson have often done, as simply revelations of their author's neurotic compulsions. The choice of material in "The Stroller's Tale," "The Convict's Return," "A Madman's Manuscript," and "The Old Man's Tale about the Queer Client" may indeed be idiosyncratic—the details about criminality, murder, imprisonment for debt, brutality towards women, wicked fathers, and abused children may indeed reflect "dark corners" of Dickens' private thoughts. Nonetheless, Dickens' purpose in presenting this material in these four tales of the uncanny appears to be the more general, artistic one of depicting "particular states of mind and processes of the imagination" which he attributed to ghost stories in his 1851 letter to Mrs. Gaskell. (Significantly, in this context, "The Old Man's Tale about the Queer Client" is mentioned in passing in *Master Humphrey's Clock* as a "ghost story" [p. 85].) These four tales, like the other tales of wonder in this novel, should be viewed as early and somewhat amateurish but still deliberate efforts to examine imaginative aberrations from everyday thinking, as Dickens had also done in 1836—in varying degrees—in the chronologically last four tales in *Sketches by Boz*. Of the three 1837 tales in *Pickwick*, "The Story of the Goblins who stole a Sexton" and "[T]he Story of the Bagman's Uncle" skillfully combine humor and forays into the world of the imagination with their respective concluding puns that the goblins who apparently kidnapped the possibly inebriated Gabriel Grub are "spirits . . . beyond proof" (p. 405) and that the ghosts of departed mail coaches naturally carry "dead letters" (p. 697). In addition, "The True Legend of Prince Bladud" seems to be a less successful effort in this humorously far-fetched vein. However, outside of *Pickwick Papers*, Dickens' work with the short story in 1837 appears to have come to a temporary standstill.

V

Evidence of this stagnation is apparent in the labored and now justifiably forgotten short writings by Dickens that appeared in 1837 and 1838 in the pages of *Bentley's Miscellany*. Of these five pieces,[50] only "Public Life of Mr. Tulrumble Once Mayor of Mudfog" (January 1837) is a fully conceived story in the sense of possessing characters, setting, plot, and conscious narrative design. It seems far less experimental than the stories in *Pickwick Papers*. Each of the tales in *Pickwick* is ostensibly introduced as a means of whiling away time—a purpose that suggests the traditionally oral nature of tales like those of Scheherazade, which eventually becomes a characteristic feature of Dickens' short stories. In contrast, "Public Life of Mr. Tulrumble" lacks this implication of oral narration. Moreover, unlike all of the tales in *Pickwick*—except "The Parish Clerk"—with their sometimes unbalanced explorations of the realm of fancy, this account of the Mayor of Mudfog's absurdities harks back to the farcical but presumably down-to-earth early tales in *Sketches by Boz*. The two sketches and two parodies of scientific meetings that Dickens subsequently published in *Bentley's Miscellany* continue in this satiric vein.

Part of the reason for Dickens' relative disinterest in experimentation with the imaginative potential of the short story at this point in his career is undoubtedly due to the multiplicity of his commitments as his fame as a novelist increased. As Angus Wilson has remarked about this period, when the popularity of *Pickwick* propelled its author upward, "in a wickedly overworked life Dickens never worked so hard again."[51] Although Dickens accepted contracts for future publications with reckless eagerness and discharged staggering obligations with apparent ease, the cost in terms of his short writing is obvious. For example, Dickens composed *Pickwick Papers* and *Oliver Twist* simultaneously for several months in 1837 and then *Oliver Twist* and *Nicholas Nickleby* simultaneously for part of 1838, as well as turning out an anonymous potboiler entitled *Sketches of Young Gentlemen* in January 1838 and editing an autobiography of Grimaldi the clown in the same month.[52] The theory that Dickens used his short pieces to pad the size of his monthly numbers has no demonstrable validity as far as *Pickwick* is concerned. Nevertheless, it does appear to have some bearing on his writings for *Bentley's Miscellany,* a journal that Dickens had not only agreed to edit but also for each monthly issue of which he had contracted to supply sixteen pages—pages that usually consisted of installments of his second novel, *Oliver Twist.* For instance, shortly before the appearance of the first installment of *Oliver Twist* in the February 1837 issue of the *Miscellany,* he wrote to Richard Bentley, the publisher whose controlling authority over the journal Dickens resented and with whom he was eventually to break, *"Oliver Twist* making nearly eleven pages, I have only five more to write for the next *Miscellany*—and those five I am compelled—*really* compelled; . . . to defer until some future opportunity, and to make up, as I am carried on by my subject." The editors of the Pilgrim edition of Dickens' letters explain that "The March *Oliver* was 12½ pp.; and by writing a second paper for the same No.—'Stray Chapters. By Boz. Chapter I. The Pantomine of Life' (7 pp.) —CD made up 3½ out of the five pages short in Feb."[53] In addition, the appearance of two interpolated tales, "The Five Sisters of York" and "The Baron of Grogzwig" in the second monthly number of *Nicholas Nickleby,* despite the absence of such tales from the remainder of the novel, can partially be explained by Dickens' complaint in a letter to Forster, "I . . . have yet 5 slips to finish, and don't know what to put in them for I have reached the point I meant to leave off with," although, as the Pilgrim editors carefully observe, "each [of the tales is] the equivalent of five slips."[54] Thus only one tale could possibly be viewed as a last minute insertion to produce the necessary amount of writing. With the exception of "The Baron of Grogzwig," a comic treatment of the subject of suicidal depression that blends humor and traditionally Gothic material to depict a supernaturally induced conversion (echoing that of Gabriel Grub in "The Story of the Goblins who stole a Sexton"), the sketches and tales that Dickens produced beyond the pages of *Pickwick Papers* in 1837, as well as in the following year, seem tired.

With the conclusion of *Nickleby* in 1839, however, Dickens returned enthusiastically to the idea of the imaginative potential inherent in writings such as the fairy tales and the tales of the uncanny which he remembered from his childhood. More specifically, he embodied this enthusiasm in his cherished scheme for what he eagerly described as "the New Work."[55]

VI

According to Forster, much of the motivation for the emergence of *Master Humphrey's Clock* at this point in Dickens' career was Dickens' desire "to discontinue the writing of a long story with all its strain on his fancy."[56] Although Forster implies and critics have generally interpreted this remark to mean that Dickens conceived *Master Humphrey's Clock*, in part, as a means of escaping from some of the labor inherent in writing a full-length novel,[57] the phrase "strain on his fancy," which Forster derives from his discussions with Dickens, seems ambiguous. Undeniably, had the idea of a periodical miscellany—filled with an assortment of short pieces eventually to be composed by divers hands—succeeded in its original form, it would have alleviated the current demands on Dickens' own creative powers. Nonetheless, in Dickens' thinking, this kind of creative holiday was linked with imaginative indulgence. As he wrote to the painter Daniel Maclise in July 1839 from Petersham (the same location from which he had, shortly before, sent his proposal for *Master Humphrey's Clock* to Forster), "I am sure we both deserve—richly deserve—a holiday by this time. Come and ruralize again, and refresh your imagination."[58] In keeping with this yearning for an imaginative idyll and lured by recollections of his childhood reading, Dickens—with *Master Humphrey's Clock*— appears to have taken his most direct and disastrous plunge into what he evidently viewed as the world of fancy.

The opening sentence of the *Clock* reveals its antifactual bias. As Master Humphrey explains at the outset, "The reader must not expect to know where I live" (p. 5). Moreover, Master Humphrey's subsequent account of himself and his companions places particular emphasis upon the fact that their thoughts are far from the ordinary world: "We are men of secluded habits, with something of a cloud upon our early fortunes, whose enthusiasm, nevertheless, has not cooled with age, whose spirit of romance is not yet quenched, who are content to ramble through the world in a pleasant dream, rather than ever waken again to its harsh realities" (p. 11).

As Andrews contends, Master Humphrey's account of the secluded nature of his life may derive in part from the description of an elderly antiquarian inhabitant of Little Britain in Washington Irving's *Sketch-Book* (1820).[59] Indeed, in 1841, Dickens wrote enthusiastically to Washington Irving in response to the latter's praise of *The Old Curiosity Shop,* "There is no living writer, and there are very few among the dead, whose approbation I should feel so proud to earn. And with everything you have written, upon my shelves, and in my thoughts, and in my heart of hearts, I may honestly and truly say so."[60] In view of Dickens' familiarity with Irving's works, numerous critics have pointed to evidence of Irving's influence on Dickens' writings.[61] However, although traces of the American writer's work may occasionally be apparent in that of the younger English author, as in the characterization of Master Humphrey and some of the Christmas scenes in *Pickwick,* Irving's effect upon Dickens appears to be primarily a generalized one —stemming from, among other analogous qualities, their similar love of old legends and the writings of the eighteenth-century English essayists and reinforcing Dickens' own desire, as in *Master Humphrey's Clock,* to produce similarly influenced tales and sketches.

In connection with his declaration of the "secluded habits" of himself and his friends, Master Humphrey explains that their stories will concern "spirits of past times, creatures of imagination, and people of to-day . . ." (p. 11). In practice, "people of to-day" receive little attention. The few stories that actually appeared in this ill-fated periodical (in addition to the two novels, *The Old Curiosity Shop* and *Barnaby Rudge,* and scattered material relating to Master Humphrey and his circle of friends), deal largely with "creatures of imagination" and "spirits of past times." The three short tales that emerge from the ruins of Dickens' scheme are all set in the past. The story appearing in the "First Night of the Giant Chronicles" opens "in the reign of Queen Elizabeth of glorious memory" (p. 21), while the period of "A Confession Found in a Prison in the Time of Charles the Second" is indicated by the title; in addition, "Mr. Pickwick's Tale" occurs under the reign of James I. Despite this conspicuous historical documentation, however, the periods involved seem to hold little importance. In the first two cases, the reigns of Elizabeth and Charles could easily be exchanged without affecting the content of the stories. "Mr. Pickwick's Tale" claims to involve the superstitions and political mysteries of the time of James I, but once again, the story does not use its particular historical setting in a precise way. The specific time in which these tales occur seems less important than their distance from the "harsh realities" of present life.

Thus, like the earlier tales introduced into *Pickwick Papers,* the material that Dickens initially designed for *Master Humphrey's Clock* seems intended to tap the world of fancy. In Master Humphrey's words, "The deaf gentleman and I first began to beguile our days with these fancies, and our nights in communicating them to each other" (p. 11). *Master Humphrey's Clock* serves more as a blueprint of this world of fancy, however, than as a detailed demonstration of Dickens' plan. The "chronicles" of the speaking giants, Gog and Magog, never provide the "tales of . . . the present, and the future" (p. 20), which are intended to appear. The uncanny "fancies . . . [which Jack Bamber] has so long indulged" (p. 86), as a resurrected Mr. Pickwick explains when he proposes this earlier narrator of "The Old Man's Tale about the Queer Client" as a potential member of Master Humphrey's circle, never—at least in *Master Humphrey's Clock*—see the light of day. Nonetheless, the blueprint remains significant. As David Sonstroem has observed in his analysis of the significance of the elusive term "fancy" in the context of *Hard Times:* "Two areas of meaning emerge. . . . The one is imaginative play: mental play unhindered by the strictures of reality. The other is fellow feeling: compassion, sentiment."[62] Both varieties of fancy— imaginative escapism and sentiment—involve a respite from grinding actuality. Their evident presence in the *Clock* explains not only its avowed unreality but also what modern readers are apt to perceive as its cloying sentimentality apparent in unwelcome details such as Master Humphrey's stress upon his sad resignation to his own deformity, his affection for his deaf companion, and his love for his antique clock. In other words, of the "three characteristic features of the *Clock,* before the novel assumed precedence: the [elegiac] tone, the retreat [from present realities], and the workings of the imagination" which Andrews has described,[63] all are related to the vital quality of fancy that Dickens promoted more effectively fourteen years later in *Hard Times.* Like that subsequent successful novel, this early, abortive "lost book" was intended to combat not only the imaginative barrenness but also the callousness that Dickens considered so dangerous in life.

Moreover, the material that Dickens included as part of the initial *Clock* apparatus demonstrates what he evidently viewed as the rightful association of short stories with this fanciful world. Part of the original design of the *Clock* appears to be a demonstration of what is and is not suitable to Master Humphrey's circle. Thus Pickwick emphasizes Jack Bamber's "dreamy" (p. 86) eccentricity when suggesting him for membership and explains that Bamber is "a strange secluded visionary, in the world but not of it; and as unlike anybody here as he is unlike anybody elsewhere that I have ever met or known" (p. 86), a recommendation with which only Mr. Miles—a retired businessman and the only vaguely practical member of Master Humphrey's coterie—finds fault. In contrast, the letter presented under "Correspondence" from a gentleman (appearing to be a kind of early version of Joey Bagstock in *Dombey and Son*) who applies unsuccessfully for one of Master Humphrey's empty chairs and offers to emend Master Humphrey's "prosy" narrative and "come in with great effect with a touch of life" (p. 32) demonstrates the kind of worldly spirit that is antithetical to Master Humphrey's group.[64] Appropriately, this gentleman's application excites the interest of no one except his jilted Belinda who responds in a subsequent epistle with a request for his place of residence. Like versions of the tales in *Pickwick* in an opposite key, these letters differ conspicuously in style and tone from the material that encompasses them. Here fancy—in the sense of both sentiment and imaginative escapism from actuality—flourishes freely in the encompassing material and is excluded from the introduced pieces. With the exception of this designedly inappropriate "Correspondence," however, the introductory remarks about Master Humphrey's reclusive life-style lead, in turn, to stories that are deliberately remote from actuality. These stories, in their own turn, confirm the out-of-the-ordinary interests of Master Humphrey and his friends.

In this fashion, this "lost book," motivated by its creator's memories of the tales told by Scheherazade and miscellanies like Goldsmith's *Bee,* delineates the outlines of the realm that Dickens viewed as that of fancy, and it reveals the strong connection in Dickens' thinking of short stories with this realm. However, the *Clock* itself, as Dickens wisely discerned, remains a failure. The primary reason for this failure seems twofold. On the one hand, as Dickens' readers made clear, the original design of *Master Humphrey's Clock* was unsuccessful simply because popular taste demanded novels. As Dickens wrote firmly to Edgar Allan Poe, explaining the impossibility of satisfying Poe's request that Dickens locate an English publisher for *Tales of the Grotesque and Arabesque,* two-and-a-half years after the *Clock's* metamorphosis into *The Old Curiosity Shop,* "the only consolation I can give you is that I do not believe any collection of detached pieces by an unknown writer, even though he were an Englishman, would be at all likely to find a publisher in this metropolis just now."[65]

On the other hand, as Dickens may have sensed, the material about Master Humphrey and his club of tale-telling companions seems inherently flawed because of its sustained remoteness from actuality. In Dickens' thinking elsewhere, escapism, such as he described in his invitation to Daniel Maclise to "refresh your imagination," was acceptable only when it was temporary. As he wrote to Wilkie Collins, in a letter outlining his ideas for the Christmas number of *Household Words* for 1858, eighteen years after his plans for the *Clock* had proved abortive, "... you can't shut out the world; ... you are in it, to be of it; ... you get into a false position the moment you try to sever yourself from it; and ... must mingle with it, and make the best of it, and make the best of yourself into the bargain."[66] Even before *Master Humphrey's Clock,* "The Five Sisters of York" in *Nicholas Nickleby*—a short story that staggers beneath the weight of anti-Catholic prejudice and is probably Dickens' least attractive early tale—stresses the conviction that one should "barter not the light and air of heaven, and the freshness of earth and all the beautiful things which breathe upon it, for the cold cloister and the cell" (p. 60). In contrast, perhaps because its author was seduced by the nostalgia with which he remembered his childhood reading, the escapism offered by *Master Humphrey's Clock* seems intended to be permanent. Master Humphrey declares that he and his friends "are content to ramble through the world in a pleasant dream, rather than ever waken again to its harsh realities" (p. 11). Even the revivified Sam Weller, although still more down-to-earth than Pickwick, is content to live with his master, in proximity to his father Tony, raising children in retirement.

Significantly, the only exception to this dominant sense of hazy unreality in *Master Humphrey's Clock*, other than the "Correspondence" and two brief anecdotes told by Sam, is the tale entitled "A Confession Found in a Prison in the Time of Charles the Second," a rapidly moving first-person account by a murderer who describes the manner in which he designed and accomplished the death of his four-year-old nephew. The narrator explains with horrifying bluntness how he buried the corpse in the garden of his estate and placed his chair upon the grave to entertain unexpected guests. The guests then apprehend him when two bloodhounds, having escaped from the person exercising them, scent the body and furiously unearth it. In this piece, once again, as in the grim tales in *Pickwick*, as well as "The Drunkard's Death" and "The Black Veil," Dickens appears to be deliberately exploring an abnormal state of mind. For example, the manner in which the thought of the child's death creeps upon the subsequent murderer is a striking illustration of Freud's attribution of the sensation of the uncanny to a feeling that things which have previously seemed unbelievable may be credible after all:

> Perhaps I hide the truth from myself, but I do not think that, when this began, I meditated to do him any wrong. I may have thought how serviceable his inheritance would be to us, and may have wished him dead; but I believe I had no thought of compassing his death. Neither did the idea come upon me at once, but by very slow degrees, presenting itself at first in dim shapes at a very great distance, as men may think of an earthquake or the last day; then drawing nearer and nearer, and losing something of its horror and improbability; then coming to be part and parcel—nay nearly the whole sum and substance—of my daily thoughts, and resolving itself into a question of means and safety; not of doing or abstaining from the deed. (P. 43)

In comparison with Dickens' mature treatment of psychological abnormality in his neglected but important short story "George Silverman's Explanation" (1868), "A Confession"—whose focus remains its sensational plot—is still an apprentice piece of writing. Nonetheless, Dickens' handling of imaginative frenzy in "A Confession" seems more controlled than in his earlier uncanny tales in *Pickwick* or "The Black Veil" and "The Drunkard's Death." (His method in "A Confession" is also more controlled than that in the concluding vignette depicting the thoughts "of a man, spending his last night on earth" [p. 212] in one of the condemned cells in the sketch entitled "A Visit to Newgate"—also published in 1836 in *Sketches by Boz* and concerned with exploring this area of the "disturbed imagination.") Not surprisingly, in a review of an American edition of *Master Humphrey's Clock,* Poe described "A Confession" as "a paper of remarkable power" (*Graham's Magazine,* May 1841). Paradoxically, the relative effectiveness of this piece appears to stem from the element of possible actuality inherent in all successful uncanny tales. In contrast, the pallid characters, limp plots, and slack descriptions that otherwise predominate at the outset of the *Clock* appear at least partially a consequence of their intended permanent detachment from ordinary life. With the exception of "A Confession," in terms of Dickens' experimentation with the short story in the early years of his career, *Master Humphrey's Clock* represents an artistic as well as a practical dead end.

In this fashion, *Master Humphrey's Clock* not only reveals Dickens' faith that short stories, like the fairy tales and tales of the uncanny that he remembered from his childhood, somehow could and should make contact with what he considered the world of fancy, but it temporarily marks the cessation of his experiments in this vein. After the *Clock's* failure, with the exception of the labored "Lamplighter's Story"— adapted from a farce written for the actor William Charles Macready (1838) and included in *The Pic Nic Papers* (1841), a work which Dickens edited for the benefit of the family of the deceased publisher John Macrone—Dickens put aside the idea of tales and concentrated on his novels. (His volume of acidic travel sketches, *American Notes* [1842], may be an effort to combine the visit to America and the "series of satirical papers" mentioned in his unfulfilled proposal for *Master Humphrey's Clock.*) Nevertheless, although the experience of the *Clock* appears to have taught Dickens that imaginative self-indulgence through the medium of the short story was financially and perhaps also artistically hazardous, the idea of the connection between stories and the element of fancy remained attractive. Three-and-a-half years after *Master Humphrey's Clock* had become simply a medium for *The Old Curiosity Shop,* Dickens returned, for the Christmas season, to the area of his self-indulgence with a more popular and practical approach.

CHAPTER 3

Storybooks in a Workaday World

... my blessing, with yours to back it, I hope, on
the Story-books, for saying anything in this
workaday world!

The Cricket on the Hearth

I

Authors, like other craftsmen, occasionally need time to reappraise
their methods. As readers have sometimes noted, the 1840s mark a
transitional period of this type in Dickens' work.[1] Evidence of this
transition is apparent not only in Dickens' novels but also in his attitude
toward the short story. Prior to his experience with the opening numbers of *Master Humphrey's Clock* in 1840, Dickens wrote short stories
readily, with an assumption that his public would automatically share
his enthusiasm for such writing. After the *Clock's* debacle, he wrote
short stories less impulsively but in many cases more determinedly,
with faith in the value of an occasional imaginative vacation in what he
had come to recognize as a pervasively unimaginative age.

One sign of this shift in Dickens' thinking about the short story is
the difference between Master Humphrey's declared aim in 1840 and
that of *Household Words*, the successful weekly journal that Dickens
established in 1850. In the earlier periodical, as this escapist narrator
openly avows, Master Humphrey's chief goal, as well as that of his
friends, is to retreat forever from contemporary reality into a private
paradise of make-believe. In contrast, one of the fundamental aims of
Household Words is to encourage the presence of fancy in the contemporary world. As the "Preliminary Word" of *Household Words* declares,

> No mere utilitarian spirit, no iron binding of the mind to grim
> realities, will give a harsh tone to our Household Words. In the
> bosoms of the young and old, of the well-to-do and of the poor, we

would tenderly cherish that light of Fancy which is inherent in the human breast; which, according to its nurture, burns with an inspiring flame, or sinks into a sullen glare, but which (or woe betide that day!) can never be extinguished. To show to all, that in all familiar things, even in those which are repellent on the surface, there is Romance enough, if we will find it out. . . . (30 March 1850)

Between these two declarations, after the *Clock's* demise, Dickens seems less concerned with writing short stories than with thinking about their value, as in the early literary experiences of Scrooge and David Copperfield—who both remember their reading of *The Arabian Nights* as a beneficent aspect of their childhood—or Paul Dombey, who vainly longs to hear old Glubb's yarns "about the deep sea, and the fish that are in it, and the great monsters that come and lie on rocks in the sun . . ." (p. 152) as a respite from relentlessly studying Latin grammar with Miss Blimber.

The primary exceptions to this general absence of short stories in Dickens' work between 1841 and 1849 are the Christmas Books, which are deeply imbued with memories of Dickens' own childhood reading. As Forster explained about these five holiday books, published annually, with the omission of 1847, from 1843 to 1848,

> No one was more intensely fond than Dickens of old nursery tales, and he had a secret delight in feeling that he was here only giving them a higher form. The social and manly virtues he desired to teach, were to him not less the charm of the ghost, the goblin, and the fairy fancies of his childhood; however rudely set forth in those earlier days. What now were to be conquered were the more formidable dragons and giants that had their places at our own hearths, . . . With brave and strong restraints, what is evil in ourselves was to be subdued; with warm and gentle sympathies, what is bad or unreclaimed in others was to be redeemed; the Beauty was to embrace the Beast, as in the divinest of all those fables; the star was to rise out of the ashes, as in our much-loved Cinderella; and we were to play the Valentine with our wilder brothers, and bring them back with brotherly care to civilization and happiness.[2]

As John Butt, Michael Slater, Harry Stone, and Kathleen Tillotson have perceptively argued in varying ways, the Christmas Books occupy an important position in Dickens' career as a novelist, for they afforded him an opportunity to experiment with techniques and topics that he subsequently used to advantage in his novels, beginning in 1846 with *Dombey and Son*.[3] However, these five diminutive volumes also serve as a significant turning point in Dickens' attitude toward and treatment of the short story. Both by their presence and their content, they illustrate his concern with the role of "story-books . . . in this workaday world."

II

Once again, the difficulty of definition inherent in the protean vitality of Dickens' language becomes evident. In Dickens' usage, the term "storybooks" is vague, in keeping with the frequent imprecision of words to which he attributed great emotional significance in his writing, but in practice, storybooks for Dickens appear equivalent to nursery tales in book form. For instance, the Smallweed family in *Bleak House* "discountenanced all story-books, fairy tales, fictions, and fables, and banished all levities whatsoever" (p. 288). The subsequent description of the literary limitations of Bart Smallweed—who "knows no more of Jack the Giant Killer, or of Sinbad the Sailor, than he knows of the people in the stars" (p. 290)—suggests that the most important storybooks of which Bart is ignorant are fairy tales. In general, according to the *Oxford English Dictionary,* the term "storybook" had a juvenile connotation in the eighteenth and nineteenth centuries: it might sometimes refer to "a novel or romance" but more commonly meant "a book containing stories, esp[ecially] children's stories."[4] Moreover, Dickens' personal use of the word "storybook" was undoubtedly affected by his recollections of the chapbooks that he had read so eagerly in his boyhood. As Earle Davis has explained,

> These little volumes, sixteen or twenty-four pages in length, were hawked about the country by peddlers and sold for anything from a penny to sixpence. They included the old fairy tales about Jack the Giant-Killer, Bluebeard, Beauty and the Beast, Valentine and Orson, Wat Tyler, Tom Thumb, Cinderella, Richard Whittington, Friar Bacon, the Wandering Jew, and endless others. Famous plays and novels were sometimes shortened and printed in digest form in the chapbooks, *Robinson Crusoe, Gil Blas, Don Quixote,* and *Gulliver's Travels* finding wide circulation in this way. . . . It is possible and even probable that Dickens became acquainted with eighteenth-century fiction in shortened form before the full texts were given to him.[5]

Thus, the designation "storybook" for Dickens seems to refer to something quite different from his own full-length, serialized novels. When Dickens uses the term he appears to have in mind an individually published short story for children or an individually published collection of such stories—in both cases, analogous to the chapbooks that he had encountered with such delight as a child.

Throughout his adult life, Dickens continued to place a premium on such freely imaginative literature. For example, he wrote in 1850 to the philanthropist Angela Burdett-Coutts, whom he was currently advising about her aid to the Ragged School movement as well as the details of her recently established home for reformed prostitutes, "It would be a great thing for all of us, if more who are powerfully concerned with Education, thought as you do, of the imaginative faculty." After mentioning firms which might publish children's books that she could examine in this context, he then commented that "Tegg of Cheapside, also published a charming collection of stories, called The Child's Fairy Library—in which I had great delight on the voyage to America."[6] In connection with this remark, it is worth noting that Dickens and his wife had left their children in England during their American visit. In other words, in 1842, as the internationally famous author of *Pickwick Papers, Oliver Twist, Nicholas Nickleby, The Old Curiosity Shop,* and *Barnaby Rudge,* Dickens evidently viewed fairy stories as ideal holiday reading for himself. Furthermore, as he demonstrated with dazzling popular success in 1843 with *A Christmas Carol,* whose separately published format resembled that of the chapbooks of his childhood, the Christmas season offered a splendid opportunity for similar indulgence.[7]

The warrant for such indulgence lies in Dickens' concept of the occasion. As Humphry House has noted, Christmas for Dickens entailed an allowable disregard of ordinary rules: "Christmas means the breakdown for a season of the restraints imposed by normal social life, a sort of psychological release, in the manner of the Saturnalia. It means release from cares that dim the affections . . . it means relaxation of the formality and strictness of business relationships. . . ."[8] In *Pickwick Papers,* for example, young and old, master and servant mingle in holiday recreation at Dingley Dell as part of an annual festival of good fellowship. The breakdown of restraint, however, is not confined to social conventions; it applies both to restrictions that inhibit human communication and to those that fetter the imagination. Thus, the celebration at Dingley Dell includes not only blindman's buff and struggles beneath the mistletoe but also the supernatural tale of "The Story of the Goblins who stole a Sexton." Similarly, as the narrator declares in Dickens' "What Christmas is, as we Grow Older" (from the holiday number of *Household Words* for 1851), Christmas is a time for reminiscing of the past, dreaming of the future, and envisioning what has never been, as well as for opening one's affections to other human beings: "Welcome, everything! Welcome, alike what has been, and what never was, and what we hope may be, to your shelter underneath the holly, to your places round the Christmas fire, where what is sits openhearted!" (*CS,* p. 23). In Dickens' terminology, this sense of emotional and imaginative release is related to the two manifestations of the vague but vital quality of fancy which, as discussed in chapter 2, David Sonstroem has discerned within *Hard Times* as "imaginative play" and "fellow feeling."

Imaginative escapism, as Dickens firmly came to believe after his experience with *Master Humphrey's Clock,* was beneficial only when it was impermanent; Harold Skimpole's perennial evasion of adult responsibility in *Bleak House* is clearly scorned. However, the lamentably transitory nature of the Christmas holiday ensures the fact that its celebrators will return refreshed to actuality, and *A Christmas Carol* offers a triumphant illustration of the elements of temporary escapism and fellow feeling which Dickens felt such seasonal fiction ideally should contain.

III

Indeed, the *Carol* focuses upon imaginative escapism and fellow feeling in its theme, for the essence of *A Christmas Carol* lies in the reeducation of Scrooge, a utilitarian businessman motivated solely by the desire for financial profit.[9] Scrooge in his counting house, when the story begins, is frozen in the world of facts: "he was a tight-fisted hand at the grindstone. Scrooge! . . . Hard and sharp as flint, from which no steel had ever struck out generous fire; . . . The cold within him froze his old features, nipped his pointed nose, shrivelled his cheek, stiffened his gait; made his eyes red, his thin lips blue; and spoke out shrewdly in his grating voice. A frosty rime was on his head, and on his eyebrows, and his wiry chin. He carried his own low temperature always about with him; he iced his office in the dog-days; and didn't thaw it one degree at Christmas" (*CB,* p. 8). As the narrator humorously explains, in preparation for Scrooge's momentary sight of the face of his deceased partner Marley where a door knocker ought to be: "It is . . . a fact . . . that Scrooge had as little of what is called fancy about him as any man in the city of London" (p. 14). When Marley's spirit enters his lodging, Scrooge struggles to maintain his factual surroundings:

> "You don't believe in me," observed the Ghost.
> "I don't," said Scrooge.
> "What evidence would you have of my reality beyond that of your senses?"
> "I don't know," said Scrooge.
> "Why do you doubt your senses?"
> "Because," said Scrooge, "a little thing affects them. A slight disorder of the stomach makes them cheats. You may be an undigested bit of beef, a blot of mustard, a crumb of cheese, a fragment of an underdone potato. There's more of gravy than of grave about you, whatever you are!" (P. 18)

As the narrator's commentary indicates, Scrooge's joke here is a good example of Freud's explanation of humor as "the ego's victorious assertion of its own invulnerability": "It refuses to be hurt by the arrows of reality or to be compelled to suffer. . . . Humour is not resigned; it is rebellious. It signifies the triumph not only of the ego, but also of the pleasure principle, which is strong enough to assert itself . . . in the face of . . . adverse real circumstances."[10] In the storyteller's words, "Scrooge was not much in the habit of cracking jokes, nor did he feel, in his heart, by any means waggish then. The truth is, that he tried to be smart, as a means of distracting his own attention, and keeping down his terror; for the spectre's voice disturbed the very marrow in his bones" (p. 18).

The fear awakened in the marrow of Scrooge's bones suggests the reorienting effect that Marley's ghost is already beginning to produce, and by the end of his experience, Scrooge has thoroughly abandoned his initial self-centered skepticism. With the help of the Spirits of Christmases Past, Present, and Yet to Come, he has returned to the sources of fancy—childhood storybooks and scenes of love—and he has seen the drab and loveless destination of his present way of life. As a beginning step in this reeducation, the Ghost of Christmas Past shows Scrooge a vision of his solitary, former self reading nursery tales for comfort when left alone at school:

> The Spirit touched him on the arm, and pointed to his younger self, intent upon his reading. Suddenly a man, in foreign garments: wonderfully real and distinct to look at: stood outside the window, with an axe stuck in his belt, and leading by the bridle an ass laden with wood.
>
> "Why, it's Ali Baba!" Scrooge exclaimed in ecstasy. "It's dear old honest Ali Baba! Yes, yes, I know! One Christmas time, when yonder solitary child was left here all alone, he *did* come, for the first time, just like that. Poor boy! And Valentine," said Scrooge, "and his wild brother, Orson; there they go! And what's his name, who was put down in his drawers, asleep, at the Gate of Damascus; don't you see him! And the Sultan's Groom turned upside down by the Genii; there he is upon his head! Serve him right. I'm glad of it. What business had *he* to be married to the Princess!" (P. 28)

As the narrator emphasizes, this vision of long-forgotten childhood reading and Scrooge's emotional involvement with the vision mark an important stage in his movement away from utilitarian practicality: "To hear Scrooge expending all the earnestness of his nature on such subjects, in a most extraordinary voice between laughing and crying; and to see his heightened and excited face; would have been a surprise to his business friends in the city, indeed" (p. 28). Likewise, the prediction of Tiny Tim's death, made by the Ghost of Christmas Present, who ironically echoes Scrooge's earlier Malthusian callousness, contributes to Scrooge's shift from good business to good fellowship: " 'If these shadows remain unaltered by the Future, none other of my race,' returned the Ghost, 'will find him here. What then? If he be like to die, he had better do it, and decrease the surplus population' " (p. 47). As a result of Scrooge's penitence, however, "these shadows" are altered. Tiny Tim lives, for Scrooge has learned to believe and has learned to love. He vows at the end to the last ghost, whose horrifying vision of Scrooge's own death—leaving a corpse ghoulishly plundered for profit and unmourned—is thus happily averted, "I will honour Christmas in my heart, and try to keep it all the year" (p. 70).

Moreover, the narrator's comments in this story not only explain but also reflect the nature of Scrooge's transformation. As Slater has perceptively noted, one of the distinguishing features of the Christmas Books is "a special intimacy of tone."[11] Slater describes this tone, with respect to *A Christmas Carol,* as "that of a jolly, kind-hearted bachelor uncle seated across the hearth from his hearers on some festive domestic occasion,"[12] and when one reads the *Carol,* the bachelor uncle sometimes appears unexpectedly nearby: "The curtains of his bed were drawn aside, I tell you, by a hand. Not the curtains at his feet, nor the curtains at his back, but those to which his face was addressed. The curtains of his bed were drawn aside; and Scrooge, starting up into a half-recumbent attitude, found himself face to face with the unearthly visitor who drew them: as close to it as I am now to you, and I am standing in the spirit at your elbow" (p. 24). As this obvious presence of the storyteller suggests, Dickens is re-creating here the sense of oral narration, which he had struggled less felicitously to achieve in the creaking machinery of *Master Humphrey's Clock* and from which most of the interpolated tales in *Pickwick Papers* and *Nicholas Nickleby* ostensibly spring. In addition, at his public readings of the *Carol,* Dickens made this sense of fireside narration even more explicit. As he urged his audience on one such occasion, "nothing would be more in accordance with his wishes than that they should all, for the next two hours, make themselves as much as possible like a group of friends, listening to a tale told by a winter fire."[13]

In Dickens' thinking, the storyteller's guiding and moderating presence was an important part of the meaning of the *Carol,* and strikingly, the narrator moves from fact to fancy in a manner that parallels the metamorphosis of Scrooge. In keeping with Scrooge's unregenerate, fact-bound personality, the narrator opens *A Christmas Carol* by attempting to establish certain fundamental areas of agreement:

> Marley was dead, to begin with. There is no doubt whatever about that. The register of his burial was signed by the clergyman, the clerk, the undertaker, and the chief mourner. Scrooge signed it. And Scrooge's name was good upon 'Change for anything he chose to put his hand to.
>
> Old Marley was as dead as a door-nail. (P. 7)

The echoes of this statement resound throughout the work and underlie its marvelous machinery. As the storyteller observes three paragraphs later:

> The mention of Marley's funeral brings me back to the point I started from. There is no doubt that Marley was dead. This must be distinctly understood, or nothing wonderful can come of the story I am going to relate. If we were not perfectly convinced that Hamlet's Father died before the play began, there would be nothing more remarkable in his taking a stroll at night, in an easterly wind, upon his own ramparts, than there would be in any other middle-aged gentleman rashly turning out after dark in a breezy spot—say Saint Paul's Churchyard for instance—literally to astonish his son's weak mind. (P. 7)

By the end of the *Carol,* however, something "wonderful" has genuinely come of the story that the narrator has related. While still sufficiently rooted in the world of actuality to make a pun about "abstinence" from "spirits" similar to that at the end of "The Story of the Goblins who stole a Sexton," the storyteller has wholeheartedly entered into Scrooge's Christmas-observing frame of mind: "He had no further intercourse with Spirits, but lived upon the Total Abstinence Principle, ever afterwards; and it was always said of him, that he knew how to keep Christmas well, if any man alive possessed the knowledge. May that be truly said of us, and all of us! And so, as Tiny Tim observed, God bless Us, Every One!" (p. 76). As the change from "he" to "us" makes clear, the storyteller has broadened the scope of his story to encompass all humanity. His own empathic shift from an emphasis on facts to an exuberant embracing of the values of fancy reveals the ideally contagious quality of Scrooge's change of heart.

Harry Stone has argued that Dickens viewed his Christmas Books as versions of fairy tales,[14] and Dickens' preoccupation in the theme of the *Carol* with the element of fancy, a quality which he believed was specifically nurtured by fairy tales, appears deliberate. John Butt has noted that *A Christmas Carol* represents a successful fusion of the form that Dickens had earlier used for "The Story of the Goblins who stole a Sexton" in *Pickwick* and the musings about selfishness, impoverished children, and employer-employee relationships which were in his mind in the fall of 1843.[15] The marked attention given to the topic of fancy in this Christmas Book suggests that this element and its vital encouragement by storybooks in a "workaday world" were also very much part of his thinking at this time. In many ways, this "Ghost Story of Christmas" is Dickens' best short story. Its form and content are supremely suited to one another and to the season that evoked it. Moreover, Scrooge's exuberant change of heart set a pattern that Dickens followed in the four subsequent Christmas Books with varying degrees of felicity.

As Stone has observed, Dickens' basic method in the Christmas Books "consists of taking a protagonist who displays false values and making him, through a series of extraordinary events, see his error."[16] In three cases, as in the *Carol,* the changes occur through supernatural means. Trotty Veck in *The Chimes* (1844) learns—with the help of the spirits of the bells—that even the most downtrodden human being is basically good rather than bad, as he had despondently come to believe. Ill-natured old Tackleton in *The Cricket on the Hearth* (1845) is converted (in a transformation which echoes that of Scrooge) to an attitude of good fellowship; however, in this instance, the supernatural beings appear to another character, the erroneously jealous John Peerybingle, and their effect reaches Tackleton only indirectly. Redlaw, the haggard professor in *The Haunted Man* (1848), discovers through what proves to be a dreadful gift of oblivion bestowed upon him by a phantom, that human beings must not forget their unhappy memories. *The Battle of Life* (1846), the only Christmas Book without supernatural machinery, teaches Doctor Jeddler that life is a serious business after all when his younger daughter takes the phenomenal step of renouncing her fiancé and disappearing for six years so that the man she loves will marry her older sister. In each book after the *Carol,* the suggestion of oral narration is, to some degree, maintained—with the exception of *The Battle of Life,* where the narrator alludes awkwardly to "my rude pen" (p. 308). Dickens' own prefatory comment about the Christmas Books underscores their common design: "My chief purpose was, in a whimsical kind of masque which the good humour of the season justified, to awaken some loving and forbearing thoughts, never out of season in a Christian land."[17] Like the kind of "masque" to which Dickens alludes in this somewhat vague yet still revealing remark, the Christmas Books are dramatizations (in fictional form) of particular ideas, often with only a thin allegorical disguise. In the course of their action, mistaken attitudes are exchanged for true ones, and foolish or misguided individuals learn to recognize the wrongness of their ways. What has not generally been noticed is the place—illustrated by Scrooge's beneficent return to childhood storybooks in the *Carol*—that reading occupies in this pattern of conversion.

IV

For Trotty Veck, the ticket porter whose renewed faith in poor people like himself forms the central subject of *The Chimes,* reading results in a problem of interpretation. As Trotty explains near the beginning of the tale, his education has been limited, and it is consequently difficult for him to evaluate what he reads: "I hadn't much schooling, myself, when I was young; and I can't make out whether we have any business on the face of the earth, or not. Sometimes I think we must have—a little; and sometimes I think we must be intruding. I get so puzzled sometimes that I am not even able to make up my mind whether there is any good at all in us, or whether we are born bad. We seem to be dreadful things; we seem to give a deal of trouble; we are always being complained of and guarded against. One way or other, we fill the papers" (*CB,* p. 87). The difficulty of properly judging the comments about the poor which "fill the papers" remains troubling to Trotty. Later in the same day, after his daughter Meg and the two visitors whom they have charitably fed and sheltered have retired to bed, his thoughts return to the same point:

> he took his newspaper from his pocket, and began to read. Carelessly at first, and skimming up and down the columns; but with an earnest and a sad attention, very soon.
>
> For this same dreaded paper re-directed Trotty's thoughts into the channel they had taken all that day, and which the day's events had so marked out and shaped. His interest in the two wanderers had set him on another course of thinking, and a happier one, for the time; but being alone again, and reading of the crimes and violences of the people, he relapsed into his former train.
>
> In this mood, he came to an account (and it was not the first he had ever read) of a woman who had laid her desperate hands not only on her own life but on that of her young child. A crime so terrible, and so revolting to his soul, dilated with the love of Meg, that he let the journal drop, and fell back in his chair, appalled!
>
> "Unnatural and cruel!" Toby cried. "Unnatural and cruel! None but people who were bad at heart, born bad, who had no business on the earth, could do such deeds. It's too true, all I've heard to-day; too just, too full of proof. We're Bad!" (P. 116–17)

As the context of this remark makes clear, Trotty's simplistic conclusion that "We're Bad!" is, in fact, thoroughly foolish. His own charitable actions—offering hospitality and food to Will Fern and his niece Lilian ("the two wanderers" who have come to London in search of work and a family friend) as well as warning them against the callous Alderman Cute—have already abundantly demonstrated Trotty's personal goodness. Nevertheless, as the narrator explains, Trotty is a "foolish little old fellow" (p. 116). The remainder of *The Chimes* is devoted to showing Trotty how he should have correctly evaluated the grim newspaper description ("of a woman who had laid her desperate hands not only on her own life but on that of her young child") which he has read.[18]

Trotty's lesson is complicated, however, by the necessity of distinguishing false teachers from true ones. His mistake in interpreting this newspaper account is in large part a consequence of the erroneous teachers who proliferate earlier in the story. For example, the small family celebration in which Trotty's daughter Meg announces her marriage to the young workingman Richard is undermined by the political economist Mr. Filer who explains that the tripe which Meg has brought to her father as a special treat "is without an exception the least economical, and the most wasteful article of consumption that the markets of this country can by possibility produce" (p. 94). This moment of festivity is further marred by the gentleman vaguely extolling "the good old times" (pp. 95, 96). He declares his indifference to Trotty's existence since the latter is not dressed like a porter "in any of the good old English reigns" (p. 96). Finally, the mood of simple joyfulness at the impending wedding is thoroughly dampened by Alderman Cute who professes knowledge of "this sort of people" (pp. 96, 97), predicts destitution and suicide for Meg and misery for Richard if they marry, and heartlessly warns, in his capacity as a Justice, that he is "determined to Put Down" (p. 99) whatever socially aberrant behavior may result from their future distress. Cute then sends Trotty with a letter to yet another false teacher, Sir Joseph Bowley, Member of Parliament, who explains to Trotty, "I do my duty as the Poor Man's Friend and Father; and I endeavour to educate his mind, by inculcating on all occasions the one great moral lesson which that class requires. That is, entire Dependence on myself" (p. 106).

The outcome in the mind of the good-natured ticket porter, when he turns to his newspaper that evening, is a depressed conviction that poor people are indeed depraved. In reaction, the spirits of the bells instruct him, in a frequently repeated refrain, to "learn from the creature dearest to your heart, how bad the bad are born" (p. 125). These spirits then show Trotty a horrifying vision of a possible future in which his own daughter Meg is left without support or shelter after his death and that of her husband Richard, whom she has finally married after a long period of misery and delay caused by fear of Cute's predictions. In this dire vision, Meg attempts to commit suicide with her infant daughter. Like the repentant Scrooge, Trotty declares in agony that the lesson has been "learnt" (pp. 150, 151) and awakens on New Year's Day, from what proves to have been a dream, to a joyful celebration of Meg's impending marriage.

As Slater has observed, *The Chimes* is "far more of a tract for the times than its predecessor" in the sense that in this second Christmas Book, Dickens is vehemently ridiculing particular well-fed approaches to the ill-fed poor common during the 1840s. In addition, Dickens is clearly placing the blame for the frequency of behavior such as prostitution, infanticide, and suicide by the poor on society's failure to help those who desperately need help.[19] In order to enhance the power of what he described to Forster as the story's "grip upon the very throat of the time,"[20] Dickens seems to have slightly marred the artistic content of his tale. Its message about the plight of the poor is so strongly expressed that it repeatedly attracts the reader's attention to the world of actuality beyond the story. Although Trotty Veck may awake on New Year's Day to a burst of celebration, the reader's thoughts remain with the desperate women, as in Trotty's dream of his daughter, without shelter on New Year's Eve. Nonetheless, although its tone is perhaps a bit too strident and its finale seems implausibly cheerful, *The Chimes* holds an important place in Dickens' work. As Slater has persuasively argued, it marks a decisive transitional point between Dickens' loosely constructed, exuberant "early" writings, which episodically attacked specific social problems, and his more tightly constructed and more somber "late" writings, most of which—like *The Chimes*—reveal a widespread "sense of something radically wrong with society."[21] Among Dickens' late writings, the affinity between *Bleak House*—which J. Hillis Miller has recently described as "a document about the interpretation of documents"[22]—and *The Chimes* appears especially striking. The technique of *The Chimes* in 1844 is far less sophisticated than the interwoven symbolism of deciphering and detection that forms the completed fabric of *Bleak House* in 1853, but the fact that Dickens has placed at the center of this pivotal Christmas Book a well-intentioned individual who needs to be taught how properly to interpret what he reads seems a further indication of the shift in Dickens' creative thinking at this time. In *The Chimes,* however, the need for interpretation is not paramount as in *Bleak House,* and at the end of *The Chimes,* Trotty's reading is abandoned. The lesson that Trotty learns "from the creature dearest to . . . [his] heart" seems to be that he should have relied on his heart from the outset and dismissed newspaper accounts that suggested anything contrary to his instinctive good nature. As Trotty awakens from his dream, "he caught his feet in the newspaper, which had fallen on the hearth" (p. 151). The newspaper here has simply become a minor impediment that keeps Trotty from embracing his daughter before her fiancé can claim her first kiss of the

New Year. The following Christmas Book presents an even more obvious devaluation of reading material which transcends the simple wisdom of the heart.

V

An indication of the devaluation of rationally demanding reading can be discerned in the often juvenile tone of Dickens' next holiday volume. The milieu of this third Christmas Book, *The Cricket on the Hearth,* seems consciously a childish one. As Slater has aptly observed, "in the *Cricket* we have found ourselves in a world of toys."[23] The characters, in Slater's words, appear to be "animated dolls,"[24] and even many of their names are childish. Dot Peerybingle, one of the major characters, has "a very doll of a baby" (*CB,* p. 164). Dot resembles a figure in a Christmas puppet show, representing a chubby, prepubescent teenager, playing at keeping house with a painted toy. This pervasive effect of make-believe is one for which Dickens seems to have strived. As Dot explains to her husband at the end of *The Cricket on the Hearth,* in one of the story's rare—and not very successful—efforts to put its details into a more serious, adult perspective, "when I speak of people being middle-aged, and steady, John, and pretend that we are a humdrum couple, going on in a jog-trot sort of way, it's only because I'm such a silly little thing, John, that I like, sometimes, to act a kind of Play with Baby, and all that: and make believe" (p. 228). In his opening inconsequential discussion of which began to sing first, the kettle or the cricket, the narrator appears to be engaging in a laboredly cute effort to establish himself on Dot Peerybingle's juvenile level:

> The kettle began it! Don't tell me what Mrs. Peerybingle said. I know better. Mrs. Peerybingle may leave it on record to the end of time that she couldn't say which of them began it; but I say the kettle did. I ought to know, I hope! The kettle began it, full five minutes by the little waxy-faced Dutch clock in the corner, before the Cricket uttered a chirp.
>
> . . . .
>
> Why, I am not naturally positive. Every one knows that. I wouldn't set my own opinion against the opinion of Mrs. Peerybingle, unless I were quite sure, on any account whatever. Nothing should induce me. But, this is a question of fact. And the fact is, that the kettle began it, at least five minutes before the Cricket gave any sign of being in existence. Contradict me, and I'll say ten.
> (P. 159)

Part of the reason for this opening emphasis on "a question of fact" is simply that both of the previous Christmas Books had begun with an emphasis on certain fundamental areas of agreement. However, unlike the talk about the fact of Marley's death at the outset of the *Carol* and, more peripherally, the remark about falling asleep at night in church where the wild wind may ring bells at the beginning of *The Chimes,* this pretended argument about whether the cricket or the kettle first began to sing bears no relationship to the events that follow. Indeed, a major weakness of *The Cricket on the Hearth* is the lack of a clear focus. Tackleton's conversion to an attitude of fellow-feeling, which the example of the previous Christmas Books indicates should be central to this work, seems an implausible afterthought. The obviously artificial juvenility of this piece (such as the narrator's remark, "Contradict me, and I'll say ten" or the recurrent details about Dot Peerybingle's childish domesticity) appears uncomfortably contrived.

In the midst of this labored emphasis on childishness, two attitudes toward the reading of books awkwardly become evident. In the main plot of the tale, the world of heart-felt, unintellectual domestic happiness represented by Dot and John Peerybingle is explicitly contrasted with a more sophisticated world evidenced by reading material in which people like Dot and John are not interested or which they cannot understand. Thus, near the opening of the story, as part of his effort to bring himself (and by extension his readers) down to the childish level of most of the details of the story, the narrator remarks about the "cosy and hilarious" sound of the kettle, "Bless you, you might have understood it like a book—better than some books you and I could name, perhaps" (p. 161). Cosy domesticity in this context is clearly superior to books that cosily domestic people cannot comprehend. A few pages later, the story makes a similar distinction—describing Dot's affectionately efficient relegation of the baby to its small nursemaid in order to welcome John into the house—when it suggests that Dot herself has become the "busy bee" about which she read in bygone days at school: "Here! Take the precious darling, Tilly, while I make myself of some use. Bless it, I could smother it with kissing it, I could! Hie then, good dog! Hie, Boxer, boy! Only let me make the tea first, John; and then I'll help you with the parcels, like a busy bee. 'How doth the little'—and all the rest of it, you know, John. Did you ever learn 'how doth the little,' when you went to school, John?" (p. 165). On an absolute scale, Isaac Watts' "Against Idleness and Mischief," memorably parodied by Lewis Carroll in the second chapter of *Alice's Adventures in Wonderland,* is hardly intellectually difficult reading. Nevertheless, as John's reply makes clear, the traditional schoolboy method of mastering this poem by memorizing it is beyond the present speaker's intellectual powers: " 'Not to quite know it,' John returned. 'I was very near it once. But I should only have spoilt it, I dare say' " (p. 165). In the world of *The Cricket on the Hearth,* however, John's imperviousness to traditional education is no disgrace. Dot simply laughs and exclaims, "What a dear old darling of a dunce you are, John, to be sure!" (p. 165), just as the narrator has earlier explained that John's intellectual slowness conceals a more genuine kind of wisdom: "so rough upon the surface, but so gentle at the core; so dull without, so quick within; so stolid, but so good!" (pp. 163–64). In turn, it is this inner goodness—like that on which Trotty Veck needed to be taught to rely—that leads John to put aside the possibility of revenge against Dot's apparent lover. Tackleton cynically reveals Dot talking affectionately in private to a person who has come into her home in the guise of a deaf old man and who emerges as a much younger man than her husband, but John eschews vindictiveness. This goodness, finally, is rewarded when the disguised young man proves to be the long-lost fiancé of Dot's friend May Fielding who, in his absence, has reluctantly become engaged to Tackleton. As the end of the story explains, the young man had decided to adopt a disguise and reveal himself initially only to Dot in order to discover if May genuinely loves Tackleton; after learning that she does not, the returned lover and May are quickly married, and the story concludes with a wedding celebration, a reunion, and general rejoicing.

While the primary plot of *The Cricket on the Hearth* seems built around this unfelicitously coy contrast between the wisdom of the heart and the wisdom of the head, a secondary plot, concerning one of the minor characters and his blind daughter, deals more effectively with a different attitude toward different books from those which the narrator dismisses at the outset of the opening chapter. As this narrator observes at the beginning of the second chapter,

> Caleb Plummer and his Blind Daughter lived all alone by themselves, as the Story-books say—and my blessing, with yours to back it, I hope, on the Story-books, for saying anything in this workaday world!—Caleb Plummer and his Blind Daughter lived all alone by themselves, in a little cracked nutshell of a wooden house, which was, in truth, no better than a pimple on the prominent red-brick nose of Gruff and Tackleton. The premises of Gruff and Tackleton were the great feature of the street; but you might have knocked down Caleb Plummer's dwelling with a hammer or two, and carried off the pieces in a cart. (P. 182)

Here, briefly, Dickens seems to have broken away from the pervasive artificiality of this work (evident even in details such as the chapter titles "Chirp the First," "Chirp the Second," etc.). The blessing that the narrator invokes "on the Story-books, for saying anything in this workaday world!" is a direct expression of the idea, as Forster explained, that lies behind all of the Christmas Books—Dickens' own cherished faith in the value of "old nursery tales" in contemporary life.

In the context of this Christmas Book, however, Dickens is primarily concerned with Caleb Plummer's misuse of the potentially beneficent faculty of fancy. Like Dickens' own original intention in the machinery of *Master Humphrey's Clock,* Caleb's manner of existence reveals an overindulgence in the kind of imaginative escapism that Dickens believed was contained in storybooks, although Caleb's excesses are now presented by Dickens simply to show their limitations. As the narrator remarks in a qualification of his initial statement: "I should have said that Caleb lived here, and his poor Blind Daughter somewhere else—in an enchanted home of Caleb's furnishing, where scarcity and shabbiness were not, and trouble never entered" (p. 182). Caleb has fallen into the habit of confusing "himself about himself and everything around him, for the love of his Blind Daughter." Later in the chapter, Caleb illustrates his customary method of concealing the unpleasantness of their life. When his daughter Bertha asks him to describe their room, Caleb responds, "It's much the same as usual. . . . Homely, but very snug. The gay colours on the walls; the bright flowers on the plates and dishes; the shining wood, where there are beams or panels; the general cheerfulness and neatness of the building; make it very pretty" (p. 189). As the narrator's commentary indicates, Caleb has deliberately departed from actuality into the world of fancy: "Cheerful and neat it was wherever Bertha's hands could busy themselves. But nowhere else, were cheerfulness and neatness possible, in the old crazy shed which Caleb's fancy so transformed" (p. 189). Like Jenny Wren, the crippled dressmaker of dolls in *Our Mutual Friend* who spins elaborate fantasies as solace in her constricted and impoverished existence, Bertha—who also works "as a Doll's dressmaker" (p. 184)—inhabits an enchanted world. In contrast to Jenny's later, artistically more sophisticated fantasies, however, the make-believe world in which Bertha dwells is not of her own making. Unlike Jenny, Bertha is both literally and metaphorically blind to the realities that surround her. Ultimately, Caleb recognizes his error when he finds that Bertha has fallen in love with the benevolent Tackleton whom he has described in the place of their bad-natured employer and has thus become grief-stricken at the news of the latter's impending marriage to May Fielding. Caleb sadly confesses to his daughter, "I have had concealments from you, put deceptions on you, God forgive me! and surrounded you with fancies" (p. 222). Bertha, softened from her initial "passion of regret" (p. 222) by the beneficent influence of the Cricket on the Hearth, then responds joyfully that her "eyes are open" (p. 223) so that she can now love her father as he truly is. In his treatment of Caleb and Bertha, Dickens seems to be working with the idea that, although the kind of temporary imaginative escapism offered by storybooks is invaluable "in this workaday world," one cannot and should not attempt to escape forever from the actualities of life. Caleb has clearly been misguided, although his error has been prompted by love. In another direction, the philosopher who is apparently intended to stand at the center of the next Christmas Book is more misguided yet.

VI

It is difficult to discern the center of Dickens' fourth Christmas Book, however, for while *The Cricket on the Hearth* lacked a definite focus, its successor, *The Battle of Life,* appears totally confused. Not surprisingly, the concept of reading is blurred in this confusion. In the *Cricket,* Dickens' repetition of the elements of supernatural machinery and a colloquial, ostensibly oral storyteller, which he had used with success in his earlier Christmas Books, had seemed jaded. In the *Battle,* Dickens dispensed with these elements without any corresponding artistic gain. The story itself is mawkishly sentimental; the plot is implausible; the characters are poorly motivated and thinly drawn. Much of this weakness stems from the difficulty that Dickens experienced in starting *The Battle of Life* and *Dombey and Son* at approximately the same time. As Dickens complained to Forster in September 1846, "The apparent impossibility of getting each into its place, coupled with that craving for streets, so thoroughly put me off the track, that, up to Wednesday or Thursday last, I really contemplated, at times, the total abandonment of the Christmas book this year, and the limitation of my labours to *Dombey and Son!* I cancelled the beginning of a first scene—which I have never done before—and, with a notion in my head, ran wildly about and about it, and could not get the idea into any natural socket. At length, thank Heaven, I nailed it all at once."[25]

Even with the opening scene "nailed," the *Battle* continued to be troublesome. Part way through the story, Dickens again complained to Forster, "to manage it without the supernatural agency now impossible of introduction, and yet to move it naturally within the required space, or with any shorter limit than a *Vicar of Wakefield,* I find to be a difficulty."[26] The allusion here to Goldsmith's novel is revealing. Slater has observed that "it is noticeable how Dickens's mind ran on Goldsmith in connection with this story,"[27] and Katherine Carolan has called attention to the similarities between *The Vicar of Wakefield* and *The Battle of Life,* which both depict two sisters of marriageable age as well as the elopement—real in the *Vicar* and feigned in the *Battle*—of one of them. Carolan contends, however, that "the . . . most important bond between the *Vicar* and the *Battle* . . . [is that] both books [are] profoundly informed with a religious spirit, in which the traditional teachings of Christianity serve as consolation and inspiration."[28] To some extent, Carolan's view is accurate. *The Battle of Life* is indeed markedly pervaded with Christian sentiment. However, Humphry House has astutely noted about Dickens that "one of the chief causes of his success as a popular moralist and reformer was the skill with which he struck a good religious note without committing himself beyond the common stock of Christian phrases."[29] Dickens seems to have primarily valued *The Vicar of Wakefield* not because of its "traditional teachings of Christianity," but simply because it was part of his own cherished childhood reading—among that small collection of books affectionately recreated in *David Copperfield* which, in David's words, "kept alive my fancy." Dickens' enthusiastic description of *The Vicar of Wakefield* to Miss Coutts in 1849 as "a book of which I think it is not too much to say that it has perhaps done more good in the world, and instructed more kinds of people in virtue, than any other fiction ever written"[30] needs to be considered in the light of his equally enthusiastic description of fairy tales four years later in "Frauds on the Fairies": "It would be hard to estimate the amount of gentleness and mercy that has made its way among us through these slight channels. Forbearance, courtesy, consideration for the poor and aged, kind treatment of animals, the love of nature, abhorrence of tyranny and brute force—many such good things have been first nourished in the child's heart by this powerful aid" (*Household Words,* 1 October 1853). Moreover, at the end of this 1853 essay, prompted by outrage at Cruikshank's tampering with "fairy text" to support contemporary propaganda, Dickens explicitly evokes Goldsmith's novel in support of his own belief in the fundamentally undogmatic nature of fairy tales: "The Vicar of Wakefield was wisest when he was tired of being always wise. The world is too much with us, early and late. Leave this precious old escape from it, alone."[31] Thus, in the context of the motif of reading, which again appears in *The Battle of Life,* the connection between this fourth Christmas Book and this fondly read novel of Dickens' own childhood warrants further exploration.

Like Goldsmith's vicar, the major character in Dickens' *Battle* is a man of learning. However, unlike Goldsmith's Doctor Primrose, who willingly acknowledges that "I was never much displeased with those innocent delusions that tend to make us more happy,"[32] Dickens' Doctor Jeddler openly expresses indifference to harmless human pleasures such as the enjoyment that his daughters find in dancing together at the opening of the story. In the words of the narrator of *The Battle of Life,* "Doctor Jeddler was . . . a great philosopher, and the heart and mystery of his philosophy was, to look upon the world as a gigantic practical joke; as something too absurd to be considered seriously, by any rational man" (*CB,* p. 243). As Carolan has observed, the contrast between the solace offered by philosophy and the more enduring comforts of religion in the sermon preached in prison by Doctor Primrose in *The Vicar of Wakefield* seems echoed in Doctor Jeddler's eventual conversion from his wrong-headed view of the world "as a gigantic practical joke."[33] However, rather than turning to traditional Christianity, Jeddler turns simply to an undogmatic attitude of fellow feeling. As Jeddler confesses at the end, "It's a world full of hearts . . . and a serious world, with all its folly—even with mine" (p. 308).

Furthermore, in depicting this change in Jeddler's personality, Dickens seems to have been influenced less by Primrose's faith in traditional Christianity than by his general attitude of benevolence and his love of books—secular as well as religious—which contribute to this benevolent frame of mind. For example, in chapter 23 of *The Vicar of Wakefield,* Primrose returns with his seduced and abandoned daughter to discover the fire that destroys his home and disables him, thus rendering him defenseless against his subsequent imprisonment for debt. He consoles himself and his family by reading "from the few books that were saved, and particularly from such as, by amusing the imagination, contributed to ease the heart."[34] In contrast, Doctor Jeddler ridicules his younger daughter's emotion at reading a sentimental passage from a book dealing with parting from home—shortly before the somewhat far-fetched plot presents her pretended elopement (and consequent victory in the "battle of life") so that her lover will marry her elder sister. As the unreformed Jeddler exclaims: "What! overcome by a story-book! . . . Print and paper! Well, well, it's all one. It's as rational to make a serious matter of print and paper as of anything else. But dry your eyes, love, dry your eyes. I dare say the heroine has got home again long ago, and made it up all round—and if she hasn't, a real home is only four walls; and a fictitious one, mere rags and ink" (p. 269). Jeddler's attitude here simply illustrates the "folly" that he ultimately renounces. Similarly, in what is apparently conceived as a humorous analogue of this central character's transformation, Jeddler's servant Benjamin Britain is at first morosely confused by Jeddler's pronouncements. However, Britain's fellow servant Clemency Newcome, "who was not much given to the study of books" (p. 255), eventually leads him out of his bewilderment by sharing with him her "pocket library" (p. 255)—a nutmeg grater bearing the motto "For-get and For-give" (p. 255) and a thimble which reads "Do as you—wold—be—done by" (p. 256). In gratitude for the change that this simplification of reading material effects in his personality, Benjamin marries Clemency and calls the inn they then keep The Nutmeg-Grater; eventually this name is changed to The Nutmeg-Grater and Thimble. Both Britain and Jeddler thus undergo a change of heart, and the alteration in their personalities is manifested in their attitude toward reading matter that inculcates fellow feeling.

The autobiographical implications of Dickens' reworking of ideas from *The Vicar of Wakefield* in this fashion are striking. Steven Marcus has provocatively suggested, prompted by Dickens' use of the letters "D.J." in Jeddler's name, that "Doctor Jeddler . . . is clearly some refraction of John Dickens"[35]—Charles Dickens' father. Besides the acknowledged problem of beginning the *Battle* in conjunction with *Dombey,* the mixed feelings toward this beloved but perennially irresponsible parent which perhaps surfaced in Dickens' depiction of the character of Jeddler—combined with the emotions undoubtedly stirred in Dickens' mind by recollections of Primrose's imprisonment for debt and the comfort the latter found in reading at a time of misfortune—may partially explain the difficulty Dickens experienced in shaping the material of this Christmas Book. Dickens' preoccupation with the traumatic experience of his childhood—his father's imprisonment and his own employment in the blacking warehouse—is evident in the autobiographical fragment that he apparently wrote, in part, in 1848.[36] In 1849, in the opening installments of *David Copperfield,* Dickens was able to distance and control this experience through the medium of fiction. In 1846, however, to the degree that they impinge upon *The Battle of Life,* these autobiographical pressures seem to be unmanageable. The *Battle* is a clear failure. It remains interesting in the context of Dickens' other Christmas Books only in terms of its treatment of the common motif of reading and its variation on the recurring topic of the value of the qualities contained in storybooks within "this workaday world."

VII

In contrast, *The Haunted Man* (which Dickens exhaustedly postponed to 1848 after his difficulty with the *Battle* in 1846) combines the motif of reading and the topic of storybooks with renewed vitality. As in *The Battle of Life,* the character who is to be converted from false values to true ones is an educated man—in this case, as the story rather melodramatically explains, "a learned man in chemistry, and a teacher on whose lips and hands a crowd of aspiring ears and eyes hung daily" (*CB,* p. 317). Once again, such learning has not taught, in Forster's words, this "over-thinking sage"[37] named Redlaw what he most needs to know. As in the *Carol*—but not in *The Battle of Life*—the customary pattern of conversion from erroneous to genuine values lies at the center of *The Haunted Man.* Here all of the details of the story are related to the metamorphosis experienced by the major character, although this change, contrary to Scrooge's exuberant transformation, is presented in subdued and psychological terms. Within this book, which has the appearance of a morality play, the forces of good and evil contend for the mastery of Redlaw's psyche. In keeping with the spirit of Christmas and the pattern of the other Christmas Books, the evil power—represented by a phantom that persuades Redlaw to relinquish his memory of "sorrow, wrong, and trouble" (p. 334)—ultimately fails to win. At the end, the power of good—represented by Milly, the gentle and innocent wife of the custodian of his college—removes the harm he has spread, restores his memory, and brings him to a better understanding of himself. As Stone has noted, Redlaw's unhappy memories of his now deceased sister's betrayal in love by Redlaw's own best friend—who then married the sweetheart whom Redlaw had hoped to wed after his rise from poverty—appear to be veiled allusions to Dickens' own early difficulties: "Redlaw's early history is a mosaic of references to Dickens' blacking-warehouse days, neglectful parents, struggles with shorthand, British Museum studies, and affair with Maria Beadnell; to sisterly Mary Hogarth's coming to live with him, taking pride in his fame, and dying in his arms expressing her love for him; and to sister Fanny's closeness to him as a child and self-effacing deathbed conversations with him."[38] However, unlike the awkward treatment of whatever autobiographical material may intrude into *The Battle of Life,* in *The Haunted Man* such references to Dickens' own life seem artistically controlled.

A primary ingredient in this control is Dickens' use of the idea of reading. Forster summarized Dickens' design, in the main plot of the story, as an underlying contrast between wisdom derived from study and wisdom derived from "the affections."[39] This contrast is made clear at the outset when Redlaw questions the extent to which forgetfulness of "sorrow, wrong, and trouble" will affect his memory of other things: "What shall I lose, if I assent to this? What else will pass from my remembrance?" (p. 335). In response, the Phantom explains that the amnesia being offered is only partial and that it will not affect the intellectual learning that Redlaw has so laboriously acquired: "No knowledge; no result of study; nothing but the intertwisted chain of feelings and associations, each in its turn dependent on, and nourished by, the banished recollections. Those will go" (p. 335). By the end of the story, the duplicity inherent in the Phantom's reassurance is apparent. Redlaw has discovered that memories of "sorrow, wrong, and trouble" are what make human beings human, and by accepting the Phantom's gift of oblivion as well as the ability to spread this gift to others, he has blighted not only himself but every human being with whom he has come in contact. In the end, Milly gently explains Redlaw's error to him in a manner that once again underscores the contrast between, in Forster's words, "the highest exercise of the intellect" and "the simplest form of the affections":

"I have no learning, and you have much," said Milly; "I am not used to think, and you are always thinking. May I tell you why it seems to me a good thing for us to remember wrong that has been done us?"

"Yes."

"That we may forgive it." (P. 393)

In other words, with his brand of what Yeats was later to describe as "blear-eyed wisdom [born] out of midnight oil," Redlaw has failed to perceive what more clear-sighted people like Milly have long since understood.

At the same time, this basic contrast between the wisdom of the head and the wisdom of the heart is explicitly linked with the concept of learning to read correctly. The motto "Lord Keep My Memory Green"—inscribed at the college beneath the portrait of "one of the learned gentlemen that helped endow us in Queen Elizabeth's time" (p. 326)—runs like a leitmotif through this Christmas Book. An important sign of Redlaw's transformation is the ability to read this motto with understanding. Early in Redlaw's career—at a time when old Philip Swidger (the former custodian of the college and father of the present custodian) recalls, "you was a student yourself, and worked so hard that you was backwards and forwards in our Library even at Christmastime" (p. 390)—it is not Redlaw but his sister who knows how to comprehend the motto. As old Philip continues his reminiscence,

One Christmas morning . . . that you come here with her—and it began to snow, and my wife invited the young lady to walk in, and sit by the fire that is always a-burning on Christmas Day in what used to be, before our ten poor gentlemen commuted, our great Dinner Hall. I was there; and I recollect, as I was stirring up the blaze for the young lady to warm her pretty feet by, she read the scroll out loud, that is underneath that picter. "Lord, keep my memory green!" She and my poor wife fell a-talking about it; and it's a strange thing to think of, now, that they both said (both being so unlike to die) that it was a good prayer, and that it was one they would put up very earnestly, if they were called away young, with reference to those who were dearest to them. "My brother," says the young lady—"My husband," says my poor wife.—"Lord, keep his memory of me green, and do not let me be forgotten!" (Pp. 390–91)

Ironically, Redlaw's memory of this sister's disappointment in love and subsequent early death is one of the sorrows that the Phantom tempts him to forget. However, by the end of his experience, as the concluding sentences make clear, he has finally learned to read this slogan with awareness: ". . . there was one thing in the Hall, to which the eyes of

Redlaw, and of Milly and her husband, and of the old man, . . . were often turned, which the shadows did not obscure or change. Deepened in its gravity by the firelight, and gazing from the darkness of the panelled wall like life, the sedate face in the portrait, with the beard and ruff, looked down at them from under its verdant wreath of holly, as they looked up at it; and, clear and plain below, as if a voice had uttered them, were the words 'Lord, keep my memory green' " (p. 398).

The motif of reading is also echoed in the subplot, dealing with the impoverished Tetterby family whose attitudes directly reflect the baneful influence of Redlaw, while he is afflicted with the Phantom's gift, and the healing counter-influence of Milly. When they are first introduced, despite their large numbers and cramped living quarters, the Tetterbys are cheerful. Mr. Tetterby, a newsvender by occupation, is attempting to read a newspaper: "A small man sat in a small parlour, partitioned off from a small shop by a small screen, pasted all over with small scraps of newspapers. In company with the small man, was almost any amount of small children you may please to name—at least, it seemed so; they made, in that very limited sphere of action, such an imposing effect, in point of numbers" (p. 339). The "small scraps of newspapers" covering Mr. Tetterby's screen prove to be clippings which he is in the habit of reading to his eight children for instructively emotional effect. Thus, after successfully subduing five boisterously exuberant sons who are supposed to be asleep as well as accidentally reprimanding and then embracing another child named Johnny, Mr. Tetterby reads to his children what he feels is an appropriate passage from the screen before settling down peacefully to his newspaper:

> "My little woman herself . . . could hardly have done it better! I only wish my little woman had had it to do, I do indeed!"
>
> Mr. Tetterby sought upon his screen for a passage appropriate to be impressed upon his children's minds on the occasion, and read the following.
>
> " 'It is an undoubted fact that all remarkable men have had remarkable mothers, and have respected them in after life as their best friends.' Think of your own remarkable mother, my boys," said Mr. Tetterby, "and know her value while she is still among you!"
>
> He sat down in his chair by the fire, and composed himself, cross-legged, over his newspaper. (Pp. 342–43)

However, after Redlaw, in possession of the Phantom's gift, visits their home on his way to see an ill student (who proves to be the son of Redlaw's own bygone sweetheart and best friend), the Tetterbys fall to wrangling. Husband and wife find fault with one another, and later in the story, Mr. and Mrs. Tetterby together quiet their brood in a scene which contrasts strikingly with the earlier one:

> Into the midst of this fray, Mr. and Mrs. Tetterby both precipitated themselves with great ardour, as if such ground were the only ground on which they could now agree; and having, with no visible remains of their late soft-heartedness, laid about them without any lenity, and done much execution, resumed their former relative positions.
>
> "You had better read your paper than do nothing at all," said Mrs. Tetterby.
>
> "What's there to read in a paper?" returned Mr. Tetterby, with excessive discontent.
>
> "What?" said Mrs. Tetterby. "Police!"
>
> "It's nothing to me," said Tetterby. "What do I care what people do, or are done to?"
>
> "Suicides," suggested Mrs. Tetterby.
>
> "No business of mine," replied her husband.
>
> "Births, deaths, and marriages, are those nothing to you?" said Mrs. Tetterby.
>
> "If the births were all over for good and all to-day; and the deaths were all to begin to come off to-morrow; I don't see why it should interest me, till I thought it was a-coming to my turn," grumbled Tetterby. "As to marriages, I've done it myself. I know quite enough about *them.*" (Pp. 381–82)

Like the unregenerate Scrooge, the disaffected Tetterby now feels that the misfortunes of others are "no business of mine." As the argument continues, moreover, this indifferent feeling of "what do I care what people do, or are done to?" extends to Tetterby's attitude toward his habit of reading to his children:

> To judge from the dissatisfied expression of her face and manner, Mrs. Tetterby appeared to entertain the same opinions as her husband; but she opposed him, nevertheless, for the gratification of quarrelling with him.
>
> "Oh, you're a consistent man," said Mrs. Tetterby, "an't you? You, with the screen of your own making there, made of nothing else but bits of newspaper, which you sit and read to the children by the half-hour together!"
>
> "Say used to, if you please," returned her husband. "You won't find me doing so any more. I'm wiser, now."
>
> "Bah! wiser, indeed!" said Mrs. Tetterby. "Are you better?"
>
> The question sounded some discordant note in Mr. Tetterby's breast.

. . . .

He turned to the screen, and traced about it with his finger, until he found a certain paragraph of which he was in quest.

"This used to be one of the family favourites, I recollect," said Tetterby, in a forlorn and stupid way, "and used to draw tears from the children, and make 'em good, if there was any little bickering or discontent among 'em, next to the story of the robin redbreasts in the wood. 'Melancholy case of destitution. Yesterday a small man, with a baby in his arms, and surrounded by half-a-dozen ragged little ones, of various ages between ten and two, the whole of whom were evidently in a famishing condition, appeared before the worthy magistrate, and made the following recital:'— Ha! I don't understand it, I'm sure," said Tetterby; "I don't see what it has got to do with us." (P. 382)

Before Redlaw's "over-thinking" mistake, in contrast to Trotty Veck in *The Chimes,* Tetterby knows how to interpret what he reads. One example of this ability to present potentially depressing material from newspapers in the beneficently human light that Dickens believed was nourished by storybooks is the way in which, as Tetterby forlornly recollects, his account of the clipping describing "a small man, with a baby in his arms, and surrounded by half-a-dozen ragged little ones" formerly could heal disagreement among his own children ("next to the story of the robin redbreasts in the wood"). Redlaw's error temporarily negates this ability. However, Milly's influence—which eventually restores harmony among the Tetterbys—presumably returns it just as her influence teaches Redlaw how to comprehend the implications of the motto beneath the ancient portrait.

The idea of reading in this Christmas Book is evident not only in the shift in Tetterby's ability to find meaning in the newspaper and Redlaw's ability to understand the often-repeated motto but in two significant references to "old nursery tales" from Dickens' own childhood. The more explicit of these two allusions derives from *The Tales of the Genii,* the didactic, pseudo-oriental collection of short stories, written in imitation of *The Arabian Nights,* which David Copperfield, less than a year after *The Haunted Man,* lists as part of his cherished library. In general, the similarity between *The Tales of the Genii* and Dickens' Christmas Books is striking. Like the basic pattern of the Christmas Books, each of the *Tales* focuses upon a misguided mortal who learns to mend his ways through supernatural means. Despite what now seem almost ludicrous weaknesses in language and characterization, the *Tales* appear to have served, at least in part, as remembered models for the kind of Christmas fiction that Dickens desired to write. At the same time, more specifically, the relationship between *The Tales of the Genii* and *The Haunted Man* is not confined to similarities of moral intention and plot. In his description of a storm at the beginning of this final Christmas Book, the narrator of *The Haunted Man* reinforces an allusion to Ali Baba's ill-fated brother (from a tale usually considered part of *The Arabian Nights*) with a reference to the less familiar merchant Abudah:

> When travellers by land were bitter cold, and looked wearily on gloomy landscapes, rustling and shuddering in the blast. When mariners at sea, outlying upon icy yards, were tossed and swung above the howling ocean dreadfully. When lighthouses, on rocks and headlands, showed solitary and watchful; and benighted sea-birds breasted on against their ponderous lanterns, and fell dead. When little readers of story-books, by the firelight, trembled to think of Cassim Baba cut into quarters, hanging in the Robbers' cave, or had some small misgivings that the fierce little old woman with the crutch, who used to start out of the box in the merchant Abudah's bedroom, might, one of these nights, be found upon the stairs, in the long, cold, dusky journey up to bed. (P. 319)

These two storybook scenes, emphasized in the original illustration at the beginning of the first chapter, make important contributions to the sense of frightening desolation pervading this description, but their function is not simply that of atmosphere. Both of these allusions suggest the danger of dissatisfaction, a fault of which "the haunted man" proves to be guilty. Moreover, the reference to "the fierce little old woman with the crutch," from the first "tale of the Genii," seems particularly linked to the alteration in Redlaw's character.

Jack Lindsay observes that the story of the merchant Abudah and the tormenting hag "lies at the heart of . . . [*The*] *Haunted Man,*"[40] but he is primarily concerned with relating this Christmas Book to Dickens' own inner turmoil, and he does not explore the implications of this remark. Nevertheless, the similarities between Abudah and "the haunted man," in both phases of his personality, are well worth exploring. Egged onward by the old woman, the merchant Abudah vainly searches for the talisman of Oromanes, "the which whoever possesseth shall know neither uneasiness nor discontent."[41] After many fruitless adventures, Abudah finally discovers "that human nature, which is imperfect, cannot attain to perfection; that true happiness, which is the real talisman of Oromanes, being immortal, can be enjoyed by immortals alone: that man, being a creature, is subject to the commands of his Creator; and therefore a knowledge of his will, and a faithful obedience to it, should be the first and last pursuit of mortality."[42] He learns "to be content,—the utmost man must expect on earth . . . to be obedient to Alla, to love and cherish . . . [his] family, and to do good to mankind."[43] Like the merchant, the protagonist of *The Haunted Man* recklessly seeks relief from disturbing thoughts—in this case, his memories of "sorrow, wrong, and trouble." Like Abudah, Redlaw learns that human beings cannot achieve happiness by attempting to escape sorrow. The unhappy chemist discovers that such memories are humanizing impulses, and they are part of "the beneficent design of Heaven" (p. 379). He resolves not to brood alone at Christmas but rather to "protect . . . teach . . . and reclaim" (p. 397) the homeless and savage child with whom he has been compared, "as Christmas is a time in which, of all times in the year, the memory of every remediable sorrow, wrong, and trouble in the world around us, should be active with us, not less than our own experiences, for all good" (p. 397). In this fashion, the seemingly casual allusion to *The Tales of the Genii* with which *The Haunted Man* begins foreshadows Redlaw's eventual transformation.

The figure of the savage child whom the reeducated Redlaw vows to educate seems less explicitly but equally closely linked to Dickens' childhood reading. As Forster noted, part of Dickens' general purpose in the Christmas Books was to encourage his readers "to play the Valentine with our wilder brothers, and bring them back with brotherly care to civilization and happiness." Although the tale of Valentine and Orson is not explicitly mentioned in this Christmas Book, it seems to underlie many of the details of *The Haunted Man.* In brief, the story of Valentine and Orson (first recorded in an early French romance), which was popular in chapbooks and collections of nursery tales in Dickens' childhood and is recollected excitedly in *A Christmas Carol* by the reforming Scrooge, describes the adventures of twin brothers. The first, Valentine, is discovered in a forest as an infant and raised at court to be a knight, while the second, Orson, is carried off by a bear and brought up in the woods. Eventually, Orson is found and civilized by Valentine.[44] In a similar fashion, Redlaw in *The Haunted Man* is repeatedly paired with the brutish child whom Milly has found and brought home to Redlaw's college—a child whom the narrator initially describes as "a baby savage, a young monster, a child who had never been a child, a creature who might live to take the outward form of man, but who, within, would live and perish a mere beast" (p. 337). To Redlaw's horror, he discovers that this child alone is impervious to the baneful gift of amnesia which he spreads wherever he goes and that, on three potentially but vainly softening occasions, as they walk beside one another on Redlaw's misguided errand to extend this noxious influence to greatly suffering individuals, "the expression on the boy's face was the expression on his own" (p. 364). Later, the Phantom emphasizes Redlaw's affinity with this "young monster" and explains, "This . . . is the last, completest illustration of a human creature, utterly bereft of such remembrances as you have yielded up. No softening memory of sorrow, wrong, or trouble enters here, because this wretched mortal from his birth has been abandoned to a worse condition than the beasts, and has, within his knowledge, no one contrast, no humanising touch, to make a grain of such a memory spring up in his hardened breast. All within this desolate creature is barren wilderness. All within the man bereft of what you have resigned, is the same barren wilderness" (p. 378).

In the depiction of the Phantom—"ghastly and cold, colourless in its leaden face and hands, but with his [Redlaw's] features, and his bright eyes, and his grizzled hair, and dressed in the gloomy shadow of his dress" (pp. 330–31)—Dickens appears to be deliberately working with the figure of the double, a type of apparition that he facetiously suggested in an anonymous review in the *Examiner* in February 1848 was "so common among learned professors and studious men in Germany, that they have no need of the Kilmarnock weaver's prayer for grace to see themselves as others see them."[45] At the same time, the details of the story suggest that not only the Phantom but also the baby savage is intended to serve as Redlaw's alter ego, and that the child is ultimately the more ominous of these other selves. As the Phantom explains, the social implications of abandoned and neglected children of this type are terrifying: "There is not . . . one of these—not one—but shows a harvest that mankind MUST REAP. From every seed of evil in this boy, a field of ruin is grown that shall be gathered in, and garnered up, and sown again in many places in the world, until regions are overspread with wickedness enough to raise the waters of another Deluge. Open and unpunished murder in a city's streets would be less guilty in its daily toleration, than one such spectacle as this" (p. 378). In this Christmas Book, Dickens appears to be mingling what he viewed as the supernatural convention of the double with the nursery-tale legend of Valentine's reclamation of his savage twin, and the traces of this nursery tale, like the allusion to Abudah's transformation, reinforce Redlaw's regeneration. In the end, like Valentine embracing Orson, Redlaw looks upon the child "with compassion and a fellow-feeling" (p. 392). Thus, this nursery tale provides a pattern for Redlaw's conversion as well as the conversion that Dickens wished his own "higher form" of nursery tale to effect in his readers' hearts.

VIII

Like *A Christmas Carol, The Haunted Man* offers a notable illustration of the fanciful values Dickens believed modern versions of "old nursery tales" could encourage. Moreover, this faith in the imaginatively and emotionally nurturing qualities of such storybooks in a "workaday world" may partially explain Dickens' enthusiastic welcome of Hans Christian Andersen during the latter's visit to England in 1847. At the time of this visit, the Danish writer was already famous as the author not only of novels but also of fairy tales like "The Little Mermaid," a story to which Dickens specifically alluded in their initial conversation.[46] Dickens greeted Andersen with eagerness, and Andersen responded to Dickens' friendship with delight. Back in Denmark once again, Andersen dedicated a volume containing "seven short stories" to Dickens, and the tone of this dedication indicates the apparent affinity that the two writers had evidently discovered between one another:

> I feel a desire, a longing, to transplant in England the first produce of my poetic garden, as a Christmas greeting; and I send it to you, my dear, noble, Charles Dickens, who by your works had been previously dear to me, and since our meeting have taken root for ever in my heart.
>
> Your hand was the last that pressed mine on England's coast; it was you who from her shores wafted me the last farewell. It is therefore natural that I should send to you, from Denmark, my first greeting again, as sincerely as an affectionate heart can convey it.[47]

It seems significant here that Andersen chose to dedicate a collection of "short stories" to Dickens "as a Christmas greeting," and Dickens seems to have reacted to Andersen at this point primarily as the author of tales resembling those that he delighted to remember from his childhood. For example, he wrote to Andersen in reply to the latter's dedication, "Your book made my Christmas fireside, happier. We were all charmed with it. The little boy, and the old man, and the pewter soldier, are my particular favorites. I read that story over and over again, with the most unspeakable delight."[48]

Even more revealingly, the books—collections primarily of short writings—which he laid out for Andersen on the latter's less successful return visit to England illustrate not only what he apparently viewed as Andersen's taste in short stories but also what the evidence of the Christmas Books and the cancelled machinery of *Master Humphrey's Clock* indicates was his own. As Andersen wrote to Henriette Wulff from Gadshill in 1857, "Here in the country books for reading were placed upon my table: 'The fairy Family', 'Arabian Nights', 'Sir Roger de Coverley by the Spectator' and 'Works of W. Irving'. You will see from this what Dickens judged to be my taste."[49] In a similar fashion, Dickens' earlier reception of Andersen in 1847 suggests Dickens' own concerns. At this stage in his career, while he was clarifying his views about the place of short stories in the contemporary world and attempting to illustrate these theories in his own storybooks for the Christmas season, Andersen's tales seem to have confirmed his faith in the potential success of the type of short fiction that he was currently creating.

However, *The Haunted Man,* in 1848, was the last of Dickens' Christmas Books. Dickens' reason for abandoning this now established form seems partly a sense, as he later wrote to W. H. Wills, that "the idea . . . was wearing out."[50] In practical terms, he was undoubtedly affected by the "growing coolness towards the series" which Slater has noted among readers and reviewers after *The Cricket on the Hearth.*[51] In artistic terms, he may have grown frustrated by a feeling (such as that about which he complained in his procrustean struggle with *The Battle of Life*) that he was attempting to force material, which might better be developed in novels, into an unsuitably short format. Also, he may simply have tired of repeating the usual pattern of the exchange of false values for true ones through supernatural means. Nonetheless, the Christmas Books occupy a critical position in Dickens' treatment of the short story. In the first of these books, *A Christmas Carol,* Dickens achieved his most enduring artistic and popular triumph in what he described in his dedication of *The Cricket on the Hearth* as a "Little Story" (p. 156). All of Dickens' Christmas writings after the *Carol* were, to some extent, affected by his and his readers' recollections of that success. Moreover, both by their presence and by their concern with the motif of reading—often explicitly linked with the topic of storybooks—the Christmas Books as a group reveal Dickens' preoccupation in the 1840s with the role of "story-books . . . in this workaday world." By 1850, Dickens' concern with nurturing the element of fancy through such storybooks was, to a great degree, incorporated in his scheme for *Household Words* (which was to be largely filled with short writing—including, in Forster's words, "short stories by others as well as himself"[52]—and which was designed to "cherish that light of Fancy which is inherent in the human breast"). Thus, Dickens may have set aside the concept of Christmas Books partly as a result of his awareness that this new periodical provided an outlet for many of the ideas that he had been attempting to express in the Christmas Book format. At the same time, in the very differently organized Christmas numbers of *Household Words* and its successor *All the Year Round,* he retained the opportunity for holiday antidotes to workaday life.

# CHAPTER 4

The Chord of the Christmas Season

And I *do* come home at Christmas. We all do, or
we all should. We all come home, or ought to
come home, for a short holiday—the longer, the
better—from the great boarding-school, where we
are for ever working at our arithmetical slates, to
take, and give a rest.

DICKENS, "A Christmas Tree"

I

As children know and adults try to remember, Christmas is a time for
games. It is a season when children yearn for grown-up pastimes, while
grown-ups delight in juvenile ones, and nowhere is this sense of play
more apparent than in Dickens' familiar descriptions of holiday festivity. At Dingley Dell, Pickwick and his friends frolic under the mistletoe
and pursue one another in blindman's buff, while, in *A Christmas Carol,*
the reformed Scrooge revels at his nephew's home in a "wonderful
party, wonderful games, wonderful unanimity, wonderful happiness!"
(*CB,* p. 75). Like too much turkey, unfortunately, even "wonderful
games" can grow tiresome. *A Christmas Carol* is a brief masterpiece,
and Dickens' holiday excursions into the world of fancy in *The Chimes*
and *The Haunted Man* well repay artistic examination. However, some
of Dickens' other Christmas writings are undeniably little more than
potboilers—created to make the most of the Christmas market—or
perfunctory holiday tributes, produced to avoid leaving "any gap at
Christmas firesides which I ought to fill."[1] Nevertheless, not all of Dickens' Christmas writings after *The Haunted Man* deserve the oblivion to
which they have customarily been consigned. Indeed, the holiday
pieces Dickens composed annually from 1850 to 1867, commonly collected under the misleading title of *Christmas Stories,* seem to have
been largely ignored in critical discussions merely because, as with
many bygone holiday pastimes, the conventions that originally gov-

erned them have largely been forgotten. In particular, the anecdotal description of two eloping children presented by the Boots at the Holly-Tree Inn, first published in the Christmas number of *Household Words* for 1855, offers a notable illustration of the unusual circumstances that gave rise to Dickens' "Christmas Stories" as well as Dickens' concept of the appropriately playful nature of Christmas fiction.

II

As the format in which it first appeared makes clear, Dickens originally conceived this piece, entitled simply "The Boots," as an enclosed Christmas tale. Although "The Boots" is now customarily contained in *Christmas Stories* as the "Second Branch: The Boots," included in a three-part work entitled "The Holly-Tree," it was initially intended to serve as the third section of a seven-part work called *The Holly-Tree Inn*, published as an extra number of *Household Words* for Christmas, 1855. All of the other writings standardly reprinted as *Christmas Stories* are detached sections of larger creations which originally appeared, beginning in 1850, as the Christmas numbers of *Household Words* and its successor in 1859, *All the Year Round.* In marked contrast to the Christmas Books which Dickens wrote in the 1840s, these later holiday productions were composite creations in which Dickens joined his own writing with that of other hands (see Appendix A). Initially, such seasonal publications were simple affairs. The Christmas number for 1850 is merely a regular issue whose contents focus on the subject of Christmas. Subsequently, however, the annual issue grew into a separate and increasingly elaborate endeavor, and Dickens gradually hit upon a scheme, which Scheherazade might well have envied, for enclosing the contributions by other authors within his own overarching designs. His customary method became one of outlining a principal narrative—standardly written by himself but in a few cases composed in collaboration with Wilkie Collins—which usually, but not always, formed the first and last chapters of the Christmas number. This framing narrative, in turn, typically gave some excuse for interpolated pieces written by various contributors and occasionally by Dickens.

Today, far removed from their original contexts and grouped under the heading of *Christmas Stories,* Dickens' portions of these productions can seem strangely constructed and mysterious, even in the case of writings like the "Three Branches" of "The Holly-Tree," which can stand to a large extent without the work of his collaborators.[2] For example, without a knowledge of the tales narrated by "The Ostler," "The Landlord," "The Barmaid," and "The Poor Pensioner" (interpolated into the framework for *The Holly-Tree Inn*, in addition to Dickens' own story "The Boots"), the extended opening chapter of this

Christmas number is apt to strike modern readers who confront it in *Christmas Stories* as an artistically unbalanced "long preamble of a tale" (in the words of Chaucer's Friar) without the stylistic excuse of the Wife of Bath's notorious loquaciousness. However, to make critical sense of the "Christmas Stories," a reader must ignore their often odd appearance in their usual collected format and concentrate instead on the individual sections composed by Dickens in light of the circumstances for which they were originally created. The majority of the "Christmas Stories" should be viewed simply as frameworks (sometimes incompletely reprinted) or detached, originally interpolated tales. Thus both the complete, customarily two-part frameworks and the individual tales can usually be analyzed as self-contained stories in Dickens' own loose sense of the short story. In this context, like "The Story of the Goblins who stole a Sexton" in *Pickwick,* "The Boots" stands as one of several interpolated tales within a larger work. As an inset tale, "The Boots" has important links with its framing narrative, but it also legitimately can and should be analyzed in its own right.

Such analysis, moreover, illuminates Dickens' view of the style and material appropriate for Christmas. Unlike the Christmas tale in *Pickwick* and the subsequent Christmas Books, which all have some obvious tie with the holiday season (a period that for Dickens extended from Christmas Eve to Twelfth Night on January 6th),[3] "The Boots" and many of the other "Christmas Stories" seemingly have little connection with the actual holiday that evoked them. Nevertheless, as Dickens explained to one contributor in 1852 who failed to understand his somewhat confusing directions, writings for the Christmas numbers were intended to contain "suitable Christmas interest" and to "strike the chord of the season."[4] Dickens' other contributions to the Christmas numbers between 1850 and 1867 will be examined in more detail later in this chapter, as well as in chapters 5 and 7. At this point, "The Boots" warrants detailed discussion. Written by Dickens out of a sense of dissatisfaction with the contributions by most of his co-authors in this holiday number for 1855,[5] "The Boots" provides an especially striking and in many ways resonant sounding of what Dickens viewed as the seasonal chord.

The underlying principle of this piece, containing the Boots' account of a remarkable juvenile elopement, as paraphrased by the first-person narrator of the framework of the Christmas number, is the contrast between the idyllic experience that it describes and the customary realities of life. Its purpose in this Christmas number is to help beguile an enforced stay at the Holly-Tree Inn by the snowbound first-person narrator. From the outset, in the paraphrased words of Boots, its central occurrence lies outside the realm of ordinary existence:

What was the curiousest thing he [Boots] had seen? Well! He didn't know. He couldn't momently name what was the curiousest thing he had seen,—unless it was a Unicorn,—and he seen *him* once at a Fair. But supposing a young gentleman not eight year old was to run away with a fine young woman of seven, might I think *that* a queer start? Certainly. Then that was a start as he himself had had his blessed eyes on, and he had cleaned the shoes they run away in—and they was so little that he couldn't get his hand into 'em. (*CS*, p. 116)

Viewed by the standards of the familiar adult world, Master Harry Walmers' romance with his beloved Norah and his ultimate decision to run away with her to be married at Gretna Green is as incongruous as the appearance of their diminutive shoes among the usual adult footgear at the inn, and much of the piece simply emphasizes this incongruity. The lovers are dwarfed by an "e-normous sofa" (p. 120), unencumbered by any practical luggage, and delayed in their matrimonial mission by an elaborate falsehood about a pony which ostensibly will take them to their journey's end. The prevailing tone—underscored by the colloquial idiom of the down-to-earth Boots, a person so thoroughly identified with his daily occupation that it serves as a substitute for his true name Cobbs—is one of wistful participation in an experience that to adult eyes can only be a "curious" event.

As discussed in chapter 3, Harry Stone has observed that Dickens conceived his Christmas Books as versions of fairy tales, and Dickens also explained that he intended "The Boots" to have "something of the effect of a Fairy Story out of the most unlikely materials."[6] As Boots explains when he recognizes the children, ascertains their intention, and sends the owner of the inn for the grown-ups who normally have them in charge, "he wished with all his heart there was any impossible place where those two babies could make an impossible marriage, and live impossibly happy ever afterwards. However, as it couldn't be, he went into the Governor's plans, and the Governor set off for York in half an hour" (p. 122). The real world, as both the listener at the Holly-Tree Inn and the reader well know, is not a fairy-tale one in which seven-year-old children can wed and "live impossibly happy ever afterwards." Indeed, their elopement has apparently been prompted by earlier adult scoffing, and they can play at preparing to keep house in this Edenic fashion only within the perimeter of the Holly-Tree Inn where they are aided by the protection and conscious deception of the overseeing Boots. Their paradise is inherently an unstable one. Even at the Holly-Tree, Norah grows irritable as time passes, and inevitably, although gently and still under the protective observation of Boots, the outside world asserts its power. The children's guardians arrive and understandingly, but firmly, return the would-be bride and groom to their respectively maturing lives. Nonetheless, the note of contrast with actuality is maintained to the end. As the first-person narrator points out, in recording this episode, "In conclusion, Boots put it to me whether I hold with him in two opinions: firstly, that there are not many couples on their way to be married who are half as innocent of guile as those two children; secondly, that it would be a jolly good thing for a great many couples on their way to be married, if they could only be stopped in time, and brought back separately" (p. 126). Like all games where adults join with children, the experience has been one in which its juvenile participants play intently while its more worldly participants play semiseriously as a temporary escape from the more complex realities which they know.

Moreover, the sense of temporary enjoyment of a normally impossible game, evident in this episode, is intimately linked with Dickens' concept of Christmas. Specifically, "The Boots" illustrates the breakdown of workaday restraint and the consequent indulgence in fellow feeling and temporary imaginative escapism which, as explained in chapter 3, Dickens believed the fanciful license of Christmas time entailed. The motif of children playing at marriage, manifested in "The Boots," is one that recurs in Dickens' short writing, from the youthful imitators of "The Young Couple" in *Sketches of Young Couples* (1840) early in his career to their somewhat cloying cousins in "Holiday Romance" (1868) near its end. For example, the narrator of "A Christmas Tree," from the Christmas number for 1850, alludes ironically to Little Red Riding Hood: "She was my first love. I felt that if I could have married Little Red Riding-Hood, I should have known perfect bliss" (*CS*, p. 7). Likewise, the narrator whose youthful memories prove to be the "ghost in Master B.'s room" in *The Haunted House* (the Christmas number for 1859) yearns nostalgically for "my little sister, . . . my angelic little wife, and . . . the boy I went to school with" (*CS*, p. 244) and amusingly recollects the pleasures and administrative problems of the make-believe seraglio which he organized with eight girls long ago at school. More occidentally but still blissfully, the concluding chapter of *Mrs. Lirriper's Lodgings* (the Christmas number for 1863) ends with a picture of happily-ever-after living envisioned by Mrs. Lirriper's adopted grandson Jemmy in which two schoolboys marry their schoolmaster's daughters and gallop away to an existence where money never vanishes and no one ever ages, quarrels, or dies. The idea seems artistically most successful when it is most clearly countered by a more worldly frame of mind, as in the allusion to Red Riding Hood, and it achieves what is perhaps its most significant expression in *The Holly-Tree Inn,* refracted through the understanding eyes of the deceivingly playful Boots. The impulse behind this recurring motif undoubtedly lies at least partly in Dickens' personal disappointments with women and the growing marital unhappiness which led him to separate from his wife in 1858. The opportunity for permissible escapism and generalized fellow feeling which he found preeminently in Christmas writing and, to a certain degree, in much of his other short work, probably goes far toward explaining the repeated image of asexual juvenile passion. In this particular case, earlier in the same year in which he wrote "The Boots," Dickens had been profoundly disappointed by the middle-aged reappearance of his lost adolescent sweetheart Maria Beadnell, and the memories stirred by this event, reflected more pessimistically in the bygone love of Arthur Clennam and Flora Finching in *Little Dorrit,* seem to have likewise prompted the romance of Master Harry Walmers and "Mrs. Harry Walmers, Junior, that was never to be" (p. 126). The primary point here, however, is not the way in which this interlude at the Holly-Tree may reflect a response to unpleasant realities in Dickens' own life but the way in which it differs from all lives and the manner in which it offers an extended version of the childhood game of playing house as suitable Christmas fare.

In the larger context of this Christmas number, the episode is part of the means by which the diffident narrator of Dickens' framework manages, at Christmas time, to overcome his "inherent bashfulness" (p. 116) and become concerned with "the lives of those by whom I find myself surrounded" (p. 129), a decision which permits him to share in the spirit of the season and ultimately leads to a resolution of the misunderstanding which initially separated him from his fiancée. The heart of *The Holly-Tree Inn,* however, is not the conventionally successful adult romance which frames it but the idyllically unsuccessful juvenile romance which is enclosed, and this enclosed romance, like all impossible dreams, paradoxically seems more genuine than the artificial conventions of the adult world. The reasons for this apparent authenticity rest in the wider knowledge of the more calculating "game" of later life with which this juvenile game is hedged. As Boots explains to his listener at the inn (as paraphrased by the first-person narrator):

> Boots don't know—perhaps I do,—but never mind, it don't signify either way—why it made a man fit to make a fool of himself to see them two pretty babies a lying there in the clear still sunny day, not dreaming half so hard when they was asleep as they done when they was awake. But, Lord! when you come to think of yourself, you know, and what a game you have been up to ever since you was in your own cradle, and what a poor sort of a chap you are, and how it's always either Yesterday with you, or else To-morrow, and never To-day, that's where it is! (P. 124)[7]

Actuality will of course intrude, and cynical readers will dismiss this episode as only holiday nonsense. Nonetheless, for a few fleeting moments, snowbound from reality and snug at the Holly-Tree Inn, "The Boots" exemplifies the note of sympathetic play that Dickens felt belonged to Christmas.

III

As Dickens well knew by the 1850s, both successful holiday celebrations and successful writing are seldom as unpremeditated as they appear. Many of Dickens' contributions during the eighteen years in which he created Christmas numbers do not "strike the chord of the season" as skillfully as "The Boots." Part of this undeniable weakness in some of Dickens' holiday work between 1850 and 1867 is undoubtedly due to intermittent feelings of the same kind of impatience on Dickens' part which he jokingly attributed to his caricature of a "Voluntary Correspondent" (an amateur author of unsolicited contributions to *Household Words*) in 1853:

> He [the "Voluntary Correspondent"] has a general idea that literature is the easiest amusement in the world. He figures a successful author as a radiant personage whose whole time is devoted to idleness and pastime—who keeps a prolific mind in a sort of corn-sieve, and lightly shakes a bushel of it out sometimes, in an odd half hour after breakfast. It would amaze his incredulity beyond all measure, to be told that such elements as patience, study, punctuality, determination, self-denial, training of mind and body, hours of application and seclusion to produce what he reads in seconds, enter into such a career. He has no more conception of the necessity of entire devotion to it, than he has of an eternity from the beginning. Correction and re-correction in the blotted manuscript, consideration, new observation, the patient massing of many reflections, experiences and imaginings for one minute purpose, and the patient separation from the heap of all the fragments that will unite to serve it—these would be Unicorns or Griffins to him—fables altogether.[8]

From time to time, Dickens apparently lost interest in what he occasionally viewed as simply a seasonal necessity. As he complained half-jokingly to Charles Fechter in March 1868, "I feel as if I had murdered a Christmas number years ago (perhaps I did!) and its ghost perpetually haunted me."[9]

Some of the lack of vitality evident at intervals in such "murdered" numbers is undoubtedly attributable to the difficulties experienced by Dickens in finding a suitable arrangement for a multi-author form of composition. As he wrote more seriously to Wills, a few months after his earlier complaint to Fechter and shortly before deciding to drop the annual production altogether, "I have been, and still am—which is worse—in a positive state of despair about the Xmas No. I cannot get an idea for it which is in the least satisfactory to me, and yet I have been steadily trying all this month. I have invented so many of these Christmas Nos. and they are so profoundly unsatisfactory after all with the introduced stories and their want of cohesion or originality, that I fear I am sick of the thing."[10] Nevertheless, in retrospect, some of Dickens' contributions to the Christmas numbers seem more satisfactory than others, and, in any case, all of his writings for these annual occasions remain significant. As K. J. Fielding has wisely commented, "Certainly Dickens cannot be fully understood without the Christmas Stories."[11] Two notable developments—technical experiments of the type which the Voluntary Correspondent would dismiss as "Unicorns or Griffins" —deserve particular attention among the Christmas numbers that Dickens "invented" during the uneasily formative, initial twelve years (1850–1861) of these holiday productions: his experimentation with depicting what he viewed as the realm of the imagination and his experimentation with a period of close collaboration with Wilkie Collins.

IV

The first of these developments stems from Dickens' belief, evident in the Christmas Books as well as "The Boots," that Christmas provided a splendid excuse for a temporary imaginative escape from everyday actuality. Indeed, "A Christmas Tree," Dickens' principal contribution to the initial Christmas number of *Household Words* in 1850, focuses directly on this idea of an imaginative vacation. In actuality, this piece is not a short story, even in Dickens' loose concept of that term. It is rather an impressionistic sketch, on the boundary between fiction and nonfiction, and it is commonly included among the "Christmas Stories" simply because it was originally published in one of Dickens' Christmas numbers. Nonetheless, it warrants an important niche in Dickens' writings, for it offers an enthusiastic catalog of what for Dickens constituted the ingredients of the world of childhood imagination.

The sketch begins with the narrator's description of a recently observed Christmas tree—lavishly trimmed with toys and other decorations—whose "motley collection of odd objects, clustering on the tree like magic fruit, and flashing back the bright looks directed towards it from every side . . . made a lively realisation of the fancies of childhood" (*CS,* pp. 3–4). He then empathically allows his own generalized recollections to enter into such early "fancies": "my thoughts are drawn back, by a fascination which I do not care to resist, to my own childhood. I begin to consider, what do we all remember best upon the branches

69

of the Christmas Tree of our own young Christmas days, by which we climbed to real life" (p. 4). The first components of this remembered world—reminiscent of the childish world that Dickens created less felicitously in *The Cricket on the Hearth*—are toys, sometimes amusing, sometimes terrifying, and sometimes both, such as "the Tumbler with his hands in his pockets, who wouldn't lie down, but whenever he was put upon the floor, persisted in rolling his fat body about, until he rolled himself still, and brought those lobster eyes of his to bear upon me— when I affected to laugh very much, but in my heart of hearts was extremely doubtful of him" (p. 4). After toys come children's books— "thin books, in themselves, at first, but many of them, and with deliciously smooth covers of bright red or green" (pp. 6–7)—and the narrator, re-creating the tactile as well as the cognitive aspects of his childhood memories, becomes more and more excited by and involved within his recollections as the world that he is describing becomes that of "the bright Arabian Nights" (p. 8):

> Oh, now all common things become uncommon and enchanted to me. All lamps are wonderful; all rings are talismans. Common flower-pots are full of treasure, with a little earth scattered on the top; trees are for Ali Baba to hide in; beefsteaks are to throw down into the Valley of Diamonds, that the precious stones may stick to them, and be carried by the eagles to their nests, whence the traders, with loud cries, will scare them. Tarts are made, according to the recipe of the Vizier's son of Bussorah, who turned pastrycook after he was set down in his drawers at the gate of Damascus; cobblers are all Mustaphas, and in the habit of sewing up people cut into four pieces, to whom they are taken blindfold. (P. 8)

The Arabian Nights are kaleidoscopically followed by "a prodigious nightmare" (p. 9) which, in turn, gives way to recollections of plays about "the devoted dog of Montargis," "poor Jane Shore, dressed all in white, and with her brown hair hanging down," and "George Barnwell [who] killed the worthiest uncle that ever man had, and was afterwards so sorry for it that he ought to have been let off," succeeded by the comforting "Pantomine—stupendous Phenomenon!—when clowns are shot from loaded mortars into the great chandelier" (p. 10) and then "the toy-theatre . . . and all its attendant occupation with paste and glue, and gum, and water colours. . . . In spite of a few besetting accidents and failures . . . a teeming world of fancies . . . suggestive and all-embracing" (pp. 10–11). Unlike the escapism advocated in *Master Humphrey's Clock,* the narrator's indulgence in such "fancies" here is clearly temporary, although, as he admits, the "bright" world can momentarily be dazzling: "Now . . . I perceive my first experience of the dreary sensation—often to return in after-life—of being unable, next day, to get back to the dull, settled world; of wanting to live for ever in the bright atmosphere I have quitted" (p. 10).

For the occasion of this Christmas sketch, however, the narrator's transitory escape from the "dull, settled world" is legitimate, and the dissolution of his personality becomes more and more apparent as he enters more and more deeply into the imaginative world that he is depicting. Part way through the sketch, the "fancy" that starts "from our Christmas Tree" flies "away into the winter prospect" and into the realm of "Winter Stories—Ghost Stories, or more shame for us—round the Christmas fire" (p. 12). It flows in and out of narrative personae. The unspecified first-person singular speaker of the initial portion of the sketch becomes a nervous observer of ghosts: "We are a middle-aged nobleman, and we make a generous supper with our host and hostess and their guests"; "we always travel with pistols"; "we are dead now" (pp. 12, 13, 14). Finally, the narrator returns to his present situation, "encircled by the social thoughts of Christmas-time" (p. 18), and his supernatural "going a visiting" (p. 12) ultimately fades into seasonal emotion with an allusion to the birth in Bethlehem for which the holiday is named: "In every cheerful image and suggestion that the season brings, may the bright star that rested above the poor roof, be the star of all the Christian world!" (p. 18). In other words, in this cinematic sketch of a thoughtful observer's shifting thoughts, Dickens has provided a glimpse into the workings of imagination as well as the toys, books, theatrical productions, fairy tales, and tales of the uncanny, which—as his earlier writings indicate—he viewed as the vital childhood roots of this imaginative realm. A number of his subsequent holiday works reveal his experimentation with ways of translating into story form this interest in depicting imagination.

His contributions to the Christmas numbers for 1851 and 1852 show this translation in progress. Like "A Christmas Tree," Dickens' 1851 holiday piece—entitled "What Christmas is, as we Grow Older"—is an impressionistic sketch narrated by an idly speculative personality whose pose resembles that of Boz. After the richly detailed picture of the "fancies of childhood" re-created in "A Christmas Tree," this piece seems somewhat diffuse and anticlimactic, but once again, the narrator attempts to give free rein to his imagination as old illusions mingle with new "Christmas castles in the clouds": "Welcome, old aspirations, glittering creatures of an ardent fancy, to your shelter underneath the holly! We know you, and have not outlived you yet. Welcome, old projects and old loves, however fleeting, to your nooks among the steadier lights that burn around us. . . . Do we build no Christmas castles in the clouds now? Let our thoughts, fluttering like butterflies among these flowers of children, bear witness!" (*CS,* pp. 22–23). In the Christmas number for 1852, *A Round of Stories by the Christmas Fire,* Dickens' earlier Christmas sketches give way to more thoroughly fictionalized stories, in the sense of possessing plot, setting, characters, and deliberate narrative design as well as some suggestion of oral narration. However, in the first of Dickens' two contributions for this year, his fascination with "Christmas castles" is notably continued. Indeed, the essence of this tale, called simply "The Poor Relation's Story," is a revelation of the fantasy life of its principal speaker, a gentle and well-meaning but imprudently trustful individual who is recognized by the family assembled around the fire at Christmas as "nobody's enemy but . . . [his] own" (*CS,* p. 29). As the poor relation explains, his life is not what it is commonly believed to be. He was not ruinously disinherited by his uncle, abandoned by the woman he loved, and deceived by his business partner; on the contrary, despite his uncle's disfavor, he retained the love of his fiancée and the loyalty of his partner, received an adequate income from his business, married his beloved Christiana, and settled in a "Castle." In the poor relation's words, "At this time of the year—the Christmas and New Year time—I am seldom out of my Castle. For, the associations of the season seem to hold me there, and the precepts of the season seem to teach me that it is well to be there" (p. 39). As he adds in response to the "grave, kind voice" (p. 39) of the family member who is serving as host for this holiday gathering, "My Castle is in the Air!" (p. 39).

In his Christmas writings after the depiction of this intentional illusionist in 1852, Dickens' concern with the landscape of castles in the air becomes more elaborate. In 1854 Dickens inaugurated his scheme, followed in most of the subsequent Christmas numbers, for enclosing the contributions by other authors within a narrative generally written by himself. The opening and closing portions of *The Seven Poor Travellers,* the Christmas number for 1854, comprise a monologue by a benevolent wanderer. This narrator provides a dinner on Christmas Eve for six poor travellers lodged at the expense of a long deceased philanthropist, listens to their stories (contributed by Dickens' co-authors) after telling a story of his own, and finally sees these six travellers resume their journeys on Christmas Day. The narrator here is depicted simply as an idly contemplative figure, "a Traveller myself, though an idle one" (*CS,* p. 69), reminiscent of the contemplative personalities that preside over Dickens' Christmas sketches in 1850 and 1851 and anticipatory of the figure of the Uncommercial Traveller (which Dickens later created to preside over the sketches published under this heading in *All the Year Round*). Nevertheless, like the poor relation in 1852, the "poor traveller" who narrates this framework in 1854 is richly endowed with the ability to daydream. As he explains after making arrangements to serve as the host for the other travellers' holiday meal:

> I went back to my inn to give the necessary directions for the Turkey and Roast Beef, and, during the remainder of the day, could settle to nothing for thinking of the Poor Travellers. When the wind blew hard against the windows . . . I pictured them advancing towards their resting-place along various cold roads, and felt delighted to think how little they foresaw the supper that awaited them. I painted their portraits in my mind, and indulged in little heightening touches. I made them footsore; I made them weary; I made them carry packs and bundles; I made them stop by finger-posts and milestones, leaning on their bent sticks, and looking wistfully at what was written there; I made them lose their way; and filled their five wits with apprehensions of lying out all night, and being frozen to death. . . . After it fell dark, and the Cathedral bell was heard in the invisible steeple . . . striking five, six, seven, I became so full of my Travellers that I could eat no dinner, and felt constrained to watch them still in the red coals of my fire. They were all arrived by this time, I thought, had got their tickets, and were gone in.—There my pleasure was dashed by the reflection that probably some Travellers had come too late and were shut out. (Pp. 73–74)

In Dickens' Christmas number for the following year, this idea of a narrator snugly seated by a winter fire, creating elaborate mental pictures, becomes intensified.

Once again, the events of this next Christmas number (1855), *The Holly-Tree Inn,* are moderated by a narrator who describes himself in a framing first-person monologue. However, this framing narrator at the Holly-Tree is more distinctly delineated than his benevolent predecessor of the previous year and more concerned with revealing the nature of his interior life. As he explains in his opening words, "I have kept one secret in the course of my life. I am a bashful man. Nobody would suppose it, nobody ever does suppose it, nobody ever did suppose it, but I am naturally a bashful man. This is the secret which I have never breathed until now" (*CS,* p. 97). Moreover, it is this bashfulness that not only results in his mistaken trip to the Holly-Tree where he becomes snowbound but that initially keeps him apart from the other people at the inn, unwilling to remain in his bedroom ("the grimmest room I have ever had the nightmare in"), reluctant to explore his drafty and cavernous sitting room (where "the drapery of the ten curtains of the five windows went twisting and creeping about, like a nest of gigantic worms"), and thus confined to his armchair ("roasting whole before an immense fire" [p. 102]). As a result, much of his monologue consists of embryonic stories about his former literal and fictitious experiences with inns, which he recounts to himself in a vain attempt "to keep my solitude out of my mind" (p. 115). However, a number of these stories are sufficient to make him "quite uncomfortable" (p. 106).

His opening tale, which bears a striking similarity to the Uncommercial Traveller's later description of Captain Murderer's culinary feats in "Nurse's Stories," provides a good example of several that follow:

> My first impressions of an Inn dated from the Nursery; consequently I went back to the Nursery for a starting-point, and found myself at the knee of a sallow woman with a fishy eye, an aquiline nose, and a green gown, whose specialty was a dismal narrative of a landlord by the roadside, whose visitors unaccountably disappeared for many years, until it was discovered that the pursuit of his life had been to convert them into pies. For the better devotion of himself to this branch of industry, he had constructed a secret door behind the head of the bed; and when the visitor (oppressed with pie) had fallen asleep, this wicked landlord would look softly in with a lamp in one hand and a knife in the other, would cut his throat, and would make him into pies; for which purpose he had coppers, underneath a trap-door, always boiling; and rolled out his pastry in the dead of the night. Yet even he was not insensible to the stings of conscience, for he never went to sleep without being heard to mutter, "Too much pepper!" which was eventually the cause of his being brought to justice. (P. 104)

After pages of such inns, and a few more inviting ones, the narrator breaks down: "What was I to do? What was to become of me? Into what extremity was I submissively to sink? Supposing that, like Baron Trenck, I looked out for a mouse or spider, and found one, and beguiled my imprisonment by training it? Even that might be dangerous with a view to the future. I might be so far gone when the road did come to be cut through the snow, that, on my way forth, I might burst into tears, and beseech, like the prisoner who was released in his old age from the Bastille, to be taken back again to the five windows, the ten curtains, and the sinuous drapery" (pp. 115–16). Hence, in the narrator's words, "A desperate idea came into my head" (p. 116). He conquers his bashfulness with a determined effort and seeks out the company of other individuals, such as the Boots, who tell him the more fully developed stories (the interpolated pieces of this Christmas number) that beguile the remainder of his stay at the Holly-Tree Inn. To an even greater degree in this framing monologue than in that which he composed for the previous year, Dickens seems to be humorously but very deliberately experimenting with depicting the results of what Garrett Stewart has recently described as "fire-gazing."[12] In this context, the "Fairy Story" about Master Harry Walmers and "Mrs. Harry Walmers, Junior, that was never to be" is, in Keats' words, "a waking dream," remembered and re-created for a few passing moments by the Boots. Dickens' design for the Christmas number for 1859 makes this link between the world of the imagination and the kind of story traditionally told around a Christmas fire even more explicit.

However, the 1859 holiday production, entitled *The Haunted House,* also underscores the importance of a twentieth-century critic's familiarity with Dickens' original Christmas numbers. As it standardly appears (in two chapters) in *Christmas Stories,* the nature of this work seems highly puzzling, for the brief concluding chapter by Dickens, which finishes the framework and places the previous portions of the entire Christmas number in perspective, is commonly omitted.[13] Nevertheless, the principle that underlies *The Haunted House* is clear. In Dickens' introductory section, "The Mortals in the House," the narrator of the framework describes the way in which he has become the tenant of the haunted house—a building which he has rented, despite its reputation of being haunted, because he is a sensible man who is skeptical about the authenticity of spiritualism or ghosts. When the servants are terrified by rumors and noises, the narrator and his equally sensible sister resolve to dismiss them and invite a group of friends to visit and share in the housework. The narrator and his guests then plan to reserve until Twelfth Night their accounts of their experiences in the house's various rooms. Dickens' brief, neglected conclusion, "The Ghost in the Corner Room," subsequently corroborates the wisdom of the narrator's initial skepticism and clarifies the nature of the different tales in prose and verse placed within the framework of this Christmas number: ". . . we lived our term out, most happily, and were never for a moment haunted by anything more disagreeable than our own imaginations and remembrances."[14] Prompted by the controversy in which he was currently embroiled with William Howitt, an outspoken believer in spiritualism,[15] Dickens seems to be explicitly using the traditional custom of what "A Christmas Tree" describes as "telling Winter Stories—Ghost Stories, or more shame for us—round the Christmas fire" to reflect his own less traditional view (as explained in his 25 November 1851 letter to Mrs. Gaskell) of "ghost-stories, illustrating particular states of mind and processes of the imagination." In the monologue that frames *The Haunted House,* with the exception of an emphasis on his debunking attitude toward supernatural phenomena, the personality of the presiding narrator is not elaborated. In contrast, in his account of his own ghostly experience in "Master B.'s Room"— Dickens' contribution to the interpolated "imaginations and remembrances" of this Christmas number—the process of the central speaker's imagination, as well as the idiosyncratic nature of his thinking, becomes evident.

The focus of this loosely organized inset piece, "The Ghost in Master B.'s Room," is the mind of its narrator. As he explains at the end, "No other ghost has haunted the boy's room . . . since I have occupied it, than the ghost of my own childhood, the ghost of my own innocence, the ghost of my own airy belief" (*CS*, p. 252). Throughout the piece, such ghosts take the form of the speaker's wandering thoughts. Master B.'s room bears the unpleasant distinction of being singled out for special ghostly attention, and, when the narrator takes possession of the room, his mind ranges wildly over the significance of the letter "B":

> When I established myself in the triangular garret which had gained so distinguished a reputation, my thoughts naturally turned to Master B. My speculations about him were uneasy and manifold. Whether his christian name was Benjamin, Bissextile (from his having been born in Leap Year), Bartholomew, or Bill. Whether the initial letter belonged to his family name, and that was Baxter, Black, Brown, Barker, Buggins, Baker, or Bird. Whether he was a foundling, and had been baptized B. Whether he was a lion-hearted boy, and B. was short for Briton, or for Bull. Whether he could possibly have been kith and kin to an illustrious lady who brightened my own childhood, and had come of the blood of the brilliant Mother Bunch?
>
> With these profitless meditations I tormented myself much. I also carried the mysterious letter into the appearance and pursuits of the deceased; wondering whether he dressed in Blue, wore Boots (he couldn't have been Bald), was a boy of Brains, liked Books, was good at Bowling, had any skill as a Boxer, ever in his Buoyant Boyhood Bathed from a Bathing-machine at Bognor, Bangor, Bournemouth, Brighton, or Broadstairs, like a Bounding Billiard Ball?[16]

As the words "speculations" and "meditations" suggest, the content of this piece is similar in some respects to that of an impressionistic sketch like "A Christmas Tree." However, the speaker here is much more complex than the generalized idly speculative persona who presides over "A Christmas Tree." The apparent supernatural phenomena encountered in Master B.'s room, unlike the conventional ghost stories briefly described in "A Christmas Tree," are clearly reflections of earlier aspects of the narrator himself.

Thus, phantoms merge with memories within the speaker's thoughts:

The first appearance that presented itself was early in the morning, when it was but just daylight and no more. I was standing shaving at my glass, when I suddenly discovered, to my consternation and amazement, that I was shaving—not myself—I am fifty —but a boy. Apparently Master B.?

I trembled and looked over my shoulder; nothing there. I looked again in the glass, and distinctly saw the features and expression of a boy, who was shaving, not to get rid of a beard, but to get one. Extremely troubled in my mind, I took a few turns in the room, and went back to the looking-glass, resolved to steady my hand and complete the operation in which I had been disturbed. Opening my eyes, which I had shut while recovering my firmness, I now met in the glass, looking straight at me, the eyes of a young man of four or five and twenty. Terrified by this new ghost, I closed my eyes, and made a strong effort to recover myself. Opening them again, I saw, shaving his cheek in the glass, my father, who has long been dead. Nay, I even saw my grandfather too, whom I never did see in my life.[17]

Like David Copperfield remembering his former embarrassment at having no need for shaving water, the speaker looks back upon his earlier self, but his recollections, unlike those of David, are presented in a manner that makes them appear supernatural. His memories are depicted not as memories but as ghostly visions in the mirror, and his reference to his father and grandfather humorously emphasizes the role of these apparitions as incarnations of previous stages of his own existence. As his conversation with the next specter indicates, the narrator then jokingly attempts to juxtapose such ghosts from the past with his later adult wisdom:

waking from an uneasy sleep at exactly two o'clock in the morning, what were my feelings to find that I was sharing my bed, with the skeleton of Master B.!

I sprang up, and the skeleton sprang up also. I then heard a plaintive voice saying, "Where am I? What is become of me?" and, looking hard in that direction, perceived the ghost of Master B.

. . . .

"Where is my little sister," said the ghost, "and where my angelic little wife, and where is the boy I went to school with?"

I entreated the phantom to be comforted, and above all things to take heart respecting the loss of the boy he went to school with. I represented to him that probably that boy never did, within human experience, come out well, when discovered. I urged that I myself had, in later life, turned up several boys whom I went to school with, and none of them had at all answered. I expressed my humble belief that that boy never did

> answer. I represented that he was a mythic character, a delusion,
> and a snare. (P. 244)

Evidently through a logic of association, the remainder of the piece concentrates on two contrasting memories of schools. When the youthful skeleton and the ghostly "customers" (p. 244) whom the narrator is doomed to shave are seen, in this fashion, as simply embodiments of his own past, the basic purpose of this seemingly digressive piece—to depict the narrator's primarily reminiscing daydreams—is apparent.

Moreover, in this work, as in the story presented by the Boots at the Holly-Tree Inn, Dickens appears to be deliberately indulging in the kind of playfulness that he felt was especially suitable to Christmas. Stylistically, as in the narrator's wildly alliterating suggestions about the possible meaning of "B," and conceptually, as in the little ghost's disconsolate yearning for "my angelic little wife," Dickens seems to be—as Forster suggested that he often did in his short stories—simply letting "loose." Here, as at the Holly-Tree, Dickens is undoubtedly rendering aspects of his own experiences and emotions in fictional disguise, although his handling of this autobiographical material does not seem as well managed as in "The Boots." Despite the anonymity of this piece, as of almost all the other contributions to Dickens' Christmas numbers, the narrator's opening pyrotechnics with the letter "B" were probably intended to be recognized by Dickens' original readers as playful reflections of his own well-known pseudonym "Boz," in a mode which anticipates his later obvious allusions to his role as editor of *All the Year Round* in *Somebody's Luggage* (1862) and *Doctor Marigold's Prescriptions* (1865). However, with "The Ghost in Master B.'s Room," such stylistic bravura does not continue past the second paragraph. In contrast, as later readers familiar with Dickens' biography are apt to sense, the remarks by the narrator about his father's death and the consequent termination of his joyful, childish school days appear to be awkward, covert allusions to Dickens' publicly concealed but privately haunting youthful experience of his father's imprisonment for debt and his own temporary employment in Warren's blacking warehouse. In the narrator's words,

> I was taken home, and there was Debt at home as well as Death, and we had a sale there. My own little bed was so superciliously looked upon by a Power unknown to me, hazily called "The Trade," that a brass coal-scuttle, a roasting-jack, and a birdcage, were obliged to be put into it to make a Lot of it, and then it went for a song. So I heard mentioned, and I wondered what song, and thought what a dismal song it must have been to sing!
> Then, I was sent to a great, cold, bare, school of big boys;

where everything to eat and wear was thick and clumpy, without
being enough; where everybody, large and small, was cruel;
where the boys knew all about the sale, before I got there, and
asked me what I had fetched, and who had bought me, and hooted
at me, "Going, going, gone!" (Pp. 251–52)

Dickens seems to be concealing fact with, in some ways, emotionally
more attractive fiction. He has substituted death for imprisonment and
an unpleasant school for the blacking warehouse, but his treatment of
this episode in "The Ghost in Master B.'s Room" seems much more
clumsy than his earlier fictional transmutation of his youthful misery in
David Copperfield. Likewise, his presentation of the motif of children
playing at marriage, emphasized in a humorous description of the seraglio which the narrator arranged with "eight of the fairest of the
daughters of men" (p. 251) in his innocent days at school before his
father's death, does not seem as artistically well balanced as in "The
Boots." Perhaps the turmoil associated with Dickens' own separation
from his wife in the previous year may be partly responsible for the
recurrence of this latter motif in "The Ghost in Master B.'s Room" as
well as his difficulty at this point in creatively controlling material so
strongly prompted by his inner life. In any case, the narrator's brief
explanatory remark that the only ghosts he has found in the room are
those of his own "childhood," "innocence," and "airy belief" does not
completely hold together the diverse elements presented in this piece.
A reader who encounters this intended but not wholly successful story
in Dickens' collected works may be left wondering why Master B.'s
room, of all the rooms in this supposedly haunted house, contains skele-
tons and ghosts. The final debunking remark in Dickens' neglected
conclusion to the entire number provides a necessary emphasis for the
point that all of the ghosts in all of the rooms derive from the thoughts
of those who describe them.

Nonetheless, in "The Ghost in Master B.'s Room," Dickens has
clearly moved from the kind of heavy-handed and highly sensational-
ized demonstration of obvious psychological abnormality evident in
early uncanny tales such as "A Madman's Manuscript" to a more subtle
revelation of the idiosyncratic vagaries of a down-to-earth and presumably normal state of mind. In "The Ghost in Master B.'s Room," Dickens
has evidently turned his attention to the fusion of past events, fantasies,
and present-day actualities that constitutes the imaginative process itself. The technical direction in which Dickens is moving here, anticipat-
ing some of James Joyce's later experimentation with verbal play and
with depicting the twists and turns of consciousness, is exciting. In some
of the writings from the Christmas numbers discussed in chapter 5,
Dickens can be seen elaborating on methods used in "The Ghost in

Master B.'s Room" in order to construct short stories whose primary purpose is a revelation of the interior, imaginative worlds of the seemingly ordinary characters who narrate them. However, this stylistic development, although clearly suggested by "The Ghost in Master B.'s Room," seems to have been to a large extent impeded during the first twelve years of the Christmas numbers by Dickens' development in another, very different direction—his increasing reliance during the latter part of this period on the help of Wilkie Collins.

V

Dickens' extensive collaboration with Wilkie Collins on all but one of the Christmas numbers between 1856 and 1860 is a remarkable experiment. Collins made his first appearance among Dickens' holiday contributors in 1854 as the author of one of the interpolated tales in *The Seven Poor Travellers,* and he contributed another interpolated tale to *The Holly-Tree Inn* in 1855. However, he soon grew to be not only one of Dickens' closest friends but the most important of his Christmas co-workers. Beginning in 1856, Collins became the only author whom Dickens permitted to work on the framing sections of the Christmas numbers in addition to himself. Moreover, in 1857 (and again in his last Christmas number a decade later), Dickens dropped the concept of framework and attached stories and simply wrote a complete number with the help of Collins alone. To modern critics trained to believe, in the words of Henry James, that "a novel is a living thing, all one and continuous, like any other organism," such attempts at fictional cloning are apt to appear unnerving. By 1868 (as his previously quoted remark to Wills makes clear), Dickens was avowedly weary with the intrinsic "want of cohesion" in his Christmas numbers. Nevertheless, with Collins at least, in the late 1850s and early 1860s, Dickens seems to have viewed the idea of joint writing not only as a valuable convenience but as a kind of creative game that he and his fellow novelist might play with one another and the reader.

For example, he wrote to Collins in 1862 to reassure the latter that if he were too ill to compose an installment of *No Name,* currently being serialized in *All the Year Round,* Dickens himself would take Collins' place:

> I was stricken ill when I was doing Bleak House, and I shall not easily forget what I suffered under the fear of not being able to come up to time.
>
> Dismiss that fear (if you have it) altogether from your mind. Write to me at Paris at any moment, and say you are unequal to your work, and want me, and I will come to London straight and do your work. I am quite confident that, with your notes and a few

words of explanation, I could take it up at any time and do it. Absurdly unnecessary to say that it would be a makeshift! But I could do it at a pinch, so like you as that no one should find out the difference. Don't make much of this offer in your mind; it is nothing, except to ease it. If you should want help, I am as safe as the bank. The trouble would be nothing to me, and the triumph of overcoming a difficulty great. Think it a Christmas number, an Idle Apprentice, a Lighthouse, a Frozen Deep. I am as ready as in any of these cases to strike in and hammer the hot iron out.[18]

The fundamental sincerity of Dickens' offer here is obvious, and its potential value is apparent. However, his assurance that "I could do it at a pinch, so like you as that no one should find out the difference" also whimsically suggests the attitude of "hide and seek," which is teasingly evident in his comment to Forster about a story composed with Collins in *The Lazy Tour of Two Idle Apprentices* (1857) "in which I think you would find it very difficult to say where I leave off and he comes in."[19] It does not seem accidental that all of the writings to which Dickens alludes in this 1862 letter to Collins—joint ventures including the plays entitled *The Lighthouse* (1855) and *The Frozen Deep* (1857), officially composed by Collins but produced under Dickens' direction and originally designed as amateur theatricals for Dickens' home—are, in various ways, holiday *jeux d'esprit*. In retrospect, unfortunately, the works that Dickens created with Collins seem well below the level of Dickens' best. Dickens' own sense of this discrepancy may be one reason why these collaborations eventually ended. In particular, an examination of their contributions to the Christmas numbers in which they worked closely together between 1856 and 1860 indicates an important difference between Collins' approach and that which Dickens had separately been evolving in his own writings for these annual productions.

As "The Ghost in Master B.'s Room" suggests, Dickens' fascination with exploring the world of the imagination in his contributions to the Christmas numbers is closely linked to his underlying interest in characterization. Thus, many of his writings for the holiday numbers between 1850 and 1856 reveal a progression in the direction of the form in which an eccentrically talkative first-person narrator presents a monologue whose primary purpose is a revelation of his or her distinctive self. In other words, just as the impressionistic sketches that Dickens produced for the Christmas numbers in 1850 and 1851 give way to the poor relation's explanation of his private daydream in 1852, so "The Poor Relation's Story," which is largely told by the poor relation himself but moderated by an omniscient narrator in the background, leads in 1853 to "The Schoolboy's Story," a monologue narrated wholly by the schoolboy. By itself, "The Schoolboy's Story" is unremarkable. Its plot is simple, consisting mainly of the discovery that a poor schoolmaster has come into a fortune, and the personality that the schoolboy reveals in the process of telling this tale is stereotypical. Nevertheless, in the context of Dickens' other writings for the Christmas numbers, it is an indication of his growing interest in the technique of self-characterization.

Even more significantly, beginning with *The Seven Poor Travellers* in 1854, Dickens not only inaugurated the idea of a framework for the Christmas number, but he introduced the method, used in many of his subsequent numbers, of composing this framework in the form of a first-person monologue by one of the characters in the work. This method, in turn, ultimately provided an occasion for the self-revealing first-person narrators who dominate most of the holiday numbers after 1861 (and perhaps helped to prepare for Dickens' sophisticated handling of the technique of first-person narrative in *Great Expectations,* begun at the end of 1860). Dickens' progression in this direction of self-characterization between 1850 and 1856 is not completely steady. Highly generalized, allegorical pieces entitled "The Child's Story" and "Nobody's Story," written in the third person, had appeared respectively in the Christmas numbers for 1852 and 1853; in both cases, Dickens seems to be somewhat heavy-handedly attempting to use the occasion of the Christmas season to evoke a sense of fellow feeling. Nonetheless, the technique of entering into the interior world of a distinctive character through the medium of a first-person monologue is one which Dickens clearly seems to be perfecting and polishing in his contributions to the Christmas numbers through 1856. As he wrote enthusiastically to Angela Burdett-Coutts about the Christmas number for this year, *The Wreck of the Golden Mary. Being the Captain's Account of the Loss of the Ship, and the Mate's Account of the Great Deliverance of Her People in an Open Boat at Sea,* "I am the Captain of the Golden Mary; Mr. Collins is the Mate."[20] However, careful comparison of Dickens' and Collins' separate contributions to this Christmas number—the first in which they had attempted to work in tandem—reveals striking differences in technique.

At the conclusion of Dickens' section of "The Wreck," the captain of the *Golden Mary* loses consciousness and the survivors of the shipwreck remain unrescued in two lifeboats in the middle of the sea. The mere fact of this unresolved ending suggests that Dickens was not primarily interested in the problem of how the castaways would extricate themselves from their dismal situation. From the opening words of the Christmas number, however, Dickens' fascination with the good-hearted, garrulous captain of the *Golden Mary* is apparent:

I was apprenticed to the Sea when I was twelve years old, and I have encountered a great deal of rough weather, both literal and metaphorical. It has always been my opinion since I first possessed such a thing as an opinion, that the man who knows only one subject is next tiresome to the man who knows no subject. Therefore, in the course of my life I have taught myself whatever I could, and although I am not an educated man, I am able, I am thankful to say, to have an intelligent interest in most things.

A person might suppose, from reading the above, that I am in the habit of holding forth about number one. That is not the case. Just as if I was to come into a room among strangers, and must either be introduced or introduce myself, so I have taken the liberty of passing these few remarks, simply and plainly that it may be known who and what I am. I will add no more of the sort than that my name is William George Ravender, that I was born at Penrith half a year after my own father was drowned, and that I am on the second day of this present blessed Christmas week of one thousand eight hundred and fifty-six, fifty-six years of age. (*CS,* p. 133)

Captain Ravender's monologue establishes the outlines of his personality—experienced, intelligent, considerate, and perhaps overly confidential. Later remarks provide further details. He is, a reader learns, aware of his role as a narrator and not wholly free from vanity. He repeatedly refers to his knowledge of books, particularly those dealing with shipwrecks, and in a more urbane fashion than Esther's somewhat awkward echoing of her own praise in *Bleak House* a few years earlier, he disclaims the esteem of others in a manner that only emphasizes their commendation. The way in which he repeats the praise of himself by the Liverpool merchant who asks him to undertake the journey in the *Golden Mary* illustrates this latter trait: " 'Now,' says he, 'you know my opinion of you, and you know I am only expressing it, and with no singularity, when I tell you that you are almost the only man on whose integrity, discretion, and energy—' &c., &c. For, I don't want to repeat what he said, though I was and am sensible of it" (p. 135). Later events indicate, however, that the merchant's high opinion is justified, and by the time that Captain Ravender lapses into unconsciousness in the bottom of the longboat, he has emerged as a good, although not faultless, human being.

John Steadiman, the chief mate who takes command after this event, appears significant throughout Dickens' section primarily to the extent that he differs from Captain Ravender. The captain is loquacious and imaginative; words spill over one another in his monologue as he utters several ideas at once. As his personality emerges from Ravender's remarks, the chief mate appears much less talkative and reflective.

Their manners of agreeing to assume the responsibility of the *Golden Mary* illustrate the difference in their characters. When the Liverpool merchant tells him that he is practically the only person who can be trusted to sail the *Golden Mary* to and from California in order to purchase gold and offers him command of the ship on very generous terms, Ravender accepts the compliment without being overwhelmed. His doubts about the undertaking remain, and he spends a great deal of time talking over the plan and imagining all its possible contingencies:

> Notwithstanding my being, as I have mentioned, quite ready for a voyage, still I had some doubts of this voyage. Of course I knew, without being told, that there were peculiar difficulties and dangers in it, a long way over and above those which attend all voyages. It must not be supposed that I was afraid to face them; but, in my opinion a man has no manly motive or sustainment in his own breast for facing dangers, unless he has well considered what they are, and is able quietly to say to himself, "None of these perils can now take me by surprise; I shall know what to do for the best in any of them; all the rest lies in the higher and greater hands to which I humbly commit myself." . . .
>
> As I was thoughtful, my good friend proposed that he should leave me to walk there as long as I liked, and that I should dine with him by-and-by at his club in Pall Mall. I accepted the invitation and I walked up and down there, quarter-deck fashion, a matter of a couple of hours; . . .
>
> All dinner-time, and all after dinner-time, we talked it over again. (Pp. 135–36)

He finally makes the decision only after he has gone to Liverpool and actually seen the ship: "We had inspected every timber in her, and had come back to the gangway to go ashore from the dock-basin, when I put out my hand to my friend. 'Touch upon it,' says I, 'and touch heartily. I take command of this ship, and I am hers and yours, if I can get John Steadiman for my chief mate'" (p. 136). John Steadiman's response, as Ravender describes it, is far more immediate and far less carefully discussed: "I told him, very gravely, what I had said to my friend. It struck him, as he said himself, amidships. He was quite shaken by it. 'Captain Ravender,' were John Steadiman's words, 'such an opinion from you is true commendation, and I'll sail round the world with you for twenty years if you hoist the signal, and stand by you for ever!'" (p. 137). Thus, in Dickens' section, John Steadiman is simply Captain Ravender's unthinking, loyal subordinate. He is a great favorite with children, and he is more popular than the captain with a little girl who is travelling aboard the *Golden Mary,* yet, on an earlier voyage, he single-handedly killed two men who were trying to murder Captain Ravender in his bed. As his name suggests, he is a steady man. Dickens explained to the Reverend James White that "John Steadiman merely came into my head as a staunch sort of name that suited the character."[21] The chief mate is conscientious and levelheaded and, undoubtedly, an excellent man for his position, but he lacks Captain Ravender's imagination and voluble eccentricity.

In the part of "The Wreck" contributed by Collins, after the heading "All that follows, was written by John Steadiman, Chief Mate,"[22] this distinction between the personalities of the captain and the chief mate is weakened. Steadiman is still the captain's subordinate, and upon occasion, he reminds the reader that he does not possess Ravender's eloquence. After discovering that the captain is still alive, he declares that his relief cannot be expressed in words—"at least, not in such words as a man like me can command" (p. 158). He concludes his description of the way in which he assumed command of the captain's boat with the qualification that "this, as well as I can tell it, is the full and true account" (p. 160). Such reminders of his own inadequacy, however, seem perfunctory, and most of this conclusion of "The Wreck" consists of Steadiman's account of his activities. While Dickens' chief mate is gifted with very little foresight, Collins' version of this character sees a distress signal from the other boat and worries that the captain may be dead. He wisely realizes that the people in each boat can only be further demoralized by the haggard appearance of the companions whom they have not seen closely since the shipwreck, and he performs the delicate maneuver of changing from one boat to the other without wasting any time. He even circumvents much of the impediment of his own established lack of eloquence by giving his information as if it were a legal deposition: "I should consider myself unworthy to write another line of this statement, if I had not made up my mind to speak the truth, the whole truth, and nothing but the truth" (p. 156). In short, under Collins' hand, John Steadiman grows more perceptive and intelligent. Significantly, the final paragraph of this section, introducing the usual assortment of interpolated stories by various authors entitled "The Beguilement in the Boats," reemphasizes Steadiman's limitations. He explains that he is adding this material because without it, his own description "would not be, in my humble estimation, complete," and he remarks to the reader that "I shall . . . ask permission, before proceeding to the account of our Deliverance, to reproduce in this place three or four of the most noteworthy of the stories which circulated among us."[23] Stone believes that this paragraph is "almost certainly by Dickens,"[24] and its awkward stress upon the chief mate's awareness of his inferiority may reflect Dickens' feeling that the contrast between Captain Ravender and his humble subordinate was beginning to disappear.

The contrast becomes even less noticeable in "The Deliverance." As Collins works out the details of the rescue, concrete problems take precedence over narrative characterization. The sentence with which John Steadiman begins "The Deliverance" provides a striking illustration of this change in emphasis: "When the sun rose on the twenty-seventh day of our calamity, the first question that I secretly asked myself was, How many more mornings will the stoutest of us live to see?"[25] The chief mate has changed from a steady subordinate, conscious of his own inadequacy, to a leader seeking an answer to a crucial question with which he is faced. Here Steadiman seems filled with ingenious suggestions. He serves all of the remaining food in the hope of encouraging his fellow sufferers, rigs up his coat as a sail, and advises his companions to shout at a barely visible ship in order to keep them from despondency. This increased activity is accompanied by a further development of his powers of imagination. In Dickens' section of "The Wreck," Captain Ravender keeps watch on board the ship and stares into darkness until his eyes "make patterns in it, and . . . flash in it, as if they had gone out of your head to look at you" (p. 142), and he imagines that the waves have an unusual sound—a suggestion that hints of the approaching disaster but which Steadiman pragmatically attributes to Ravender's state of exhaustion: "Rely upon it, Captain Ravender, you have been without rest too long, and the novelty is only in the state of your sense of hearing" (p. 142). In "The Deliverance," however, Steadiman's earlier resistance to imaginative suggestion has been forgotten, and the night in which he and his companions shout at the distant ship appears as dreadful to him as it might have been to Captain Ravender:

> The wind seemed to whirl our weak cries savagely out of our mouths almost before we could utter them. I, sitting astern in the boat, only heard them, as it seemed, for something like an instant of time. But even that was enough to make me creep all over—the cry was so forlorn and fearful. Of all the dreadful sounds I had heard since the first striking of the ship, that shrill wail of despair —rising on the wave-tops, one moment; whirled away, the next, into the black night—was the most frightful that entered my ears. There are times, even now, when it seems to be ringing in them still.[26]

John Steadiman thus becomes perceptive as well as active. His earlier phrases of self-deprecation disappear, and his words seem adequate expressions of his ideas. Collins has transformed Ravender's loyal subordinate, distinctive in terms of his difference from the captain, into a conventional leader capable of bringing a satisfactory outcome to the wreck of the *Golden Mary*. This new John Steadiman is suitable for Collins' purpose, but Dickens' subtle characterization of the chief mate through his contrast with the captain has been lost.

Collins' goal in "The Deliverance," however, appears to be not so much characterization as the achievement of suspense. At the end of "The Wreck," he keeps his readers in doubt for several paragraphs about whether or not the captain is really dead, and he arouses anxiety even more effectively in "The Deliverance." The awful question with which this section opens—"How many more mornings will the stoutest of us live to see?"—rivets the reader's attention upon the answer to this problem, while the question becomes more and more acute as the difficulties of the situation become more obvious. Even the apparent climax of the story, when the sail of a ship is sighted, fails to resolve the tension, for the possibility quickly arises that the ship may miss the castaways in the night. The long-awaited appearance of dawn illustrates Collins' method of heightening anticipation:

> It came at last—that grey, quiet light which was to end all our uncertainty; which was to show us if we were saved, or to warn us if we were to prepare for death. With the first streak in the east, every one of the boat's company, except the sleeping and the senseless, roused up and looked out in breathless silence upon the sea. Slowly and slowly the daylight strengthened, and the darkness rolled off farther and farther before it over the face of the waters. The first pale flush of the sun flew trembling along the paths of light broken through the grey wastes of the eastern clouds. We could look clearly—we could see far; and there, ahead of us—O! merciful, bountiful providence of God!—there was the ship![27]

The one word, "ship," which indicates whether or not the survivors will be rescued, is tantalizingly withheld until the last possible moment. On first reading, the suspense in this paragraph grows almost unbearable, but it is merely a culmination of the approach used by Collins throughout his contribution to this Christmas number.

The phrase "on first reading" is an important one, for Collins' method of telling the story is the kind that works well only once. Unlike Dickens, he concentrates upon events rather than personalities. In his treatment of John Steadiman, he seems less interested in character than in plot.[28] The increase in Steadiman's ability to imagine in Collins' section of this work appears to be simply a way of heightening the horrifying impact of the events that he is experiencing rather than being, as in the case of Captain Ravender in Dickens' portion of "The Wreck," a distinctive trait important in its own right. The inimitable

Captain Ravender, in turn, remains in a state of unconsciousness or quiet recuperation throughout "The Deliverance," although Stone conjectures that Dickens was responsible for the paragraph containing Steadiman's recollections of the way in which Ravender and two female passengers were taken on board the rescuing vessel.[29] On subsequent readings, when the safety of almost all the passengers and crewmen is assured, Collins' sections seem less and less appealing.

In the Christmas numbers after 1856, the impact of Collins' approach is clearly visible in terms of Dickens' experimentation with the technique of a first-person monologue in which a storyteller displays his own distinctive personality in the process of telling his story. For example, in *The Perils of Certain English Prisoners, and Their Treasure in Women, Children, Silver, and Jewels*—the Christmas number for the following year—the effect of Collins' concern with plot is even more pronounced than in *The Wreck of the Golden Mary*. The designedly sensational but now unmemorable subject of this holiday production in 1857 is the bravery and resourcefulness shown by most members of an English settlement in South America when their island, which is used to store silver from an inland mine, is invaded by pirates. The work lacks the usual inset pieces and consists simply of three chapters. In the first, "The Island of Silverstore," Dickens describes the settlement through the person of Gill Davis—an honest but illiterate man who comes with a group of marines to protect this island colony, enviously begrudges the apparently soft life of its inhabitants, falls in love with a lady of the colony from whom he is hopelessly separated by his social class, discovers with shame and amazement that the women as well as the men on the island are far more courageous than he had believed, and finally succumbs to the pirates when they overrun the fort. As in *The Wreck of the Golden Mary*, once Dickens has worked his characters into a seemingly impossible situation, Collins takes over. Collins' chapter, "The Prison in the Woods," describes the march that the prisoners are forced to make on the mainland. In the interior, they are confined by the pirates in an ancient ruined palace. Here, the women and children are held as hostages while the strongest men are set to work chopping down trees and making planks—which they sensibly turn into rafts and thereby escape with their fellow prisoners by floating down a convenient river. Dickens' concluding chapter, "The Rafts on the River," describes this trip by water as well as the reunion of the escapees with the members of a rescue party and the safe return of all to the island. At the very end, the perspective of this Christmas number shifts to the point at which it began—that of Gill Davis, in old age, dictating his account of this adventure to "my Lady" (*CS*, p. 208).

As this brief summary suggests, the narrator's personality is largely submerged by the events that he relates. Initially, while brooding about the hardships of his life, he seems to be a man of complex dimensions, but this complexity quickly settles into two major traits. First, as one of the pirates remarks, Gill Davis "is a determined man" (p. 181). Second, despite his lowly social station, he worships Miss Maryon, later Lady Carton, who—in a curious gesture of generosity—finds him in old age and brings him to her husband's home, where she takes down his story from dictation. Dickens' opening and closing efforts to deal with Lady Carton's suppressed attachment toward Gill Davis while describing the social and intellectual inferiority of "her poor, old, faithful, humble soldier" (p. 208) seem strained. More strikingly, as William Oddie has noted, the emphasis on self-sacrifice by most of the men and women of the colony, as well as the use of the name "Carton," looks forward to *A Tale of Two Cities.* [30] The ambivalently renunciatory relationship between Davis and Lady Carton may also reflect Dickens' growing romantic interest in Ellen Ternan, with whom he had recently acted in *The Frozen Deep.* Here, however, as Oddie has demonstrated, Dickens' primary purpose was to write a Christmas story that would reflect the heroism of Englishmen and particularly Englishwomen in India during the insurrection there in 1857.[31] The relationship between Davis and Lady Carton seems peripheral to the actions that Davis relates, and the comparative unimportance of Davis' personality in this Christmas number as a whole indicates the result of Dickens' increased reliance on Collins' style of writing.

The effects of Collins' concern with plot on Dickens' concern with characterization are equally apparent in the remaining Christmas numbers between 1858 and 1860. With *A House to Let* (1858), Dickens returned to the established form of framework and interpolated contributions. However, Collins' influence on the production is marked. As Stone has noted, Dickens wrote both sections of the frame with Collins. Although the passages in this framework which Stone believes are "probably" by Dickens frequently enhance the idiosyncratic yet good-natured personality of the elderly old maid who narrates it,[32] the work as a whole reflects Collins' general interest in shaping material to focus attention on the outcome of events. The interpolated stories are only three in number. The fourth interpolated section, "Trottle's Report" by Collins alone, provides essential information for the central narrative—explaining why the house to let across from the elderly lady's residence in London remains unrented. Thus, Dickens' inset "Going into Society," about a showman who formerly rented the house in question along with a dwarf who later won a fortune in a lottery, is not so easily detached from its setting as some of the pieces interpolated into earlier Christmas numbers. This fact explains its somewhat curious appearance as it is usually reprinted out of context in *Christmas Stories*—ending with a discussion about the house by characters belonging to the omitted central narrative.

In contrast, Collins' influence is clearly lessened in *The Haunted House* (1859), the first Christmas number of *All the Year Round.* Here, for the first time since 1855, Collins simply contributed an interpolated story, and the plot of Dickens' framework is correspondingly much less complex and suspenseful than that developed in the numbers between 1856 and 1858. As discussed earlier, the down-to-earth nature of the narrator's personality becomes easily apparent in his framing monologue, while his private brand of "imaginations and remembrances" emerges readily in his interpolated "Ghost in Master B.'s Room."

Less felicitously, *A Message from the Sea* (1860), the first of the Christmas numbers with a framework written in the third person rather than the first, once again relies heavily on Collins' help in presenting an adventure story whose outcome is held in suspense. Unfortunately, the adventure itself seems uninspired, although its ingredients are complex. (See Appendix A for a discussion of Dickens' and Collins' respective contributions.) In brief, as the section entitled "The Village" explains, a Yankee sea captain comes to an English fishing village in search of a family named Raybrock. His errand, described in "The Money," is to deliver a message found in a bottle—a message that proves to be a letter to Alfred Raybrock from his missing brother, suggesting that a legacy from their deceased father is, in fact, stolen money. Captain Jorgan and Alfred Raybrock then undertake to solve the mystery by tracing clues deciphered from the letter. In "The Club-Night," Jorgan and Raybrock travel to another village, enter an inn, and find themselves in the midst of a club whose members entertain themselves by telling stories—a circumstance that provides an excuse for the usual interpolated contributions. In "The Seafaring Man," the mystery of the money is partly unravelled, and the seafaring man, who arrived at the inn shortly before Raybrock and Jorgan, proves to be Alfred's missing brother Hugh. "The Restitution" concludes the unravelling process, clears the name of the deceased Raybrock, reunites Hugh with his wife and child, and makes possible the wedding of Alfred and his sweetheart which has been postponed during the investigation. Even more noticeably than the Christmas numbers of 1857 and 1858, *A Message from the Sea* illustrates the deleterious effect of a strong interest in plot on the emerging fictional form to which Dickens' monologues belong.

As this overview suggests, the general impact of Dickens' effort at tandem writing with Wilkie Collins in the Christmas numbers between

1856 and 1860 seems artistically regrettable, although Dickens' willingness to experiment with the idea of joint composition in this remarkable fashion only underscores his feeling that in short stories, such as those in his Christmas numbers, he could indeed "let himself loose." Moreover, this period of close collaboration in the holiday numbers should not be neglected in assessments of Collins' role in Dickens' career. Earle Davis has thoughtfully discussed the extent of Collins' effect on Dickens' novels after *David Copperfield* and concluded that "the long-existing impression that Wilkie was responsible for Dickens' obsession with plot structure and unified organization of his novels—that is the Collins myth, [is] completely unjustified by the facts."[33] Davis' conclusion is undoubtedly true as far as Dickens' novels are concerned. It is difficult to believe that Collins' friendship with Dickens could account for the mature, carefully developed symbolism of novels such as *Bleak House* and *Little Dorrit.* However, in the majority of the Christmas numbers between 1856 and 1860, Dickens does seem to have increasingly submerged his own previously evolving interest in characterization through the monologue of a distinctive first-person narrator in favor of Collins' concern with plot. Nevertheless, in *Tom Tiddler's Ground,* at the end of the first twelve years of the Christmas numbers, a slightly awkward but still significant turning point is evident.

VI

One sign of this shift (as Appendix A indicates) is the general absence of Wilkie Collins' hand in the Christmas numbers from *Tom Tiddler's Ground* (1861) to *Mugby Junction* (1866). Yet, despite the fact that Collins contributed only one interpolated story to the holiday production for 1861—and nothing to those for the next five years—Dickens did not return immediately to the concept of a framing first-person monologue. *Tom Tiddler's Ground* continues in the form of a third-person narrative, although its central plot lacks the heavy-handed effort at suspense of *A Message from the Sea.* In essence, the method of *Tom Tiddler's Ground* is more starkly moralistic than that of any other Christmas number. Ideas of right and wrong behavior conflict in a manner similar to that of a morality play.

Dickens' opening section, entitled "Picking up Soot and Cinders," establishes this conflict. In this first chapter, the principal character, a wanderer called Mr. Traveller, learns of the existence of Mr. Mopes the Hermit and his willfully ruined estate, which has gained the name of Tom Tiddler's ground. Mr. Traveller visits Mr. Mopes and makes no secret of his antipathy toward the Hermit's squalid and selfish life— antipathy with which the omniscient narrator evidently concurs. To prove his point that one cannot turn one's back on society, the Traveller resolves to ask each person entering the Hermit's gate to recount some personal experience:

> ". . . it is a moral impossibility that any son or daughter of Adam can stand on this ground that I put my foot on, or on any ground that mortal treads, and gainsay the healthy tenure on which we hold our existence."
> "Which is," sneered the Hermit, "according to you—"
> "Which is," returned the other, "according to Eternal Providence, that we must arise and wash our faces and do our gregarious work and act and re-act on one another, leaving only the idiot and the palsied to sit blinking in the corner." (*CS*, pp. 299–300)

Although most of the stories supplied by other writers do not deal directly with this issue, Dickens' contribution—"Picking up Miss Kimmeens"—again focuses on the question of social and antisocial behavior. In marked contrast to the designedly permanent reclusiveness of Master Humphrey and his group of friends twenty-one years earlier, Miss Kimmeens' experience underscores the moral of this Christmas number: when she is left alone at school, the child degenerates toward the hermit level and thinks increasingly bitter thoughts, but through a kind of intuitive wisdom, she rushes out of doors in order "to emerge from her unnatural solitude, and look abroad for wholesome sympathy, to bestow and to receive" (p. 310). Miss Kimmeens' action brings the interpolated stories to a close, and Dickens' final section, "Picking up the Tinker," emphasizes the conviction that pervades this work. As the narrator concludes, echoing the words of the Tinker who has observed the Hermit with disgust, ". . . the moral with which the Tinker dismissed the subject was, that he said in his trade that metal that rotted for want of use, had better be left to rot, and couldn't rot too soon, considering how much true metal rotted from over-use and hard service" (p. 313). With *Tom Tiddler's Ground*, Dickens seems to have returned to the method of dramatizing a conflict of ideas which he had used previously in the Christmas Books. Unlike Scrooge, however, Mr. Mopes is not transformed, and the only reformation worked is that which may or may not be achieved within a reader's heart.

Tom Tiddler's Ground is unusual among Dickens' Christmas numbers. It lacks Collins' type of sensational plot, and it does not turn to the monologue for inspiration. Here, once again, Dickens is explicitly working with the idea of a children's game. As the Landlord of the Peal of Bells alehouse explains when Mr. Traveller inquires why the name "Tom Tiddler's ground" is commonly given to the Hermit's property: " 'Because he scatters halfpence to Tramps and such-like,' returned the

Landlord, 'and of course they pick 'em up. And this being done on his own land . . . why it is but regarding the halfpence as gold and silver, and turning the ownership of the property a bit round your finger, and there you have the name of the children's game complete' " (p. 289). However, in contrast to the earlier pervasive playfulness of "The Boots," this later allusion to the game of Tom Tiddler's ground is not developed beyond the Landlord's opening explanation or integrated into the theme and tone of the remainder of this Christmas number. The narrator's infusion of life into the buildings of the village outside the Peal of Bells alehouse is presented in Dickens' best animistically descriptive style, but generally, Dickens seems to be groping for an effective approach to the problem of what had by 1861 evidently become a perennial holiday obligation.

At the same time, to some extent at least, *Tom Tiddler's Ground* marks a culmination of Dickens' Christmas numbers to this date. In most of his contributions to these holiday productions between 1850 and 1861—despite his personal use of such occasions to experiment with ways of depicting the imagination or trying to write "so like . . . [Collins] as that no one should find out the difference"—Dickens seems to be largely composing to satisfy his readers' expectations—expressing familiar Christmas feelings or developing more or less exciting plots which might be understood by all. *Tom Tiddler's Ground,* with its earnest Victorian emphasis on the necessity of work and social involvement, epitomizes this intention, although Dickens' own cherished faith in the value of a temporary vacation from workaday actuality emerges in the Tinker's example of resting after completing one job and before turning to another. In contrast, in many of his paradoxically highly popular contributions to the Christmas numbers after 1861, Dickens seems to be taking advantage of an artistic version of this kind of holiday respite and creating to please himself.

CHAPTER 5

Public Entertainment

The Lion looked at Alice. . . . "Are you animal—or vegetable—or mineral?" he said. . . .

"It's a fabulous monster!" the Unicorn cried out, before Alice could reply.

"Then hand round the plum-cake, Monster," the Lion said.

CARROLL, *Through the Looking-Glass*

I

Like doors flying open to welcome holiday visitors, much of Dickens' Christmas writing between 1862 and 1866 explodes with festival exuberance. To readers who base their assessment of Dickens primarily upon his novels, such ebullience in the midst of his so-called dark period may seem anachronistic. Nonetheless, perhaps because he found in his Christmas writings a kind of creative antidote to the disillusionment apparent in *Great Expectations* or the somberness of *Our Mutual Friend* (perhaps also because his pace of producing novels had slowed and the worst of his domestic storm had passed), Dickens turned to his Christmas pieces during these years with zest. As he wrote to Forster about the Christmas number for 1864, "I can report that I have finished the job I set myself, and that it has in it something—to me at all events —so extraordinarily droll, that though I have been reading it some hundred times in the course of the working, I have never been able to look at it with the least composure, but have always roared in the most unblushing manner."[1] As in many of Dickens' previous Christmas writings, childhood games proliferate in the pieces he contributed to his Christmas numbers during this period—*Somebody's Luggage, Mrs. Lirriper's Lodgings, Mrs. Lirriper's Legacy, Doctor Marigold's Prescriptions,* and *Mugby Junction.* However, with *Somebody's Luggage,* the Christmas number of *All the Year Round* for 1862, such playfulness acquires new dimensions. Specifically, the concept that recurs in many of the holiday games of this period is the striking one of entertaining the public.

II

As the narrator of "His Leaving it till called for" and "His Wonderful End" (the chapters that Dickens wrote as a framework for *Somebody's Luggage*) indicates at the outset of his monologue, he is a waiter upon whatever members of the public frequent his place of work: "The writer of these humble lines being a Waiter, and having come of a family of Waiters, and owning at the present time five brothers who are all Waiters, and likewise an only sister who is a Waitress, would wish to offer a few words respecting his calling" (*CS,* p. 317). As his use of the literary cliché "these humble lines" in his opening sentence (combined with his echoing of the idea of respect in the words "respecting" and "respected" three times in his first two sentences) suggests, his tone as a writer resembles the attitude which he later describes as the customary one for a "Waiter of my standing" (p. 321). In both cases, this attitude is one of humorously adopted but conventionally established deference toward the people in whom it is his "business . . . to take a personal interest and sympathy" (p. 320). In the course of his soliloquy, this sixty-one-year-old headwaiter named Christopher provides details about himself and his profession. For example, he explains that his earliest recollections are of "uncongenial cruets, dirty plates, dish-covers, and cold gravy" (p. 318). Similarly, he emphasizes some of the peculiarities of the waitering life, such as his mother's concealment of her private existence and his infant presence: "for a Waitress known to be married would ruin the best of businesses,—it is the same as on the stage" (p. 318).

After this meandering introduction, he describes his purchase of "somebody's [abandoned] luggage," presents the assorted stories which he finds in various articles of that luggage, and fearfully confesses to the rightful owner of the property that he has sold these stories for publication. The rightful owner, in turn, proves to be a comically stereotypical author who scribbles constantly, bites his fingernails, smears ink on himself and "every undeserving object" (p. 329), and expresses his gratitude to Christopher in deeply purple prose. The journal that purchases the stories is none other than *All the Year Round,* conducted by a gentleman whose praises—according to several footnotes—are "editorially struck out" (pp. 358*n*, 359*n*, 365*n*). Christopher sees no incongruity in his transition from waiter to writer. He declares categorically that "you cannot lay down the tailoring, or the shoemaking, or the brokering, or the green-grocering, or the pictorial-periodicalling, or the second-hand wardrobe, or the small fancy businesses,—you cannot lay down those lines of life at your will and pleasure by the half-day or evening, and take up Waitering" (pp. 317–18). However, his pun on "wait" suggests no difficulty on his own part—"having . . . offered such observations as I felt it my duty to offer . . . on the general subject [of waitering]"—in proceeding smoothly as writer "to wait on the particular question" (p. 323). As author, Christopher is far better at presenting literature for public consumption than the madly scribbling Somebody who concealed his compositions in his luggage. In Christopher's words, "If there should be any flaw in the writings, or anything missing in the writings, it is Him as is responsible—not me."[2]

In contrast, while Christopher displays his congenial relationship with the public, the narrator of one of Somebody's writings, supposedly found in "His Brown-Paper Parcel," deliberately withdraws from public recognition. As this "young man in the Art line" repeatedly complains, "If there's a blighted public character going, I am the party" (pp. 348, 358), and his monologue is largely a description of two withering incidents. By occupation, he is a sidewalk artist, although he prefers to remain anonymous and let others rent the privilege of displaying his creations. However, on the two occasions he describes, he loses a friend and a sweetheart because he cannot control his antagonism toward the individuals who take credit for his work. The source of his "blight" is his refusal to merchandise his art. As he notes bitterly at the end of his description of the way in which impersonators appeal for support with his productions, "Such is genius in a commercial country. I am not up to the shivering, I am not up to the liveliness, I am not up to the wanting-employment-in-an-office move; I am only up to originating and executing the work" (p. 358). Whatever sympathy this monologue may elicit by its first-person nature is undercut by the outrageously obvious laziness of its speaker who describes himself as "a young man of that easy disposition, that I lie abed till it's absolutely necessary to get up and earn something, and then I lie abed again till I have spent it" (pp. 349–50). Moreover, Dickens' tongue-in-cheek characterization of this speaker is intended. By 1862, the basic format of Dickens' Christmas numbers had become well established, and *Somebody's Luggage* was conceived as an elaborate spoof of the problems inherent in this annual production; as Dickens wrote to Wilkie Collins, it was designed as "a comic defiance of the difficulty of a Xmas No., with an unexpected end to it."[3] Thus, in the description of Somebody, the account of the circumstances under which Christopher brought the writings to publication, and the "editorially" censored allusions to the conductor of the journal that put these writings into print, Dickens is visibly poking fun at his contributors and his own activities as editor of *All the Year Round.* The unrecognizability of this paranoid, "blighted public character" may also be a joking allusion to the customary anonymity of contributors to *Household Words* and *All the Year Round,* which occasionally resulted in the work of other writers being mistaken for that of Dickens. At the same time, in this speaker's exaggerated avoidance of the kind of publicity that Christopher accepts, Dickens appears to be consciously playing with what he evidently viewed as the intrinsically public aspect of the successful artist's role.

Unlike *Somebody's Luggage,* the Christmas numbers for the following years are not designedly parodic. Nonetheless, in the holiday productions between 1863 and 1866, the idea of entertaining the public —in different ways—recurs. In Dickens' frameworks for *Mrs. Lirriper's Lodgings* (1863) and *Mrs. Lirriper's Legacy* (1864), the primary narrator is a widowed, lodginghouse keeper named Mrs. Lirriper, "a lone woman with a living to get" (p. 369). The opening portions of her monologues in both Christmas numbers are filled with a flood of associatively connected details about the difficulties of her life as the operator of a London boarding house in which paying customers, hopefully, will wish to lodge. Mrs. Lirriper's distinctive characteristic is her unusual style of speaking which, in the opening portions of her monologues, transcends that of Flora Finching in *Little Dorrit.*[4] As one of her remarks in *Mrs. Lirriper's Lodgings* indicates, she is able to comprehend matters as seemingly diverse as teeth, hired girls (including the willingness of such girls to work), and the genteel assumptions of her lodgers within a single thought:

> Girls as I was beginning to remark are one of your first and your lasting troubles, being like your teeth which begin with convulsions and never cease tormenting you from the time you cut them till they cut you, and then you don't want to part with them which seems hard but we must all succumb or buy artificial, and even where you get a will nine times out of ten you'll get a dirty face with it and naturally lodgers do not like good society to be shown in with a smear of black across the nose or a smudgy eyebrow. (Pp. 372–73)

The framing narrator of *Doctor Marigold's Prescriptions* (1865) is even more sensitive to the inclinations of the people whom it is his business to please and even more conscious of his public role. Doctor Marigold, the central speaker in this case, is a "cheap jack," a peddler of cheap goods, who travels about the countryside in a cart. As he explains, he has become "King of the Cheap Jacks" (pp. 446, 471) by consciously perfecting the impact of his style of speech on his audience: "I have worked at it. I have measured myself against other public speakers, Members of Parliament, Platforms, Pulpits, Counsel learned in the law

—and where I have found 'em good, I have took a bit of imitation from 'em, and where I have found 'em bad, I have let 'em alone."[5] Marigold is acutely aware that public accomplishments may not correlate with personal happiness. As he observes when he describes the discrepancy between his outward success at the cheap-jack trade and his private misery caused by the consecutive deaths of his dearly loved child, his emotionally disturbed wife, and his dog: "That's often the way with us public characters. See us on the footboard, and you'd give pretty well anything you possess to be us. See us off the footboard, and you'd add a trifle to be off your bargain" (p. 446). Nevertheless, "at selling times" (p. 446) and after adopting a previously neglected deaf and dumb girl to raise in his daughter's place, Marigold conquers his depression. Thus, he proves almost as resilient as the irrepressible Boy at the unrefreshing refreshment room at Mugby Junction, in one of the pieces Dickens wrote for the Christmas number the following year, whose operating principle—in outrageous contrast to the attitudes of Doctor Marigold, Mrs. Lirriper, and Christopher—is a determination to "Keep the Public Down" (p. 519).

Dickens' preoccupation with the idea of public entertainment during this period is not surprising. The reactions of his readers were never far from his thinking as a writer. Fielding's famous narrative pronouncement at the opening of *Tom Jones* that "an author ought to consider himself, not as a gentleman who gives a private or eleemosynary treat, but rather as one who keeps a public ordinary, at which all persons are welcome for their money"—quoted by Dickens in his 1841 preface to *The Old Curiosity Shop*[6]—provides a humorous but convenient summary of Dickens' basic view of the novelist's role. Moreover, in the last twelve years of his career, his decision to give paid, professional readings from his works brought this question of his relationship with his public into even greater prominence in his mind. In 1858, asking advice about the wisdom of undertaking his first series of such readings, Dickens urged Forster, who vainly expressed his disapproval of the scheme, to consider the plan "apart from all personal likings and dislikings, and solely with a view to its effect on that particular relation (personally affectionate and like no other man's) which subsists between me and the public."[7] As Philip Collins has observed, Dickens evidently viewed his readings at this time of domestic crisis as a source of "some of the emotional nourishment which he could not now find in his marriage."[8] His subsequent remark to Forster about his 1861 readings— "everywhere I have found that peculiar personal relation between my audience and myself on which I counted most when I entered on this enterprise"[9]—indicates that his expectations of this kind of emotional sustenance were not disappointed. Indeed, his seemingly hysterical insertion of a statement about his separation from Catherine Dickens in the 12 June 1858 issue of *Household Words* may have been partially prompted by a fear that gossip about his marriage might erode this other, vital relationship with his public. As Forster noted about Dickens' insistence on printing such a comment, "he had now publicly to show himself, at stated times, as a public entertainer, and this, with his name even so aspersed, he found to be impossible."[10] The piece entitled "Going into Society" in the Christmas number for 1858 *(A House to Let)* —depicting a dwarf's melancholy conclusion, shortly before his death, that life as an admitted public performer passing a saucer after each entertainment is preferable to life as a member of "Society" composed of unadmitted performers repeating his act for higher stakes—undoubtedly reflects some of Dickens' current uneasy attention to his own public role.[11] By 1862, however, whatever fears Dickens might have had about the enduring and satisfying nature of his public status were thoroughly allayed. His position as an outstandingly successful performer as well as the preeminently popular novelist of the age was a secure one.[12] Like wisecracks about sports events made by a winning athlete, the subject of public entertainment was one about which he could confidently joke.

The eventual similarities are obvious between Doctor Marigold's situation as a successful jester and performer, despite his concealed sorrows, and Dickens' personal situation, hiding his private discontent and his surreptitious liaison with Ellen Ternan. In his well-known "Two Scrooges" essay, Edmund Wilson suggests a somewhat strained biographical interpretation of this piece.[13] The primary significance of the framework for *Doctor Marigold's Prescriptions* and the other "Christmas Stories" between 1862 and 1866 which turn on the idea of public entertainment, however, lies not so much in what they imply about Dickens' personal life as in what they display about themselves.[14] In the pieces of this period dealing specifically with public entertainment, Dickens seems to be explicitly flaunting what he recognized as an essential feature of the writer/public reader's art. Moreover, like toys which open to reveal yet other toys, within this playfulness with the idea of public entertainment, other types of play become apparent.

III

In these stories, the general subject of catering to the public is repeatedly linked with the topic of literary composition. In *Somebody's Luggage,* such playful self-consciousness about the literary act is unmistakable. As a writer, Christopher relies heavily on clichés, occasionally mixed with colloquialisms or otherwise incongruously combined. Thus, he speaks of "my artless narrative,"[15] alludes to "the language of the

Bard of A. 1." (p. 325), and refers to "the finger of Fate and Conscience, hand in hand" (p. 359). Furthermore, enclosed within Christopher's words are three other specimens of artistic activity. In the first of these instances, as Christopher complains, the Somebody who left his writings in the luggage lacked any sense of order: "He had put no Heading to any of his writings. Alas! Was he likely to have a Heading without a Head, and where was *his* Head when he took such things into it! The writings are consequently called, here, by the names of the articles of Luggage to which they was found attached. In some cases, such as his Boots, he would appear to have hid the writings: thereby involving his style in greater obscurity. But his Boots was at least pairs—and no two of his writings can put in any claim to be so regarded."[16] His appearance, as Christopher observes when Somebody finally comes into the coffee room at the end of this Christmas number, confirms this image of disarray:

> the gentleman had gone up to the mantelpiece, right in front of the fire, and had laid his forehead against the mantelpiece (which it is a low one, and brought him into the attitude of leap-frog), and had heaved a tremenjous sigh. His hair was long and lightish; and when he laid his forehead against the mantelpiece, his hair all fell in a dusty fluff together over his eyes; and when he now turned round and lifted up his head again, it all fell in a dusty fluff together over his ears. This give him a wild appearance, similar to a blasted heath. (P. 361)

Secondly, while Somebody is merely disorganized, the "young man in the Art line" who narrates "His Brown-Paper Parcel" is malevolent. As he cautions the reader at the outset of his narrative, "Let us have it down in black and white at the first go off, so that there may be no unpleasantness or wrangling afterwards. And this is looked over by a friend of mine, a ticket writer, that is up to literature" (p. 348). As his departing former friend Mr. Click warns him, using hackneyed quotations from Shakespeare's *Othello* and Isaac Watts' "Against Idleness and Mischief":

> Thomas, beware of envy. It is the green-eyed monster which never did and never will improve each shining hour, but quite the reverse. I dread the envious man, Thomas. I confess that I am afraid of the envious man, when he is so envious as you are. Whilst you contemplated the works of a gifted rival, and whilst you heard that rival's praises, and especially whilst you met his humble glance as he put that card away, your countenance was so malevolent as to be terrific. Thomas, I have heard of the envy of them that follows the Fine-Art line, but I never believed it could be what yours is. I wish you well, but I take my leave of you. And if you

should ever get into trouble through knifeing—or say, garotting,
—a brother artist, as I believe you will, don't call me to character,
Thomas, or I shall be forced to injure your case. (P. 353)

Finally, the persona of Dickens himself, the conductor of the journal that purchases Somebody's writings, provides a kind of norm. This persona accepts Christopher's cliché-ridden but humorously practical presentation of the writings both to "A. Y. R." (pp. 359, 360) and to the reader, ignores Somebody's incomprehensible corrections of the proofs, and lacks the malevolence of the reclusive "young man in the Art line." As Christopher explains at the end of his description of Somebody's glee at finding his writings at last in print,

> He [Somebody] smeared himself and he smeared the Proofs, the night through, to that degree, that when Sol give him warning to depart (in a four-wheeler), few could have said which was them, and which was him, and which was blots. His last instructions was, that I should instantly run and take his corrections to the office of the present Journal. I did so. They most likely will not appear in print, for I noticed a message being brought round from Beaufort Printing House while I was a throwing this concluding statement on paper, that the ole resources of that establishment was unable to make out what they meant. Upon which a certain gentleman in company, as I will not more particularly name—but of whom it will be sufficient to remark, standing on the broad basis of a wave-girt isle, that whether we regard him in the light of—* laughed, and put the corrections in the fire.
>
> *The remainder of this complimentary parenthesis editorially struck out.[17]

Within the comprehensive joke about entertaining the public on which this Christmas number turns, Dickens spins proliferating jokes about the creative (extending to the editorial) process itself.

For the next three Christmas numbers, this playful self-consciousness of the art of fiction is less conspicuous but still present. In the first Christmas number over which she presides, Mrs. Lirriper urges her friend and long-term lodger Major Jemmy Jackman to write down the stories told to him by other lodgers as a way of working out of his depression when Jemmy—Mrs. Lirriper's adopted grandson and the major's godson—goes away to school. As a result, "the Major was another man in three days and he was himself again in a week and he wrote and wrote and wrote with his pen scratching like rats behind the wainscot" (p. 396). He proves to be so prolific a writer that his stories supply material for the Christmas number for 1864 as well as that for 1863. In the holiday production for 1865, when his adopted daughter leaves his care in order to extend her education, Doctor Marigold also turns to the remedy of literary composition—"a . . . scheme . . . which, as it turned out, kept my time and attention a good deal employed, and helped me over the two years' stile" (pp. 451–52). In Marigold's case, the work is editorial as well as creative. He decides to "have a book new-made express for her" and "considering that I was in the habit of changing so much about the country, and that I should have to find out a literary character here to make a deal with, and another literary character there to make a deal with, as opportunities presented, I hit on the plan that this same book should be a general miscellaneous lot" (p. 452). However, the "new-made" book is to begin with an account by Marigold of himself, a section which he finds far more difficult than organizing the rest of this production: "This same book took up all my spare time. It was no play to get the other articles together in the general miscellaneous lot, but when it come to my own article! There! I couldn't have believed the blotting, nor yet the buckling to at it, nor the patience over it. Which again is like the footboard. The public have no idea" (p. 453).

Although Marigold claims that it is "no play" to organize the articles of his co-authors, it is clear that Dickens is playing exuberantly with this narrator's occupation, and Dickens' original readers would have been fully conscious of the game. Marigold's scheme, like that of Mrs. Lirriper, provides the excuse for the customary additional pieces by diverse contributors to the holiday number. Thus, Marigold's "general miscellaneous lot" is, in fact, an accurate description of the Christmas number for 1865. In a similar vein, the last paragraph of his opening monologue (like the allusions to "A. Y. R." at the end of *Somebody's Luggage*) reflects the original circumstances of publication of these holiday creations:

> Now I'll tell you what I am a-going to do with you. I am a-going to offer you the general miscellaneous lot, her own book, never read by anybody else but me, added to and completed by me after her first reading of it, eight-and-forty printed pages, six-and-ninety columns, Whiting's own work, Beaufort House to wit, thrown off by the steam-ingine, best of paper, beautiful green wrapper, folded like clean linen come home from the clear-starcher's, and so exquisitely stitched that, regarded as a piece of needlework alone, it's better than the sampler of a seamstress undergoing a Competitive examination for Starvation before the Civil Service Commissioners—and I offer the lot for what? For eight pound? Not so much. For six pound? Less. For four pound. Why, I hardly expect you to believe me, but that's the sum. Four pound! The stitching alone cost half as much again. Here's forty-eight original

pages, ninety-six original columns, for four pound. You want more for the money? Take it. Three whole pages of advertisements of thrilling interest thrown in for nothing. Read 'em and believe 'em. More? My best of wishes for your merry Christmases and your happy New Years, your long lives and your true prosperities. Worth twenty pound good if they are delivered as I send them. Remember! Here's a final prescription added, "To be taken for life," which will tell you how the cart broke down, and where the journey ended. You think Four Pound too much? And still you think so? Come! I'll tell you what then. Say Four Pence, and keep the secret. (P. 455)

In editions of the collected *Christmas Stories*, the playfulness inherent in Marigold's marketing of his prescriptions is commonly diluted —a situation that once again illustrates the importance of a modern critic's familiarity with the original nature of Dickens' Christmas numbers. However, with *Doctor Marigold's Prescriptions* as well as some of the related Christmas writings dealing with the idea of public entertainment, Dickens seems to have been partly responsible for this alteration of effect. In 1867, as Harry Stone has observed in connection with *Household Words*, Dickens detached most of his contributions to several of the Christmas numbers from their initial contexts in order to allow these writings to be collected in the Diamond edition of his works, published in the United States at the time of his second American visit.[18] In the course of Dickens' changes on this occasion, Marigold's extended comic allusion to the *All the Year Round* format was deleted. In addition, among Dickens' revisions, the framework of *Doctor Marigold's Prescriptions* became a single monologue, and the word "prescriptions" vanished from the title along with the humorous chapter headings "To Be Taken Immediately" and "To Be Taken for Life"— modifications that weaken the joke about Marigold's medical skills on which the work is based. The fundamental nature of this work is only confused by the custom, in many modern editions, of restoring these chapter headings without returning the word "prescriptions" to the general title (combined with the practice of enclosing Marigold's humorous reference to *All the Year Round* in brackets).[19] Some of Dickens' changes in 1867 were undoubtedly made in order to render the stories comprehensible to American readers who might not have encountered them in their original format. Nevertheless, Dickens also omitted the readily detachable piece by the "young man in the Art line" from *Somebody's Luggage*, although this story contains no explicit reference to the circumstances of its publication. The latter deletion suggests Dickens may have felt that, once divorced from the *All the Year Round* context, any manifestation of artistically self-conscious playfulness ought to be toned down. In contrast, he could and occasionally did—with evident delight—indulge in jokes about the creative process in the pages of *All the Year Round.*

IV

Such joking, moreover, is never far removed from the sense of sympathetic indulgence in children's play which Dickens felt was especially suitable to Christmas. The second chapter of his opening narrative for *Mugby Junction,* the Christmas number for 1866, makes this connection between playing and storytelling explicit. Here a little girl named Polly teaches a misanthropic character named Barbox Brothers a fairy tale (humorously reminiscent of Captain Murderer's more bloodthirsty culinary activities in "Nurse's Stories") as part of his process of emotional and imaginative rejuvenation:

> Whereupon Polly, giving her hand a new little turn in his, expressive of settling down for enjoyment, commenced a long romance, of which every relishing clause began with the words: "So this," or, "And so this." As, "So this boy;" or, "So this fairy;" or, "And so this pie was four yards round, and two yards and a quarter deep." The interest of the romance was derived from the intervention of this fairy to punish this boy for having a greedy appetite. To achieve which purpose, this fairy made this pie, and this boy ate and ate and ate, and his cheeks swelled and swelled and swelled. There were many tributary circumstances, but the forcible interest culminated in the total consumption of this pie, and the bursting of this boy. (P. 504)

Polly, in turn, requires Barbox Brothers to repeat the story to her shortly thereafter as a kind of examination of his degree of fanciful development: "There was a want of breadth observable in his rendering of the cheeks, as well as the appetite, of the boy; and there was a certain tameness in his fairy, referable to an under-current of desire to account for her. Still, as the first lumbering performance of a good-humoured monster, it passed muster" (p. 505).

In the case of this diligently learned fairy tale, however, Dickens' opening narrative for *Mugby Junction* seems somewhat strained. The three previous Christmas numbers deal much more easily with the idea of juvenile play. In the sentimental piece contained in "His Boots" from *Somebody's Luggage,* the loving playfulness of a French corporal with a child named Bebelle ("a playful name for Gabrielle" [p. 340]) prompts the Englishman who observes them to take Bebelle into his own care when the corporal dies. The Englishman then seeks a reconciliation with his own daughter as a result of his softened feelings. In Mrs. Lirriper's two narratives, Jemmy and the major play at a variety of games, from make-believe means of transportation to enjoyable means of mastering mathematics. The two stories by Jemmy which conclude the Christmas numbers for 1863 and 1864 also emerge from their context as an elaborate kind of game in which adults participate with children. Both stories—reflecting Jemmy's youthful illusions—are told to entertain Mrs. Lirriper and Major Jackman, against the background of the compassionate but more practical knowledge of Mrs. Lirriper and the major.

Subsequently in 1865, Marigold rests the book that he is assembling on an extended joke about his ostensible medical abilities. (In fact, he received his name from his own parents "out of gratitude and compliment to" the doctor who delivered him "in consequence of his being a very kind gentleman, and accepting no fee but a tea-tray" [p. 435].) Marigold's purpose here is a way of playfully measuring his adopted daughter's growth in understanding after her years at school. As Marigold explains, he wishes to see "if she catches the idea that my only Prescriptions are for her amusement and interest" (p. 453). Thus, the punning use of the term "prescriptions" in his title allows Marigold and his daughter to transform into a game a mistake into which she had fallen in her childhood. In this fashion, they engage delightedly in that feat of mental acrobatics which Huizinga has deemed necessary for poetic understanding: "donning the child's soul like a magic cloak and . . . forsaking man's wisdom for the child's."[20]

V

Ultimately, Dickens' playing with the ideas of public entertainment, literary creation, and the games of children in these Christmas pieces leads to a marked degree of stylistic experimentation. The first-person monologues by Christopher, Mrs. Lirriper, Doctor Marigold, the "young man in the Art line," and the Boy at Mugby go far beyond the efforts by some of the speakers in Dickens' earlier Christmas numbers to characterize themselves. Unlike the first-person speakers in uncanny pieces like "A Madman's Manuscript" or "A Confession Found in a Prison in the Time of Charles the Second," these narrators are not simply vehicles for revealing some abnormal or unnatural event. Rather, they are preoccupied with bringing their distinctive existences into general view. For example, Mrs. Lirriper introduces herself in her second monologue in a passage that briefly rivals the free associations of Joyce's Molly Bloom:[21]

> Being here before your eyes my dear in my own easy-chair in my own quiet room in my own Lodging-House Number Eighty-one Norfolk Street Strand London situated midway between the city

and St. James's—if anything is where it used to be with these hotels calling themselves Limited but called unlimited by Major Jackman rising up everywhere and rising up into flagstaffs where they can't go any higher, but my mind of those monsters is give me a landlord's or landlady's wholesome face when I come off a journey and not a brass plate with an electrified number clicking out of it which it's not in nature can be glad to see me and to which I don't want to be hoisted like molasses at the Docks and left there telegraphing for help with the most ingenious instruments but quite in vain—being here my dear I have no call to mention that I am still in the Lodgings as a business hoping to die in the same and if agreeable to the clergy partly read over at Saint Clement's Danes and concluded in Hatfield churchyard when lying once again by my poor Lirriper ashes to ashes and dust to dust. (Pp. 405–6)

Doctor Marigold's style is less elliptical than that of Mrs. Lirriper but no less idiosyncratic. In place of Mrs. Lirriper's seemingly haphazard ramblings, Doctor Marigold uses cheap-jack patter. His description of his own courtship and marriage, illustrating his fundamental tendency to view life in cheap-jack terms, is worth quoting at length:

I courted my wife from the footboard of the cart. I did indeed. She was a Suffolk young woman, and it was in Ipswich market-place right opposite the corn-chandler's shop. I had noticed her up at a window last Saturday that was, appreciating highly. I had took to her, and I had said to myself, "If not already disposed of, I'll have that lot." Next Saturday that come, I pitched the cart on the same pitch, and I was in very high feather indeed, keeping 'em laughing the whole of the time, and getting off the goods briskly. At last I took out of my waistcoat-pocket a small lot wrapped in soft paper, and I put it this way (looking up at the window where she was). "Now here, my blooming English maidens, is an article, the last article of the present evening's sale, which I offer to only you, the lovely Suffolk Dumplings biling over with beauty, and I won't take a bid of a thousand pounds for from any man alive. Now what is it? Why, I'll tell you what it is. It's made of fine gold, and it's not broke, though there's a hole in the middle of it, and it's stronger than any fetter that ever was forged, though it's smaller than any finger in my set of ten. Why ten? Because, when my parents made over my property to me, I tell you true, there was twelve sheets, twelve towels, twelve table-cloths, twelve knives, twelve forks, twelve tablespoons, and twelve teaspoons, but my set of fingers was two short of a dozen, and could never since be matched. Now what else is it? Come, I'll tell you. It's a hoop of solid gold, wrapped in a silver curl-paper, that I myself took off the shining locks of the ever-beautiful old lady in Threadneedle-street, London city; I wouldn't tell you so if I hadn't the paper to show, or you mightn't believe it even of me. Now what else is it? It's a man-trap and a handcuff, the parish stocks and a leg-lock, all in gold and all in one. Now what else is it? It's a wedding-ring. Now I'll tell you what I'm a going to do with it. I'm not a going to offer this lot for money; but I mean to give it to the next of you beauties that laughs, and I'll pay her a visit to-morrow morning at exactly half after nine o'clock as the chimes go, and I'll take her out for a walk to put up the banns." *She* laughed, and got the ring handed up to her. When I called in the morning, she says, "O dear! It's never you, and you never mean it?" "It's ever me," says I, "and I am ever yours, and I ever mean it." So we got married, after being put up three times —which, by the bye, is quite in the Cheap Jack way again, and shows once more how the Cheap Jack customs pervade society. (Pp. 440–41)

Marigold's increasingly comprehensible answers to the rhetorical question "what is it"—leading up to the final explanation that "it's a wedding ring"—demonstrates the way in which, as a successful cheap jack, he gradually leads the audience in his own direction and the manner in which his professional role swallows up his private life. He sells himself in place of his usual merchandise and barters the wedding ring for a bride. When the marriage turns out badly, he expresses his grief in similarly professional terms: "She wasn't a bad wife, but she had a temper. If she could have parted with that one article at a sacrifice, I wouldn't have swopped her away in exchange for any other woman in England. Not that I ever did swop her away, for we lived together till she died, and that was thirteen year" (p. 442).

In these monologues, whether their words flow glibly like Doctor Marigold's or sourly like those of the "young man in the Art line," the narrators' utterances reveal the texture of their minds. We see not only the daily events of their lives, but also their unconscious foibles and faults. The affectations and self-regard of the waiter in *Somebody's Luggage* are minor weaknesses, but those of his younger counterpart in the railroad refreshment room at Mugby Junction verge upon juvenile delinquency. The latter depicts his exploits with such gusto, nevertheless, that it is impossible to deny him the kind of sympathy which Dickens himself must have felt when he signed a letter to his friend Thomas Beard "The Boy (at Mugby)."[22] In such pieces, Dickens approaches the problem of conflicting evaluations of a speaker's words explored by his contemporary Robert Browning in some of his best poems.[23] The Boy at Mugby displays his outrageous attitude with such unfaltering confidence that a reader hesitates to condemn him as he deserves. Other narrators of Dickens' monologues are not so zestfully reprehensible. Mrs. Lirriper's wandering thoughts, minor jealousies, and uneducated errors are a far cry from the Boy's high-spirited pursuit of public disservice. Whatever response Dickens' speakers ultimately elicit, however, their words reveal their unique perspectives on their audience's everyday world. Their distinctive manners of speaking reflect their modes of thinking, and particularly in Mrs. Lirriper's case, Dickens seems to be stylistically playing with ways of rendering the operation of the imagination itself.

VI

In these holiday pieces, the playfulness that lies at the heart of Dickens' Christmas writings reaches its culmination. In the enthusiasm with which Christopher, Mrs. Lirriper, Doctor Marigold, and the Boy at Mugby pursue their forms of public entertainment, Dickens, at least temporarily, has achieved the spirit that Mrs. Lirriper discerned in her holiday in Paris of "everybody seeming to play at everything in this world" (p. 422). One of the inherent features of these stories, as of all of Dickens' Christmas writings, is a probing of the nature of reality— of an awareness that the faculty Dickens called fancy can transform the uncharitable, unimaginative workaday world into something other than what it is. This awareness is linked with a sense that such an apparent metamorphosis in Christmas writings is only a holiday game. The supernatural tale about "The Signalman" which Dickens added to *Mugby Junction* (as well as the "prescription" by Doctor Marigold entitled "To Be Taken with a Grain of Salt," which Dickens, at least partially, may also have composed)[24] turns openly on the question of the distinction between actuality and make-believe. Moreover, in his monologues from *Somebody's Luggage* to "The Boy at Mugby," this playing with the relationship between reality and artifice becomes even more obviously self-conscious. Here, through the stylistic play with which he characterizes his speakers, Dickens mingles childhood games with an exuberant flaunting of artistic activities within the larger context of public entertainment which he evidently perceived as a fundamental feature of his own publicly oriented art. Dickens' subsequent Christmas writing is less successful. *No Thoroughfare*—the Christmas number for 1867 in which he once again relied heavily on the help of Wilkie Collins—is a technically unremarkable tangle of mistaken identity, murder, love, and larceny. Its form is that of a single story, narrated in the third person, without any interpolated pieces. Its characterization seems generally uninspired. In addition, except in the tangential sense of presenting a supposedly exciting adventure in a quasi-theatrical fashion (with chapters entitled "Acts" and headings such as "The Curtain Rises" and "The Curtain Falls"),[25] it does not deal with the idea of play. In 1868, Dickens abandoned the idea of the Christmas number altogether. However, with the figures of Christopher, Mrs. Lirriper, and Doctor Marigold—conceived against the strikingly dissimilar background of *Great Expectations* and *Our Mutual Friend*—Dickens triumphed over the annual challenges of the Christmas number. The entertainment that these individuals set before the public, in comic contrast to that which the Boy at Mugby and the "young man in the Art line" perversely decline to offer, is—as Marigold would say—worth the price.

HAPTER 6

Murder and Self-Effacement

Well did the Wisest of our time write: "It is only
with Renunciation . . . that Life, properly
speaking, can be said to begin."

CARLYLE, *Sartor Resartus*

I

As the previous chapters indicate, Dickens' work with short stories
illuminates a number of his general authorial concerns. By 1865, he was
supremely confident, as he observed ironically in his postscript to *Our
Mutual Friend,* that "an artist . . . may perhaps be trusted to know what
he is about in his vocation" (p. 821). His exuberant playing with the idea
of public entertainment in the Christmas numbers between 1862 and
1866 is a manifestation of this self-confidence. Despite the importance
of his contributions to the Christmas numbers, Dickens' experimentation with the short story between 1850 and 1868 was not confined to the
Christmas season. Most outstandingly, on two occasions unrelated to
Christmas (in 1857 and 1868 respectively), Dickens used short stories
with significant results to probe psychologically abnormal states of
mind. One of these pieces—narrated by a phantom and enclosed within
a larger work entitled *The Lazy Tour of Two Idle Apprentices*—is stylistically awkward, while the other—"George Silverman's Explanation"—
is masterfully designed. However, both stories offer unusual perspectives on the ideal of renunciation which recurs in many of Dickens'
novels (for example, Little Nell's disregard for herself in her concern for
her grandfather in *The Old Curiosity Shop* and Sydney Carton's substi-
tution of himself for the condemned Charles Darnay in *A Tale of Two
Cities*). Thus, both brief stories are worth examining at length.

II

The supernatural tale told by a murderer set within *The Lazy Tour of
Two Idle Apprentices* is one of the strangest and least discussed of
Dickens' writings. A reader who happens upon this piece at the end of

the volume of *Christmas Stories,* where it often appears in editions of Dickens' collected works, may feel as if he has awakened on the morning after Christmas with blurred vision and an aching head. To critical eyes, this story of a man who murders his ineffectual, almost nervelessly submissive wife simply by repeatedly telling her to die is apt to seem bizarre. To modern sensibilities, the tale is likely to appear puzzlingly constructed. It shifts inexplicably from third to first-person narrative, and a number of its details are entangled with those of its framework —an impressionistic description of a joint excursion to the north of England, which Dickens wrote in collaboration with Wilkie Collins and published in *Household Words* in October 1857. Such uneasiness is partly justified. The story is by no means one of Dickens' best or even better short works, and it illustrates the way in which the sense of imaginative unrestraint, which Dickens attributed to the short story, can occasionally lead to a regrettable lack of control. At the same time, excess is sometimes more illuminating than moderation. In the context of Dickens' concern with the value of self-sacrifice in his other literary productions, the picture of the misuse of the human will presented in this tale seems too significant to ignore.

Like many of the interpolated tales in *Pickwick Papers,* this piece, which Dickens left untitled but which may conveniently be called "The Bride's Chamber" from the setting of its major events,[1] is a story in the tradition of Gothic terror, placed within a somewhat more realistic frame. Unlike the wife-slaying narrator of "A Madman's Manuscript" in *Pickwick Papers,* ringing his madhouse chain and gamboling on his bed of straw, the unnamed old man who dominates the action of "The Bride's Chamber" is never explicitly described as mentally deranged. Nonetheless, his "second pursuit" (*CS,* p. 729)[2] of the widowed and now wealthy woman who had previously rejected him in order to marry a man with more money, his cold-blooded forgery of her signature to a document leaving everything to her ten-year-old daughter and naming himself the girl's guardian when the mother dies unexpectedly, and his molding of the daughter's mind like "soft white wax" (p. 729) over a period of eleven years (to regard him as "the one embodiment her life presented to her of power" until, when she reaches twenty-one, he makes her "his half-witted, frightened, and submissive Bride" [p. 730]) represent a desire for self-satisfaction carried to a pathological degree surpassed only by his subsequent treatment of the Bride. After their marriage, the girl's "half-witted" efforts to elicit kindness from her husband with groundless pleas for forgiveness only evoke his scorn:

> "O Sir! . . . look kindly on me, and be merciful to me! I beg your pardon. I will do anything you wish, if you will only forgive me!"

> That had become the poor fool's constant song: "I beg your pardon," and "Forgive me!"
>
> She was not worth hating; he felt nothing but contempt for her. (P. 730)

He coerces her into conveying her property to him should she die and then relentlessly kills her by an exercise of his will:

> "Now, die! I have done with you." She shrunk, and uttered a low, suppressed cry. "I am not going to kill you. I will not endanger my life for yours. Die!"
>
> . . . .
>
> Shut up in the deserted mansion, aloof from all mankind, and engaged alone in such a struggle without any respite, it came to this—that either he must die, or she. He knew it very well, and concentrated his strength against her feebleness. Hours upon hours he held her by the arm when her arm was black where he held it, and bade her Die! (Pp. 731–32)

Eventually her feebleness, visually emphasized by her light hair and characteristic white dress, cannot withstand his strength. As the old man narrating the tale, who proves to be the now eternally restless ghost of this wife-murdering husband, describes his annihilation of the Bride: "Her large eyes strained themselves with wonder and fear; wonder and fear changed to reproach; reproach to blank nothing. It was done" (p. 732).

In contrast to "the unhappy man whose ravings are recorded" (*PP*, p. 146) in "A Madman's Manuscript," the central character in "The Bride's Chamber" never loses his ability to function as a sane member of society, in his own eyes as well as those of others. When he impulsively throws a billhook that splits the skull of the boy who accuses him of the Bride's murder, the man buries the body carefully and then successfully goes about his business, turning "his Money over and over, and still over" until "he had increased his fortune, Twelve Hundred Per Cent" (p. 736). The boy's skeleton is discovered only by accident, when lightning strikes the tree by which the body is buried, and a bribed servant allows scientific investigators to examine the tree's roots. Even after this discovery, to his chagrin, the man is treated and executed only as a common criminal. He is "hanged at Lancaster Castle with . . . his face to the wall" for "the real" (p. 737) murder of the boy, but he is also erroneously accused of poisoning the Bride rather than being considered, as he feels he should be, an unjustly persecuted individual whose wife has died through no fault of his own:

> . . . see the justice of men, and how it was extended to him! He was further accused of having poisoned that girl in the Bride's Cham-

ber. He, who had carefully and expressly avoided imperilling a hair of his head for her, and who had seen her die of her own incapacity! (P. 737)

In this tale, Dickens appears to be using the imaginative license which he associated with the short story to explore an abnormal state of mind. In the section of *The Lazy Tour* immediately before "The Bride's Chamber," Mr. Goodchild, the persona adopted by Dickens in this work, describes a visit to a lunatic asylum and (in a more comprehensive version of James' later artistic image of "the figure in the carpet") remarks about his resulting sense of "fellow-feeling" (p. 725) with a patient whom he encountered there, a man perpetually attempting to trace the pattern in a mat upon the floor. In Mr. Goodchild's words, "I thought how all of us, God help us! in our different ways are poring over our bits of matting, blindly enough, and what confusions and mysteries we make in the pattern" (pp. 724–25). Extending this sense of "fellow-feeling" with a conventionally unacceptable mental condition into "The Bride's Chamber," Dickens has moved from the clear-cut distinction between sanity and insanity apparent in "A Madman's Manuscript" at the beginning of his career to a more sophisticated awareness of the abnormal extremes into which seemingly normal attitudes—in this case ordinary self-assertiveness—may merge.[3]

The biographical implications of "The Bride's Chamber" are readily apparent. The kind of relentless determination to destroy an impeding "weak, credulous, incapable, helpless nothing" (p. 728) which it demonstrates was undoubtedly latent in Dickens' own strong-willed personality. (In Forster's words, Dickens possessed "a sense that everything was possible to the will that would make it so.")[4] Less than a year after the composition of "The Bride's Chamber," Dickens formally separated from his own, no-longer-wanted wife. In fact, part of Dickens' purpose behind his ostensibly "lazy tour" with Collins in September 1857 was an effort to deaden the unhappiness caused by his sense of hopeless marital incompatibility combined with his extramarital interest in eighteen-year-old Ellen Ternan.[5] "The Bride's Chamber"—showing an older man who psychologically murders his encumbering wife and physically murders the young admirer of this girl, named Ellen, although usually termed "the Bride"—seems symptomatic of Dickens' own current inner conflict (as wife-abusing husband as well as ineligible lover). Harry Stone, the only critic to give extended attention to this piece, has accurately analyzed it in this vein.[6] Like the story about the tiny woman and the shadow told to Maggy by Little Dorrit—simultaneously betraying and concealing her love for Arthur Clennam—which Barbara Hardy has described as "perhaps closest to Dickens's own habitual modes of fantasy,"[7] "The Bride's Chamber" seems to reveal some of Dickens' own forbidden yearnings while masking them with fiction. As Hardy notes about Little Dorrit's tale to Maggy, "As Dickens knew so well, the secret life presses hard."[8] Nevertheless, as a mask as well as a relevation, "The Bride's Chamber" deserves examination. Such examination reveals significant affinities with the work which excited Dickens' imagination just prior to *The Lazy Tour,* Collins' play *The Frozen Deep.*

Although this play was officially billed as written by Collins alone, the version that Dickens produced in 1857 was very much a collaborative creation. This version was performed on several occasions in January, as an elaborate Twelfth Night entertainment in Dickens' home, and then in July and August, as benefits for the wife and unmarried daughter of the recently deceased author Douglas Jerrold. As Robert Louis Brannan has demonstrated, Dickens not only apparently suggested the basic idea for *The Frozen Deep* to Collins but heavily revised Collins' text to suit his own concept of the play and then feverishly threw himself into supervising every aspect of its production.[9] In this activity, as well as in his own electrifying performance in the leading role of Richard Wardour, Dickens found a temporary means of satisfying his current restlessness, although his growing romantic attachment to Ellen Ternan, one of the group of professional actresses who had replaced the amateur ones in the August performances, only exacerbated this restlessness when the relief provided by his involvement in *The Frozen Deep* had passed. As Dickens wrote to Collins in March 1858, more than half a year after the last performance of the play, "The domestic unhappiness remains so strong upon me that I can't write, and (waking) can't rest, one minute. I have never known a moment's peace or content, since the last night of The Frozen Deep."[10]

At the same time, as Brannan has perceptively argued, Dickens apparently viewed *The Frozen Deep,* and the role of Wardour in particular, as more than an escape valve for the steam of his domestic discontent. As his complaint in an 1856 letter to Forster indicates, Dickens' sense of frustration during this period was compounded by his belief that the readers of his novels forced him to depict "unnatural" heroes and would not let him show "any of the experiences, trials, perplexities, and confusions inseparable from the making or unmaking of all men!"[11] In the potentially villainous but at last triumphantly self-sacrificing Wardour, Dickens apparently felt that he had an opportunity to present this more natural kind of hero.[12] Contemporary viewers of the play, including Queen Victoria, responded favorably to Wardour's inner "trials. " Although the Queen felt that she could not give her support to a benefit, she agreed to attend a special production on 4 July 1857 just prior to the Jerrold performances; her enthusiastic reaction to the character of Wardour, described in a letter to Dickens by her equerry, Colonel C. B. Phipps, sounds almost like a rebuttal of Dickens' earlier complaint to Forster: "There was every temptation to an author to increase the effect of the play by representing the triumph of the evil passions, but it was particularly pleasing to Her Majesty to find a much higher lesson taught in the victory of the better and nobler feelings and of the reward—the only one he could obtain—to Richard, in his self content before his death."[13] As Brannan has noted, Dickens' successful performance as Wardour evidently allayed his fear that mid-Victorian audiences would not accept a hero torn by a conflict between "evil passions" and "nobler feelings" and prepared for the depiction in his later novels of Sydney Carton, Pip, and Eugene Wrayburn—heroes beset by "unmaking" impulses over which they eventually triumph.[14]

The creative connection between "The Bride's Chamber" and *The Frozen Deep* is close. Written a few weeks after the last performance of *The Frozen Deep*, the story, like the play, stems from a collaborative enterprise with Collins. Moreover, as Dickens explained in a letter to Georgina Hogarth, when Collins sprained an ankle attempting to descend a mountain in the rain on the intended vacation described in *The Lazy Tour*, Dickens reenacted the climax of *The Frozen Deep* where, as Wardour, he had staggered on stage with Collins, in the role of Frank Aldersley, in his arms: "How I enacted Wardour over again in carrying him down, and what a business it was to get him down . . . . and now I carry him to bed, and into and out of carriages, exactly like Wardour in private life."[15] Thus, the play was clearly part of the imaginative matrix of "The Bride's Chamber," at the conclusion of which, in terror at its phantom narrator, Mr. Goodchild acted the role of Wardour and "caught up Mr. Idle [the persona adopted by Collins in *The Lazy Tour*] from the sofa and rushed downstairs with him" (p. 741). In the story, however, Dickens presents the murderous "evil passions"—surmounted in the play—in a different light.

The similarities in the general outlines of these two works are striking. Both the play and the story are dominated by a single powerful character—Wardour in *The Frozen Deep* and the murderous husband in "The Bride's Chamber"—and both depict a triangular relationship in which this older, central character vies with a younger, weaker, but more appropriate suitor for a woman whom each wishes to possess. Both works focus on an overriding lust for revenge. In *The Frozen Deep*, when Richard Wardour discovers that Clara Burnham—the woman whom he loves and whom he believed was pledged to him—has become engaged in his absence to Frank Aldersley, he vows vengeance against his then unnamed rival. A contemporary reviewer hailed Dickens' performance of Wardour's role in Act II, lost with his fellow explorers in the Arctic wastes but sustained through all hardships by this unsatisfied desire for revenge, as "the most perfect representation of dogged vindictiveness that the imagination could conceive."[16] Dickens' imagination, however, could conceive an even more vicious representation of vindictiveness, for the husband's calculated, psychological murder of his wife in "The Bride's Chamber" is presented as a visitation upon the second generation of a scheme of revenge originally directed toward an earlier one. As this central character explains about his former relationship with the Bride's mother: "He had been put aside for the flaxen-haired, large-eyed man (or nonentity) with Money. He could overlook that for Money. He wanted compensation in Money" (p. 728). Unlike her daughter, however, the Bride's mother is an equal match for her calculating suitor and "cheated him" by death: "In one of her imperious states, she froze, and never thawed again" (p. 729). The language used by Dickens here strikingly resembles that of the prologue to *The Frozen Deep* in which the audience is asked to give its attention to the play where

> the secrets of the vast Profound
> Within us, an exploring hand may sound,
> Testing the region of the ice-bound soul,
> Seeking the passage at its northern pole,
> Soft'ning the horrors of its wintry sleep,
> Melting the surface of that "Frozen Deep." (P. 97)[17]

This echo underscores the relationship between these two works. In both "The Bride's Chamber" and *The Frozen Deep,* Dickens seems concerned with "exploring . . . the region of the ice-bound soul." His revisions in Collins' draft of the play, which make Wardour seem like a man whose rational powers are temporarily shaken rather than the conventional maniac whom Collins had envisioned,[18] appear deliberately designed to present Wardour, like the old man in "The Bride's Chamber," as an individual whose apparently normal—and, in Wardour's case, evidently noble—impulses can freeze into "ice-bound" ones. However, the consequences of Dickens' explorations of this area of the soul in the play and in the story are significantly different.

Although both works deal with a triangular relationship, the results of this relationship contrast conspicuously with one another. In *The Frozen Deep,* Wardour ultimately sacrifices himself in order to unite the young lovers. When he learns his rival's identity and finds that circumstances have put them together in the Arctic wastes, he eventually saves young Aldersley's life at the cost of his own—giving, in Aldersley's words, "all his strength to my weakness" (p. 159)—and substitutes a fraternal passion toward Clara for his earlier romantic one. "The Bride's Chamber," on the contrary, lacks either romantic or fraternal kisses; in this case, the central character sacrifices the young lovers in the course of asserting his own ego. After the psychological struggle in which he destroys the Bride, he kills her young admirer, who has emerged unexpectedly and charged him with the crime. The latter murder takes place on an impulse, apparently prompted by "the youth's abhorrence, openly expressed in every feature of his face and limb of his body, and very hard to bear" (p. 734). The young man has watched the relentless destruction of the Bride from a tree outside the window of the Bride's chamber and has now begun to watch her husband from this same position in order to acquire evidence of the murderer's method. However, the method of the Bride's death is such that the conventional "proofs and traces of . . . guilt" (p. 734) sought by the young man cannot be found. The language used by the narrator to describe the second, unnecessary murder suggests that it stems simply from an irrational wish to counter "the youth's abhorrence" with a violent assertion of himself.

While a fierce desire for revenge is apparent in both works, *The Frozen Deep* and "The Bride's Chamber" depict opposite responses to this desire. In *The Frozen Deep,* Wardour's rage is chivalrously directed not toward the woman whom he believes has wronged him but rather toward his rival. More importantly, as Wardour explains at the end of the play, he eventually triumphs over his strong temptation to destroy this rival despite the suitability of the setting in which they find themselves:

> Never let Frank know it! There was a time when the fiend within me hungered for his life.
>
> . . . .
>
> I took him away alone—away with me over the waste of snow—he on one side, and the tempter on the other, and I between them, marching, marching, till the night fell and the camp-fire was all aflame. If you can't kill him, leave him when he sleeps—the tempter whispered me—leave him when he sleeps! I set him his place to sleep in apart; but he crept between the Devil and me, and nestled his head on *my* breast, and slept *here*. Leave him! Leave him!—the voice whispered—Lay him down in the snow and leave him! Love him—the lad's voice answered, moaning and murmuring *here*, in his sleep—Love him, Clara, for helping me! love him for my sake!—I heard the night-wind come up in the silence from the great Deep. It bore past me the groaning of the ice-bergs at sea, floating, floating past!—and the wicked voice floated away with it—away, away, away for ever! (Pp. 158–59)

In "The Bride's Chamber," on the contrary, the desire for revenge is rampant, and it encompasses not only the woman who had "put [him] aside for . . . the man (or nonentity) with Money" but also the unfortunate Bride whom the old man views as a reflection of her father's personality. Moreover, unlike Wardour, the central character here does not hesitate to carry out his scheme of vengeance. Even the Bride's young lover, who vows to her husband, "I can know no relenting towards you" (p. 734), shares in the pervasive vindictiveness of the story's uncharitable world. The focus of "The Bride's Chamber," nonetheless, remains the personality of the old man who narrates the tale. The young lover's horrified cry when his collar is seized by this man, "I would as lieve be touched by the Devil!" (p. 733), like Dickens' description of this tale to Angela Burdett-Coutts as "a bit of Diablerie,"[19] suggests that "the fiend within" Wardour has here become visibly apparent.

Hence, in "The Bride's Chamber," Dickens appears to be deliberately inverting the doctrine of renunciation apparent in *The Frozen Deep*. Both the old man and Wardour possess tremendous will power, but the old man uses this power for self-gratifying ends while Wardour ultimately uses it for selfless ones. In Dickens' ethos, although modern readers might yearn to reverse these priorities, such selfishness is evil, while selflessness of this sort is good; Quilp, despite his comic attractiveness, is a villain, while Little Nell is intended to verge upon the condition of a saint. Moreover, the preoccupation with the power of the human will epitomized by "The Bride's Chamber" and *The Frozen Deep* is part of a larger concern with this same subject in Dickens' fiction. As Fred Kaplan has recently argued, "the Dickens world is populated with threats of domination and exploitation,"[20] and Dickens' fiction is filled with relationships between domineering figures and those whom they hold or wish to hold in their power—such as the relationships between Sikes and Nancy, Quilp and Little Nell, Jonas and Mercy Chuzzlewit, and Mr. Murdstone and Clara Copperfield—which have an implicit sexual basis. For Kaplan, the extreme manifestation of this self-gratifying urge to dominate and exploit a weaker human object of attraction is John Jasper's drive for absolute control of Rosa Bud in *The Mystery of Edwin Drood*.[21] In "The Bride's Chamber," the relationship between the husband and his Bride "formed in the fear of him, and in the conviction, that there was no escape from him" (p. 729) offers no evidence of sexual attraction. In this case, even sexual passion seems to have frozen in the ice generated by the old man's calculating determination to secure "the ascendency over her weakness" (p. 730) and bend the Bride to his wishes in order to obtain her wealth. Nevertheless, in this much neglected short story, which Kaplan like most of the other critics of Dickens' novels does not mention, Dickens has offered a kind of unsettling but significant parable of the abuse of the power of the human will—of the impulse to assert one's ego, to grab rather than to renounce—which goes far beyond his later presentation of Jasper's intense but unfulfilled desires.

The affinity between this short story and *The Mystery of Edwin Drood,* Dickens' uncompleted final novel, is not confined to their similar concern with the misuse of energy by energetic men. The structure of "The Bride's Chamber" resembles that of a series of Chinese boxes. The central, homicidal action, described in the third person, is enclosed within an eventually first-person account by the murderer—now a phantom. This encompassing narrative deals with the murderer's sensation of his execution and his punishment of haunting the Bride's chamber. As part of his punishment, for one month each year, his personality and inner pain are duplicated with each stroke of the clock until he becomes "Twelve old men. . . . Every one of the Twelve, with Twelve times my old power of suffering and agony" (p. 738), and he desperately yearns to confess his crime "to two living men together" (p. 739) in order to achieve peace. Mr. Goodchild serves as such a listener, but Mr. Idle, like the second member of every pair to whom the phantom attempts to make his "quite useless confession" (p. 740), has fallen asleep. Artistically, the shift in point of view is jarring—as the old man describes the crime and then identifies himself with the criminal:

> There was doubt for which of the two murders he should be first tried; but, the real one was chosen, and he was found Guilty, and cast for Death. Bloodthirsty wretches! They would have made him Guilty of anything, so set they were upon having his life.
> His money could do nothing to save him, and he was hanged.
> *I* am He, and I was hanged at Lancaster Castle with my face to the wall, a hundred years ago! (P. 737)

Despite its awkwardness, however, this shift from third to first-person narrative is significant. By having the murderer initially present his tale as if its events were unrelated to himself, Dickens has partly anticipated here what, twelve years later, he outlined to Forster as his plan for the ending of *The Mystery of Edwin Drood:* "the originality of which was to consist in the review of the murderer's career by himself at the close, when its temptations were to be dwelt upon as if, not he the culprit, but some other man, were the tempted. The last chapters were to be written in the condemned cell, to which his wickedness, all elaborately elicited from him as if told of another, had brought him."[22] The parabolic tale, with its one-dimensional characters, lacks the sophistication of the later novel, and there is no sense of ambiguous temptation in the old man's motives as there is in Jasper's apparent covert crime.

Nonetheless, here as elsewhere in his short stories, Dickens can be seen experimenting with subjects and techniques which go far beyond his current practices in his longer works.

The experimental nature of "The Bride's Chamber," as well as its fanciful freedom to experiment, is suggested by the comment with which Dickens directed attention to it in a letter to Wills: "A very odd story, with a wild, picturesque fancy in it."[23] In this "very odd" tale, Dickens seems to be making use of the short story to depict a normally concealed frame of mind. The idea of Bluebeard-like brutality suggested here is one that recurs in Dickens' writing. The story of Bluebeard is one of the fairy tales that Dickens remembered with delight from his own childhood, but the analogous situations presented in his work suggest that his adult fondness for "the great original Blue Beard" may not have been as ingenuous as it superficially appears.[24] As Kaplan has indicated in other terms, an awareness of the darker side of what Kate Millett has described as "sexual politics"[25] surfaces repeatedly in Dickens' writing from the descriptions of working-class husbands abusing their wives in some of the pieces collected in *Sketches by Boz* to the picture of Jasper controlling Rosa's will at the piano in *The Mystery of Edwin Drood*. It does not seem surprising that, at this time of marital crisis, the idea should appear in intensified form in his short work where he felt free to "let himself loose" just as, in the unhappiness of his last years, he threw himself into performing the murder of Nancy by Sikes in his public readings.[26] This motif seems artistically most attractive when it is touched with humor as in the scene in *The Old Curiosity Shop* where Quilp "ate hard eggs, shell and all, devoured gigantic prawns with the heads and tails on, chewed tobacco and water-cresses at the same time and with extraordinary greediness, drank boiling tea without winking, bit his fork and spoon till they bent again" (p. 40) as part of his method of terrifying his wife and mother-in-law into submission or in the description of the more refined taste of Captain Murderer, the memorable nursery-tale villain. As the narrator of "Nurse's Stories" explains, "This wretch must have been an offshoot of the Blue Beard family, but I had no suspicion of the consanguinity in those times. . . . Captain Murderer's mission was matrimony, and the gratification of a cannibal appetite with tender brides" (*UT & RP*, p. 150). Captain Murderer continues this "mission," transforming his successive brides into meat pies, until one resourceful bride swallows poison to obtain revenge for her twin sister's death at his culinary hands: "and Captain Murderer had hardly picked her last bone, when he began to swell, and to turn blue, and to be all over spots, and to scream. And he went on swelling and turning bluer, and being more all over spots and screaming, until he reached from floor to ceiling and from wall to wall; and then, at one o'clock in the morning, he blew up with a loud explosion!" (P. 152.) Such humor is lacking in "The Bride's Chamber," a fact that makes its obsessive nature more apparent. However, regardless of the extent to which the state of mind explored in this tale might have fascinated Dickens personally or become apparent in his own behavior on occasions such as his separation from his wife, it remained clearly evil in his own humanitarian terms. As the appropriate demise of Captain Murderer illustrates on a comic, miniature scale, for Dickens as for Browning's Pope in *The Ring and the Book,* treatment like Guido's plan for Pompilia—"His slave, his chattel, to use, then destroy"—was ethically abhorrent.

"The Bride's Chamber" thus stands as a kind of deliberately designed illustration of the misuse of the human will and the moral consequences of such misuse. In contrast to *The Frozen Deep,* it shows no conflict between "evil passions" and "nobler feelings." In the play, the nobler feelings appropriately triumph, in keeping with the Christmas celebration of Twelfth Night for which *The Frozen Deep* was originally conceived, while, in the story, evil passions are paramount and nobler feelings are suppressed. Admittedly, to modern tastes, both *The Frozen Deep* and "The Bride's Chamber" remain unpalatably melodramatic. Although Dickens' personal performance as Wardour may have redeemed the bathetic quality of the play, the supposedly demonic energy released in the story seems uninspired. The plot of "The Bride's Chamber" is implausible; its narrative technique is awkward; despite the psychological insight into the old man's personality and his formation of the Bride's character that the tale reveals, its figures are thinly drawn. Nevertheless, the picture of murderous self-affirmation at the cost of a weaker human being graphically demonstrates Dickens' use of the short story to explore not only holiday retreats from actuality but also what he termed, in "Nurse's Stories," "the dark corners" of the human mind (p. 150). In other stories, he explores such corners more successfully although less starkly. However, "The Bride's Chamber" should not be forgotten by readers temporarily charmed by the eloping children at the Holly-Tree Inn.

III

A decade after "The Bride's Chamber," "George Silverman's Explanation" again reflects Dickens' use of the short story to examine mental "dark corners." In this late piece, murderous self-assertion is replaced by willing self-effacement. In contrast to "The Bride's Chamber," the ambiguity inherent in the central character's presentation of his actions is pronounced. Fundamentally, "George Silverman's Explanation" is one of Dickens' most sophisticated short works.

This tightly constructed and pessimistic story, which first appeared in the *Atlantic Monthly* in 1868 near the end of Dickens' career, differs strikingly from the loosely knit, happily ended novels like *Pickwick Papers* and *Oliver Twist* with which Dickens achieved his early reputation. Its neurotically insecure first-person narrator seems less like Esther Summerson, Pip, and David Copperfield than like Dostoevsky's underground man and Eliot's J. Alfred Prufrock. Nevertheless, "George Silverman's Explanation" has only recently begun to receive the attention that it deserves. George Saintsbury dismissed it as "almost worthless,"[27] while, in his introduction to the volume of Dickens' works in which this piece appears, Andrew Lang sweepingly declared, "there is nothing of interest to be said about George Silverman."[28] Subsequent scholarship frequently seems to have followed Lang's suggestion. Many notable studies of Dickens' fiction, including those by Edmund Wilson, J. Hillis Miller, and Taylor Stoehr, say nothing about "George Silverman's Explanation"; other studies, such as those by Sylvère Monod and K. J. Fielding, mention it only in passing.[29]

Against the background of this widespread neglect, a few critics have offered thought-provoking analyses. Harry Stone considers "George Silverman's Explanation" to be Dickens' "most unequivocal and uncompromising picture of frail humanity engulfed in a tragic universe."[30] Barry Bart sees it as "Dickens' deepest examination of the consequences of the ethic [of] renunciation"[31] implicit in the conclusions reached by Pip in *Great Expectations,* Arthur Clennam in *Little Dorrit,* and Eugene Wrayburn in *Our Mutual Friend.* Dudley Flamm, who basically agrees with Stone and Bart, contends that through the narrative technique of this work "Dickens . . . reveals his bleakest view regarding self-extrication from guilt, because he seems to say that once the prosecutor has moved wholly within the accused's mind, there may be no possible extrication."[32] Q. D. Leavis discusses this piece as a "demonstration of a child whose conditioning is similar to Pip's but whose reactions to it were almost the opposite."[33] However, Stone, Bart, Leavis, and, to a large extent, Flamm view "George Silverman's Explanation" primarily in the context of Dickens' novels;[34] in this context, they see Silverman's dilemma as that of a basically innocent man who has been victimized by his surroundings.[35] When "George Silverman's Explanation" is examined in connection with some of Dickens' other experiments with the short story, its equivocal nature becomes more apparent and the issue of Silverman's innocence becomes more difficult to resolve.

Prior to the publication of "George Silverman's Explanation," as the earlier chapters of the present study indicate, Dickens had produced a number of other brief prose works narrated in the first person by their central characters. Some of these works, such as "A Madman's Manuscript" in *Pickwick Papers* or "A Confession Found in a Prison in the Time of Charles the Second" in *Master Humphrey's Clock,* are early stories that merely present sensational situations; their narrative technique serves little function beyond that of lending a contrived illusion of authenticity to the material they contain. Later, however, Dickens often used the confessional or self-explanatory mode for short stories whose narrative method focuses attention upon the distinctive personalities of their speakers. Although most of his stories in this latter vein appeared in his Christmas numbers, two nonseasonal monologues of this type are particularly relevant to "George Silverman's Explanation."

The more familiar of the two for readers of Dickens' novels is "The History of a Self Tormentor," Miss Wade's manuscript of self-justification in *Little Dorrit.* As her words reveal, Miss Wade's vision of the world is jaundiced. She begins with the assumption that she can cut through disguising appearances to underlying "truth," and she assimilates all of her experience to this overruling impression. She asserts at the beginning of her manuscript: "I have the misfortune of not being a fool. . . . If I could have been habitually imposed upon, instead of habitually discerning the truth, I might have lived as smoothly as most fools do" (p. 663). This impression is like a colored glass through which she persistently looks at life. As a child, she misinterprets the kindness of the girls with whom she is raised, and, like Browning's Duke who executes his Duchess for smiling indiscriminately, Miss Wade interprets any kindness shown to others by her "chosen friend" as an act of disloyalty to herself (p. 663). As she grows older, her actions are no less biased by her peculiar impression of what is truth. She loathes the good-natured nurse of the family in which she first serves as a governess, and she quarrels with the mistress of the household who tries to make her position easy. In another family, again as a governess, she becomes engaged to her employers' nephew, but she scorns his open admiration of her, concludes that his attachment makes her appear ridiculous, favors another man, quarrels with her fiancé's aunt, and angrily departs. The events which she describes are clearly open to more interpretations than the one she puts upon them. Her fierce attachment to her childhood friend and her identification with the girl whom she later takes to live with her seem at least implicitly lesbian, and such details combine to suggest that her particular "truth" is a delusion. Nonetheless, her *idée fixe* is a powerful one; it governs her behavior and distorts her life.

At the same time that a reader recognizes Miss Wade's delusion, there is also an awareness of the sources of her personal torment. Lionel

Trilling remarks that it is impossible "to read Miss Wade's account of her life . . . without an understanding that amounts to sympathy."[36] As her self-history demonstrates, several important reasons for her bitterness lie wholly or largely beyond her control. She is apparently illegitimate, and much of her misery as a child and as a woman stems from the accident of her birth. In her girlhood, she is innocently deceived by the woman who pretends to be her grandmother. In later years, she is cynically deceived by the man who encourages her to break her engagement and then abandons her in order to court another woman. In the rest of *Little Dorrit,* Miss Wade is a mysterious but clearly unpleasant person; Pancks, a character who has a slight business connection with her, remarks that "a woman more angry, passionate, reckless, and revengeful never lived" (p. 540). Miss Wade's manuscript provides a different perspective upon her personality. It not only displays her faults but it arouses sympathy for her suffering, and the resulting conflict between compassion and condemnation produced by her explanation resembles "the tension between sympathy and moral judgment" which Robert Langbaum has termed the hallmark of the dramatic monologue.[37] In her manuscript, Miss Wade reveals that her view of herself is seriously distorted, but she presents her case in such a fashion that it cannot be automatically assessed.

"The History of a Self Tormentor" is not an isolated example of Dickens' experimentation with this kind of fictional disequilibrium outside of his Christmas numbers. A relatively obscure short work entitled "Holiday Romance"[38] focuses even more directly on this split between a reader's knowledge and that of the characters involved. As Dickens conceived it, this composition was designed as a joke whose humor was to come from the clash between adult wisdom and childish naïveté.[39] Three of the four "romances" that it contains are third-person fantasies, pictures of the world as children presumably would like it to be, while the "Introductory Romance from the Pen of William Tinkling, Esq." is a first-person monologue whose eight-year-old narrator, like the speakers in some of Browning's best monologues, is supremely unconscious of the limitations of his point of view. "Holiday Romance" is far from being one of Dickens' most successful works. For instance, a reader of Tinkling's section cannot escape the sensation that the youthful narrator—who expresses himself in what is supposedly a childish prattle—is being manipulated: he is given a designedly cute name and forced to say the kinds of banalities that entertain doting grandparents. Tinkling's monologue is not a genuine treatment of the problem of a child in an adult world like that presented in *David Copperfield* or Joyce's "Araby." It is rather an adult's

semiserious creation of what childhood might resemble, and its resulting tone, like that of *The Cricket on the Hearth,* is uncomfortably coy.
Dickens' humorous intention seems to have led him into overempha-
sizing the conflict between speaker and reader inherent in this piece.
The split between different degrees of knowledge, which was so effective in Miss Wade's monologue, here becomes simply strained. However, the very fact that this type of conflict is used to excess in Tinkling's remarks indicates Dickens' willingness to experiment with the
technique of contrasting attitudes within a first-person narrative.

Thus, Flamm's comment about "George Silverman's Explanation"
that "no other Dickens story told in the first person derives so much of
its effect from the difference between what the reader is aware of and
what the character-narrator is aware of" is perceptive but incorrect.[40]
The discrepancy between different levels of awareness is crucially important in the monologues of Miss Wade and William Tinkling, and both
of these pieces are closely related to "George Silverman's Explanation."
Like Miss Wade, George Silverman believes that he has been misunder-
stood by the world, although Miss Wade is far more bitter than Silverman about this misunderstanding. In a manner resembling that of his
female predecessor, he gives vent to his feelings in a manuscript designed as an explanation of himself. Like "Holiday Romance," "George
Silverman's Explanation" was produced shortly before Dickens' second
visit to America;[41] the "queer combination of a child's mind with a
grownup joke,"[42] implicit in the one work and manifested in Tinkling's
monologue, was undoubtedly in his thoughts as he composed the other.
In the context of these relationships, George Silverman's narrative deserves careful reconsideration.

As in the monologues of Miss Wade and William Tinkling, the focus
of "George Silverman's Explanation" lies on the personality of its narrator. Like these pieces, it exploits a duality implicit in its speaker's words.
Edgar Johnson's passing comment calls attention to this double effect:

> The narrator of the story, rescued from a slum childhood and
> brought up as a clergyman, seems to himself always to be acting
> with the most nobly disinterested of motives, but is constantly
> striking others as selfish and disingenuous. . . . Believing himself
> cruelly misjudged, Silverman at the same time has a lurking suspi-
> cion of his own guilt. What sort of man is he, really? These am-
> biguities, in fact, represent the very point of the story, and one
> feels as if it were haunted by Dickens' troubled consciousness of
> ambiguities within himself. But he could not grapple successfully
> with the theme; it wavers half-heartedly between apologia and
> accusation, an unresolved conflict.[43]

To a certain extent, this conflict is indeed unresolved. Unlike William Tinkling's romance, "George Silverman's Explanation" ends with no suggestion that the speaker will outgrow his present attitude. Unlike Miss Wade, the narrator does not invite condemnation upon himself by luring another person to share his unhappy life. However, the essential ambiguity of "George Silverman's Explanation" is not necessarily a flaw, and it can be understood without recourse to Dickens' personal state of mind. It is, I believe, the consequence of Dickens' success in sustaining two contrasting attitudes throughout a first-person monologue.

George Silverman receives his impressions through the haze of his own personality. His abortive opening chapters reveal his insecurity:

FIRST CHAPTER

It happened in this wise—
But, sitting with my pen in my hand looking at those words again, without descrying any hint in them of the words that should follow, it comes into my mind that they have an abrupt appearance. They may serve, however, if I let them remain, to suggest how very difficult I find it to begin to explain my explanation. An uncouth phrase: and yet I do not see my way to a better.

SECOND CHAPTER

It happened in *this* wise—
But, looking at those words, and comparing them with my former opening, I find they are the self-same words repeated. This is the more surprising to me, because I employ them in quite a new connexion. For indeed I declare that my intention was to discard the commencement I first had in my thoughts, and to give the preference to another of an entirely different nature, dating my explanation from an anterior period of my life. I will make a third trial, without erasing this second failure, protesting that it is not my design to conceal any of my infirmities, whether they be of head or heart. (*UT & RP*, p. 729)

Not until the third chapter does he "begin to explain . . . [his] explanation," and he achieves his goal only by approaching it from an oblique direction: "Not as yet directly aiming at how it came to pass, I will come upon it by degrees" (p. 730). The words with which he ends the piece make clear that this "explanation" arises only from an overpowering urge to give expression to his confusion: "I pen it for the relief of my own mind, not foreseeing whether or no it will ever have a reader" (p. 756). As this tortuous beginning and diffident conclusion indicate, his angle of vision is a peculiar one. In his manner, he resembles a person like the humble Mr. Smith, from "Thoughts about People" in *Sketches by Boz*, given the opportunity to attempt to justify himself.

When he is a child in a Preston cellar, Silverman's impoverished mother calls him "a worldly little devil" (p. 730), and the sting of this rebuke haunts him as he greedily yearns for shelter, clothing, and food. In reaction, after his parents die of fever and he has been rescued from the family lair, he becomes shyly altruistic—the attitude that dominates the backward perspective of his monologue. While staying at an old farmhouse in order to recover from possible contamination, Silverman asks himself, "How not to be this worldly little devil?" (p. 736), and the remainder of his piece recounts his efforts to avoid any possible imputation of worldly aspiration. His dilemma, as Johnson observes in the passage quoted earlier, lies in the fact that he "is constantly striking others as selfish and disingenuous." Subsequent events show, on an ever-increasing scale, the conflict between his efforts to be unworldly and the assumption of the world that he is very worldly indeed. At the farmhouse, when he avoids the girl to whom he is attracted for fear that he may spread contamination, her family accuses him of moroseness and a lack of sociability. Later, when he has won a fellowship to Cambridge, he suspects that Verity Hawkyard, the religious hypocrite who first sent him to school, has suppressed an inheritance due to him from his grandfather. Instead of demanding his property in a worldly fashion, however, he effectively relinquishes all claim to it in a voluntary letter of gratitude for Hawkyard's charity to him. In return, Hawkyard and his congregation rant through a service for the benefit of "our poor, sinful, worldly-minded brother here present" whose "now-opening career . . . might lead to his becoming a minister of what was called 'the church.' . . . Not the chapel, Lord. The church" (p. 744). In due time, Silverman does become a minister of the church. The mother of a former pupil presents him a modest living and persuades him to serve, without additional payment, as her private secretary and as her daughter's tutor. Once again, the fear of worldliness infects Silverman's peace of mind. In a grand gesture of self-effacement, when he discovers that he and his lady's daughter mutually love one another, he quietly transfers the affection of his beloved Adelina to another pupil whom he views as a worthier man. He marries the couple and breaks the news to Adelina's mother, who promptly accuses him of worldliness and of having arranged the marriage for financial gain. She forces him to resign the living, stains his reputation, and hounds him into seclusion. Only through the efforts of the few people who stand by him does he finally receive "a college-living in a sequestered place," and from this place, he explains, "I now pen my explanation" (p. 756). Silverman's remarks are dominated by the distorting influences of his childhood and the peculiar bent of his gradually emerging personality. His overriding desire to appear unworldly lies at the center of his impressions.

In the context of his monologue, however, this overriding desire appears to be an obsession, and it soon becomes clear that George Silverman's behavior is confined by neuroses as restrictive as those that form the prison of Miss Wade. From his own prevailing point of view, he is a well-intentioned and much-maligned individual. Nevertheless, the framework of good intentions which he constructs for himself rests on several questionable assumptions. M. K. Bradby contends that an important motive behind Silverman's supposedly self-effacing actions is egotism:

> The first factor which troubles George Silverman is a subtle pervading egotism in his attitude towards other people. At each crisis in his life, what concerns him most is that he, George Silverman, shall do the lofty-minded thing. Compared with this it is a small matter that the little girl at the farm should feel snubbed, or her father led to judge unjustly; or that Brother Hawkyard should succeed in his fraud; or even that the adored Adelina should suffer the pangs of a first love unrequited. He cannot put himself into other people's places and realise that their feelings are as poignant as his own.[44]

This comment is perceptive. As his dealings with Adelina, Brother Hawkyard, and the family at the farmhouse demonstrate, Silverman is less concerned with love, justice, and friendship than with living up to his own exalted standards. Like the bashful narrator in Dickens' framework for *The Holly-Tree Inn,* Silverman cannot commune with his fellow human beings. Unlike this earlier speaker, however, he does not fully recognize his own limitations. Although he can refer to his abnormal sensitivity toward the idea of being considered worldly as "the delicate, perhaps the diseased, corner of my mind" (p. 744), he does not fully realize that he, as much as the wretched hermit in *Tom Tiddler's Ground,* has a responsibility toward society. Despite his claim that he has chosen a religious career because he considers himself "qualified to do my duty in a moderate, though earnest way, if I could obtain some small preferment in the Church" (p. 746), Silverman gives no evidence of enthusiasm for ministering to someone else's day-to-day human problems. His professional efforts at helping others appear confined primarily to a small number of pupils, and he tells us more about Hawkyard's religious activity, which he despises, than his own. At the end of his monologue, he has retreated to the kind of isolation that his predecessor in *The Holly-Tree Inn* contemplated but did not carry out. In other words, while consciously calling attention to his generosity, George Silverman unconsciously reveals that he has created a private and self-centered world for himself.

Any final assessment of this speaker must take both elements of his personality into consideration. George Silverman should be understood not only as the shy and much-maligned altruist that he presents himself as being, but as the unsocial and neurotically self-centered individual that his remarks and behavior show him to be. As in the case of Browning's Andrea del Sarto, we see both what he believes and what he demonstrates about himself. Indeed, both of these figures self-deludingly attribute their problems to a combination of their own loving sacrifice and the failure of others to understand them. Just as Andrea del Sarto blames his personal failure to achieve artistic greatness on his passion for his wife and comforts himself with the conviction that "I am something underrated here," so George Silverman excuses his withdrawal from society on the basis of his unwordly desire not to take advantage of anyone and explains that he possesses "a timidly silent character under misconstruction" (p. 738). Silverman's description of himself at the farmhouse near the ruined Hoghton Towers, watching the birthday celebration which he has refused to attend, provides a striking illustration of the two components of his character:

> Ah! if they could have seen me next day, in the ruin, watching for
> the arrival of the cart full of merry young guests; if they could have
> seen me at night, gliding out from behind the ghostly statue,
> listening to the music and the fall of dancing feet, and watching
> the lighted farm-house windows from the quadrangle when all the
> ruin was dark; if they could have read my heart, as I crept up to
> bed by the back way, comforting myself with the reflection, "They
> will take no hurt from me,"—they would not have thought mine
> a morose or an unsocial nature. (Pp. 737–38)

On the surface, this passage merely demonstrates Silverman's growing diffidence and his willingness to sacrifice his own happiness to protect those for whom he cares. Nevertheless, the words which he chooses for this description contain disturbing connotations. The young girl whom Silverman admires would hardly have felt easy if she could have seen him "gliding out from behind the ghostly statue," peeping at her birthday festivities from the darkened ruin, and secretively creeping up the stairs to his bed. Had the farmer who scolds him for not being sociable actually been able to read George Silverman's heart, he undoubtedly would have wondered why the boy did not discuss his fear of contamination openly or at least find a better alternative to the party than Hoghton Towers after dark. Silverman himself considers this episode a significant one, and he uses it as an analogy for the life which he remembers at college:

> I can see others in the sunlight; I can see our boats' crews and our athletic young men on the glistening water, or speckled with the moving lights of sunlit leaves; but I myself am always in the shadow looking on. Not unsympathetically,—God forbid!—but looking on alone, much as I looked at Sylvia from the shadows of the ruined house, or looked at the red gleam shining through the farmer's windows, and listened to the fall of dancing feet, when all the ruin was dark that night in the quadrangle. (P. 746)

Once again, Silverman peers out of darkness at the activities of others. The sense of himself as "always in the shadow looking on" indicates the angle from which he forever gathers his impressions of life. Although he claims that his attitude is sympathetic, the basis of his claim and even the validity of his wish to interact with people only as a sympathetic observer remain dubious. Like a voyeur, he shrinks from involvement while he maintains that his intentions are harmless. His mental position is pathetic, but it is not entirely free from blame.

The ambiguities of Silverman's attitude result from the fact that he is his own advocate. In a letter to Wills, the sub-editor of *All the Year Round,* Dickens commented about his fascination with the narrative technique of this monologue at the same time that he called attention to the seminal importance of the scene in Hoghton Towers which I have just discussed:

> Upon myself, it has made the strangest impression of reality and originality!! And I feel as if I had read something (by somebody else) which I should never get out of my head!! The main idea of the narrator's position towards the other people, was the idea I *had* for my next novel in A. Y. R. But it is very curious that I did not in the least see how to begin his state of mind, until I walked into Hoghton Towers one bright April day with Dolby.[45]

In the context of this letter, it is significant that George Silverman remembers himself in this location not on a "bright . . . day," but in the dark. This small change emphasizes the peculiarity of "the narrator's position towards the other people." Despite his diffidence, George Silverman is intelligent. Once he has conquered his initial problem of beginning his explanation, he presents his view of his life persuasively, and a reader's final judgment remains in doubt. It is never completely clear what part of his disinterestedness is genuine selflessness and what part is the rationalization of an abnormally introverted man.

Consequently, I believe that the case for Silverman as the innocent victim of injustice cannot be made as convincingly as may at first appear. Indeed, Dickens' original idea of saving Silverman's "position towards" others for his "next novel" in *All the Year Round* links this ambiguous speaker with the openly reputable and secretly murderous Jasper, whose divided personality is apparently the crux of the following, uncompleted *Mystery of Edwin Drood*.[46] It is far too easy for a literary critic to assume that Dickens' sympathy for the dilemma of this quiet, university-educated scholar is unqualified and to forget, as Philip Collins correctly observes, that "few of his characters are intellectuals, and most of those who are he presents as ludicrous or detestable."[47] Even Pip and David Copperfield do not receive a university education although, as Collins notes, "both can command in their later boyhood sufficient funds to get as good an education as Dickens cares to give them."[48] Such evidence, in conjunction with his practice in the monologues of William Tinkling and Miss Wade, suggests that Dickens intended a reader to see through at least part of Silverman's explanation and to recognize not only the extent to which this narrator has been victimized by society but the astigmatism inherent in his point of view.

In Silverman's monologue, however, neither judgment nor sympathy ultimately predominates. A reader's awareness of Silverman's limitations is balanced by compassion for his problems. In this piece, as in *The Frozen Deep* and, inversely, in "The Bride's Chamber," Dickens has dealt with one of his favorite situations—that of self-sacrificing renunciation[49]—but here he has intentionally complicated the reader's understanding of this situation through his chosen narrative technique. Like Conrad's Jim, Dickens' Silverman seems designed to remain forever enigmatic. The equivocal nature of his explanation reflects the ambiguity of human life.

CHAPTER 7

Unrestrained Invention

> When I wake in bed, at daybreak, on the cold
> dark winter mornings, the white snow dimly
> beheld, outside, through the frost on the
> window-pane, I hear Dinarzade. "Sister, sister, if
> you are yet awake, I pray you finish the history of
> the Young King of the Black Islands."
> Scheherazade replies, "If my lord the Sultan will
> suffer me to live another day, sister, I will not only
> finish that, but tell you a more wonderful story
> yet." Then, the gracious Sultan goes out, giving no
> orders for the execution, and we all three breathe
> again.
>
> DICKENS, "A Christmas Tree"

Like the tales of Scheherazade, Dickens' short stories contain a deep-breathing quality. In works as disparate as "The Black Veil" and *A Christmas Carol*, "The Boots" and "George Silverman's Explanation," Dickens seems to be deliberately using his stories to emphasize, to experiment, to exaggerate, and to explore. As he remarked near the end of his career to Bulwer-Lytton, in the context of an objection that the latter had raised to a portion of *Our Mutual Friend*, "I . . . never give way to my invention recklessly, but constantly restrain it," although, as he then admitted, "I think it is my infirmity to fancy or perceive relations in things which are not apparent generally. Also, I have such an inexpressible enjoyment of what I see in a droll light, that I dare say I pet it as if it were a spoilt child."[1] In his stories, unlike his usual practice in his novels, Dickens apparently believed that he could "give way to . . . invention" without restraint. Thus, in this short writing, he felt free to indulge, recklessly and shamelessly, in the kind of delighted enjoyment in perceiving "relations in things which are not apparent generally" that is often characteristic of scientists and poets

—including Albert Einstein and T. S. Eliot—as well as masters of the art of fiction. Readers who yearn, less recklessly, for Horatian moderation are apt to conclude that the consequences of this indulgence in Dickens' stories are indeed "spoilt" children, but even the least manageable offspring of a literary master should not be wished away. As the pieces analyzed in this study demonstrate, Dickens evidently viewed his short stories as an opportunity, in Forster's words, to "let himself loose"—to express the vital quality that Dickens described as fancy in concentrated form.

Like so many other words in Dickens' emotionally charged vocabulary, the term "fancy" remains fundamentally vague. As Dickens commonly used it, the word is approximately synonymous with "imagination" (although he sometimes employed it as the equivalent of "perception" as in the paragraph above) and comprehensively antithetical to fact. In practice, nevertheless, in the context of Dickens' short stories and as I have used it in this study, the word "fancy" has two primary meanings: imaginative escapism (which for Dickens, after the failure of *Master Humphrey's Clock,* was acceptable only when it was temporary) and fellow feeling. *A Christmas Carol,* for example, teaches Scrooge the value of a fairy-tale respite from workaday actuality as well as the value of human compassion. Likewise, the term "imagination," as Dickens employed this word and its cognates, is imprecise. In general, "imagination" for Dickens (as in the "wandering imagination" with which the young doctor muses before his fire at the outset of "The Black Veil") seems simply to describe the day-dreaming faculty that allows the mind to escape from the limits of the immediate workaday world, and "processes of the imagination" (as Dickens used the phrase in his 25 November 1851 letter to Mrs. Gaskell) are the workings of the mind through which such escapist fantasies are produced. Dickens himself, however, would have had as little patience with such explanations as with Bitzer's famous definition of a horse. Indeed, Dickens seems to have cherished his short stories, like the acts in Sleary's circus, largely because of their refusal to conform to logical restrictions.

Nonetheless, as discussed in chapter 1, Dickens' awareness of this freedom and, consequently, of the value of short stories in the context of his other writings developed gradually. At the outset of his career— as explained in chapter 2—prompted by his love of tales like those of Captain Murderer and Little Red Riding Hood, Dickens actively, although somewhat unsteadily, wrote short stories until the failure of his initial scheme for *Master Humphrey's Clock* in 1840 demonstrated the dangers of overindulgence in what had been deliberately designed as a kind of imaginative never-never land. Thereafter, Dickens confined his creation of short stories to special occasions, the most special of which was Christmas. In particular, in his five Christmas Books in the 1840s, as explained in chapter 3, Dickens seems to be consciously refining and then reflecting his theories about the role of "story-books . . . in this workaday world." Thus, *A Christmas Carol* explicitly and the other Christmas Books implicitly reveal Dickens' preoccupation with the element of fancy—an element that he believed flourished beneficently and freely in the storybooks which he remembered from his childhood and which *Household Words,* inaugurated in 1850, was avowedly intended to contain.

By the 1850s, Dickens was fully conscious of the imaginative license provided by short stories, and his brief writings for *Household Words* and its successor *All the Year Round* contain some of his most notable works in this mode. Thus, as discussed in chapters 4 and 5, his contributions between 1850 and 1867 to the Christmas numbers of *Household Words* and *All the Year Round*—customarily collected as *Christmas Stories*— show him recurringly concerned with reflecting the fanciful, and in Dickens' thinking, suitably seasonal topics of imaginative escapism and fellow feeling. However, even more significantly, these writings reveal his fascination with stylistic experimentation—with ways of depicting imagination, with joint writing with Wilkie Collins, and, most extraordinary of all (in the dazzling monologues of Christopher the waiter, Mrs. Lirriper, Doctor Marigold, and the Boy at Mugby), with a self-consciously playful flaunting of the concept of public entertainment which he viewed as a fundamental feature of his own writer/public reader's art. In the remarkably varied, sometimes haphazard, and sometimes highly sophisticated course of Dickens' short stories from 1833 to 1868, two major types of stories developed, classified in my edition of Dickens' *Selected Short Fiction* as "Tales of the Supernatural" (analogous to the uncanny tales and fairy tales that Dickens absorbed so eagerly as a child) and "Dramatic Monologues" (prose versions of the kinds of poems that Dickens' contemporary Robert Browning made famous). Chapter 6, focusing on the sensational "The Bride's Chamber" in 1857 and the more sophisticated "George Silverman's Explanation" in 1868, shows Dickens using each of these types of stories, on occasions unrelated to Christmas, to explore normally hidden states of mind.

The two pieces that Dickens wrote as addenda to the central narrative of *Mugby Junction* in 1866—the last Christmas number to contain such attached contributions—can usefully serve as an ending to this study, for they illustrate the distinction between these two types of stories that had evolved by the end of Dickens' career. Also, these two pieces show an underlying similarity with Dickens' other short stories from the time of early tales such as "The Black Veil" and "The Bagman's Story" in 1836. As suggested in chapter 5, the first of these pieces,

"Main Line. The Boy at Mugby," is a dramatic monologue, evoking a conflict between judgment and sympathy by the reader. As the Boy delightedly observes in his opening words,

> I am The Boy at Mugby. That's about what *I* am.
> You don't know what I mean? What a pity! But I think you do. I think you must. Look here. I am the Boy at what is called [T]he Refreshment Room at Mugby Junction, and what's proudest boast is, that it never yet refreshed a mortal being.
> Up in a corner of the Down Refreshment Room at Mugby Junction, in the height of twenty-seven cross draughts (I've often counted 'em while they brush the First-Class hair twenty-seven ways), behind the bottles, among the glasses, bounded on the nor'-west by the beer, stood pretty far to the right of a metallic object that's at times the tea-urn and at times the soup-tureen, according to the nature of the last twang imparted to its contents which are the same groundwork, fended off from the traveller by a barrier of stale sponge-cakes erected atop of the counter, and lastly exposed sideways to the glare of Our Missis's eye—you ask a Boy so sitiwated, next time you stop in a hurry at Mugby, for anything to drink; you take particular notice that he'll try to seem not to hear you, that he'll appear in a absent manner to survey the Line through a transparent medium composed of your head and body, and that he won't serve you as long as you can possibly bear it. That's Me.[2]

Like the narrator in Burgess' *Clockwork Orange,* who enjoys preying upon society, the Boy at Mugby revels in his chosen occupation as "a most highly delicious lark" (p. 519). At the same time, the Boy describes himself with an exuberance and a consistency that undermines a reader's condemnation. Like the Artful Dodger on trial in *Oliver Twist,* the Boy never falters in his attitude of aggravation, and he seems happily at home in his milieu. The story is a comic masterpiece which, along with the other humorous monologues that Dickens produced in his Christmas contributions to *All the Year Round* between 1862 and 1866, illustrates the error of assuming, as critics who concentrate exclusively on Dickens' novels have often done, that the somberness increasingly apparent in his late novels shadowed all aspects of his art. In addition, the high-spirited humor, as well as the stylistic experimentation (both in terms of the technique of the monologue and in terms of the playfulness with the concept of public entertainment), evident in this piece clearly reveals Dickens' sense that in such work he could "let himself loose" in directions that he currently felt unable or unwilling to pursue in his longer work.

The second attached story that Dickens wrote for *Mugby Junction,*

"No. 1 Branch Line. The Signalman," also suggests this sense of letting loose, although, in contrast to the exuberant humor of its companion piece, the tone of "The Signalman" is eerie.[3] In this latter case, temporary abandonment of workaday restraint takes the form of a foray into the realm of the supernatural. Historians of the short story have sometimes called attention to "The Signalman" for special, if somewhat biased, praise as the only one of Dickens' stories that, in the words of Henry Canby, "employed the technique of Poe with ease and effectiveness."[4] However, as the highly dissimilar but chronologically and contextually parallel "Boy at Mugby" indicates, Dickens' basic view of the short story, even at the end of his career, remained fundamentally very different from that of Poe. In Dickens' thinking, "The Signalman" was simply one more tale of the uncanny, similar to but somewhat more sophisticated than "A Confession Found in a Prison in the Time of Charles the Second" in *Master Humphrey's Clock.* Along with "The Boy at Mugby," "The Signalman" is a piece collected by the reforming misanthrope who serves as the central character in Dickens' opening portion of this Christmas number, and who has gathered stories about several of the railway lines radiating out from Mugby Junction which he then relates to the crippled daughter of a railway attendant. In contrast to the irrepressible Boy at Mugby, whose central purpose is a revelation of his own conflictingly aggravating and attractive personality to the reader, the first-person speaker in "The Signalman," like that of "A Confession," is primarily a vehicle for revealing an extraordinary experience toward which the reader's response and his own ultimately concur. At the same time, as in "A Confession," Dickens seems to be using not only the general license that he attributed to all short stories but also the specific mandate to illustrate "particular states of mind and processes of the imagination" which he attributed to tales of the uncanny as a means of exploring a disordered mental condition.

As the narrator of "The Signalman" makes clear at the outset, the distinguishing feature of the individual whom he is describing is the latter's obviously overwrought mental state. When the narrator hails the man tending a signal at the mouth of a tunnel in a lonely railroad cutting between two steep walls of stone, "Halloa! Below there!," the speaker is immediately struck by the manner in which the signalman responds to his call: ". . . he turned himself about, and looked down the Line. There was something remarkable in his manner of doing so, though I could not have said for my life what. But I know it was remarkable enough to attract my notice" (*CS*, p. 524). When the signalman subsequently explains that he is haunted by an apparition, the narrator, like Scrooge dismissing Marley's ghost as the result of indigestion, initially insists that the specter is simply an illusion: "Resisting the slow touch of a frozen finger tracing out my spine, I showed him how that this figure must be a deception of his sense of sight; and how that figures, originating in disease of the delicate nerves that minister to the functions of the eye, were known to have often troubled patients, some of whom had become conscious of the nature of their affliction, and had even proved it by experiments upon themselves" (p. 530). Gradually, however, both for the narrator and for the reader, the sense of "a frozen finger" along the spine becomes more and more difficult to resist. Events in the story move inexorably from the ordinary to the extraordinary world—an effect foreshadowed by the narrator's first response to the setting in which he finds the signalman:

> His post was in as solitary and dismal a place as ever I saw. On either side, a dripping-wet wall of jagged stone, excluding all view but a strip of sky; the perspective one way only a crooked prolongation of this great dungeon; the shorter perspective in the other direction terminating in a gloomy red light, and the gloomier entrance to a black tunnel, in whose massive architecture there was a barbarous, depressing, and forbidding air. So little sunlight ever found its way to this spot, that it had an earthy, deadly smell; and so much cold wind rushed through it, that it struck chill to me, as if I had left the natural world. (Pp. 525–26)

Nonetheless, even after the signalman explains that the apparition has twice appeared as a prelude to some railway disaster and that it now haunts him again, calling "Below there! Look out! Look out!" (p. 532) and gesticulating wildly, the narrator clings, as firmly as he is able, to familiar, factual experience. He suggests to the signalman that the ringing of the latter's bell, which the signalman has heard but the narrator has not, stems simply from the fact that "your imagination misleads you" (p. 532), and he compassionately but rationally attempts to analyze the signalman's frame of mind:

> "If I telegraph Danger, on either side of me, or on both, I can give no reason for it," he went on, wiping the palms of his hands. "I should get into trouble, and do no good. They would think I was mad. This is the way it would work,—Message: 'Danger! Take care!' Answer: 'What Danger? Where?' Message: 'Don't know. But, for God's sake, take care!' They would displace me. What else could they do?"
>
> His pain of mind was most pitiable to see. It was the mental torture of a conscientious man, oppressed beyond endurance by an unintelligible responsibility involving life. (Pp. 533–34)

Finally, when he recognizes the impossibility of attempting "to reason . . . [the signalman] out of his conviction," the narrator decides simply "for the poor man's sake, as well as for the public safety, what I had to do for the time was to compose his mind" (p. 534). Rather than succumb to unnerving suggestions, the narrator resolves, as a rational middle course between ignoring the incident and reporting the signalman to his railway superiors, to return on the following evening and suggest that he and the signalman go together "to the wisest medical practitioner we could hear of in those parts, and . . . take his opinion" (p. 535). Such rationality is eerily undermined on the narrator's subsequent visit, when he returns to find that the signalman is dead. The latter has been killed by a train that ran him down despite frantic efforts to warn him by the engine-driver, who shouted and, ironically, covered his face and waved his arm in the manner of the apparition that the harried signalman had grown accustomed to viewing as an ominous but insubstantial ghost. Even more disturbingly, as the narrator emphasizes in his last sentence, the words exclaimed by the engine-driver ("For God's sake, clear the way!") to the ill-fated signalman who fails to heed them are those which the narrator alone—and as he stresses "that only in my own mind" (p. 536)—had associated with the arm-waving of the apparition which the signalman had previously imitated.

In contrast to John Harmon's symbolic but only apparent resurrection in *Our Mutual Friend,* which Dickens completed in the previous year, the question of whether or not a specter from some world beyond the visible one actually appeared to the signalman is left unresolved. At the end of the story, still struggling to keep his bearings in the world of actuality, the narrator explicitly refuses the temptation of "prolonging the narrative to dwell on any one of its curious circumstances more than on any other" (p. 536). However, the climactic coincidence which he notes in conclusion (calling attention to the correspondence between the engine-driver's vain cry at the time of the signalman's death and the words that the signalman had earlier claimed to hear from the specter, plus those which the narrator had privately attributed to the signalman's enactment of the haunting figure's gesture) strongly suggests that elements which rational people dismiss as preposterous may indeed have been at work. Dickens has skillfully depicted in the central character of "The Signalman" the unsettling, uncanny sensation that the incredible may, after all, be credible and then reproduced this sensation for the narrator and, ultimately, the reader.

In this fashion, like its very different companion piece "The Boy at Mugby," "The Signalman" reveals Dickens' indulgence in the sense of temporary imaginative license which he gradually came to perceive as an underlying feature of his short stories. In both of these pieces, as in all of his brief stories in varying directions and degrees, he is willingly letting loose. Lack of inhibition is often dangerous, and some of Dickens' short stories might be gladly wished away. However, others—as diverse, yet as analogous, as "The Boy at Mugby" and "George Silverman's Explanation"; "The Signalman" and *A Christmas Carol; The Haunted Man* and the monologues of Christopher the waiter, Mrs. Lirriper, and Doctor Marigold—well repay examination, and all of them, in keeping with all of Dickens' other short writings, must be remembered for a thorough comprehension of Dickens' work.

Familiarity with Dickens' short stories enriches a reader's understanding of Dickens' writing as a whole. In his stories, often far more freely than in the novels that he was currently producing, Dickens can be seen attempting to escape momentarily from actuality, to lighten the workaday world with humor or soften it with emotion, to experiment with unusual techniques through which the familiar world might be rendered, and to explore normally hidden corners of the human mind. Dickens' stories thus provide an important perspective from which his novels can be examined. More immediately, like all extraordinary perspectives, they are well worth viewing in themselves.

Appendix A

Contributors to the Christmas Numbers
of *Household Words* and
All the Year Round, 1850–1867

The difficulty of determining Dickens' collaborators in the Christmas numbers that he produced annually in *Household Words* and *All the Year Round* throughout most of the latter part of his career may be one reason why these works have been so widely neglected. With the exception of *Mugby Junction* and *No Thoroughfare,* they were published anonymously, and only *Mugby Junction* appeared with the names of the authors given for each section. Most of Dickens' own contributions are included in his collected works under the misleading title of *Christmas Stories,* but his co-authors have generally slipped from anonymity into oblivion. Many of them undoubtedly deserve this obscurity, but such historical amnesia can easily lead to the unsatisfactory situation in which Dickens' parts are mistaken for their larger wholes. It can further lead to the even more deplorable situation in which someone else's anonymous handiwork is erroneously taken for that of Dickens himself.[1] Blunders of this kind are not only confusing but unnecessary, for, although the endeavor is difficult, it is not impossible to discover Dickens' fellow-writers.

Most contributors to *Household Words* can be identified on the basis of the account book used in the office of the periodical.[2] In his edition of *Charles Dickens' Uncollected Writings from "Household Words,"* Harry Stone makes extensive use of this book, as well as other evidence, to identify writing previously not attributed to Dickens; in the course of his work, he deals with the authorship of several of the Christmas numbers. The issue of identification in *All the Year Round* is more complicated because its Office Book has disappeared.[3] However, while the attribution of some of the writing in *All the Year Round* is at present impossible to establish, the Christmas numbers fortunately occupy a special category. In 1868 Chapman and Hall conjointly with the *AYR* office, and in 1907 Chapman and Hall alone, published what are now very scarce editions of the Christmas numbers from *All the Year Round* in which they named the authors of the various parts of these annual productions.[4] In the following tables, on the basis of these sources, I have listed the contributors to Dickens' Christmas numbers. Wherever possible, I have attempted to supply brief distinguishing material about these co-workers, many of whom today seem unfamiliar even when their names are known.[5] I have indicated information derived from the *Household Words* Office Book with an asterisk (*)[6] and information derived from Stone's *Uncollected Writings* with a dagger (†). The symbol (‡) designates attributions based on the above mentioned editions of the Christmas numbers from *All the Year Round.* I have given no special designation to writing which is standardly attributed to Dickens or to the contents of *Mugby Junction* which are listed by author at the beginning of this holiday production *(All the Year Round, XVI).* My remarks about the authorship of *No Thoroughfare* are based on its headnote in the Gadshill edition of Dickens' works.

I have not attempted to go beyond these identifications to determine exactly where Dickens' hand stops and those of his collaborators begin. As Harry Stone has observed, Dickens "often interpolated passages—sometimes opening or concluding paragraphs—into works that are not designated by the Contributors' Book as collaborative,"[7] and, in the Christmas numbers, he was particularly apt to supply transitional passages incorporating the stories of other writers within his framework.[8] The kind of editing that Stone provides for the four framework numbers in *Household Words* undoubtedly needs to be extended to those in *All the Year Round,* but such an undertaking lies outside the scope of this Appendix.[9] The purpose of the following lists is not so much to ascribe as to provide a convenience for the reader. I have concentrated upon assembling previously scattered information that is essential to an understanding of the nature of these Christmas numbers.[10]

HOUSEHOLD WORDS

THE CHRISTMAS NUMBER (1850)

A Christmas Tree	Charles Dickens
Christmas in Lodgings	W. B[lanchard] Jerrold, and W[illiam] H[enry] W[ills]*
Christmas in the Navy	J[ames] Hannay*
A Christmas Pudding	Charles Knight*
Christmas Among the London Poor and Sick	F[rederick] K[night] Hunt*[11]
Christmas in India	Joachim Heyward Siddons ("J. H. Stocqueler")*[12]
Christmas in the Frozen Regions	Charles Dickens and Dr. Robert McCormick†*
Christmas Day in the Bush	S[amuel] Sidney*
Household Christmas Carols	R[ichard] H[enry] Horne*

As this initial table of contents indicates, the contributors to the Christmas numbers included some names that are relatively familiar in the history of nineteenth-century journalism and others that now seem virtually impossible to trace. The first writer mentioned here, W. Blanchard Jerrold (1826–1884; *DNB*), was the oldest son of the author Douglas Jerrold, one of Dickens' close friends. Blanchard Jerrold became an active journalist who eventually wrote a number of books on a variety of subjects, including *London: A Pilgrimage,* illustrated by Gustave Doré (1872). His collaborator in this case, William Henry Wills (1810–1880; *DNB*), is familiar to followers of Dickens' periodicals as the invaluable sub-editor of *Household Words* and later *All the Year Round*. Charles Knight (1791–1873; *DNB*), editor and then publisher for the Society for the Diffusion of Useful Knowledge (1828–1846), spent most of his literary career in projects designed to make general information and good literature inexpensively available to the public—a laudable aim which probably explains the tendentious didacticism of "A Christmas Pudding." The contributions by James Hannay, Joachim Heyward Siddons, Dr. Robert McCormick, and Samuel Sidney also reflect their authors' personal concerns. Hannay (1827–1873; *DNB*) spent five dissatisfied years in the navy before being court-martialled in 1845, whereupon he turned his attention to journalism and, in addition to a variety of other work, wrote novels and sketches about navy life. Siddons—who often used the pseudonym "J. H. Stocqueler"—(1801?–1885; *DNB*), a journalist who lived in India for approximately twenty years, became known as a lecturer and writer on subjects dealing with India after his return to England *ca.* 1841. McCormick (1800–1890; *DNB*), a naturalist as well as a naval surgeon, based "Christmas in the Frozen Regions" on his own experiences with an Antarctic expedition.[13] Sidney (1813–1883; *DNB*) seems to have been inspired by his brother's return from Australia in 1844, and he subsequently wrote extensively about "the Bush." Richard Henry (who later changed his name to Hengist) Horne (1803–1884; *DNB*), was a prolific and talented writer as well as a flamboyant individual. In 1852, Horne went to Australia with the understanding that he would supply *Household Words* with a series of sketches about his experiences, but he failed to keep his agreement, and his friendship with Dickens disintegrated.[14] Frederick Knight Hunt (1814–1854; *DNB*), a doctor and journalist, met an untimely death from typhus; in 1850, he was sub-editor of the *Daily News* and the person who solicited McCormick's contribution to this Christmas number.[15]

EXTRA NUMBER FOR CHRISTMAS (1851)

What Christmas is, as we Grow Older	Charles Dickens
What Christmas is to a Bunch of People	[Richard Henry] Horne*
An Idyl for Christmas In-doors	[Edmund] Ollier*
What Christmas is in Country Places	[Harriet] Martineau*
What Christmas is in the Company of John Doe	[George Augustus] Sala*
The Orphan's Dream of Christmas	[Eliza] Griffiths*
What Christmas is after a Long Absence	[Samuel] Sidney*
What Christmas is if you Outgrow it	[Theodore William Alois] Buckley*
The Round Game of the Christmas Bowl	[Richard Henry] Horne*

As before, the mixture of writers in this Christmas number is strikingly eclectic. Included among the authors on this occasion are two remarkably different examples of the Victorian lady of letters. Eliza Griffiths, who is listed for this holiday number in the *Household Words* Office Book simply as Miss Griffiths, eludes more specific identification; she seems to illustrate the legion of aspiring authoresses who dabbled in the backwaters of Victorian journalism, often under assumed names. Harriet Martineau, on the contrary, steered a more conspicuous course. During her long life (1802–1876; *DNB*), she wrote voluminously on a variety of subjects, ranging from fiction to philosophy. At first, she contributed frequently to *Household Words,* but she eventually objected to what she felt was its anti-Catholic and anti-feminist bias.[16] In 1855–56, she became publicly involved in a controversy with Dickens about a series of articles in *Household Words* expressing concern for the victims of factory accidents; her own biased statements enraged Dickens and finished their relationship.[17] The rest of Dickens' new Christmas writers were less controversial. Edmund Ollier (1827–1886; *DNB*), a poet and journalist who turned to writing books on historical subjects in the 1870s and 1880s, apparently derived his literary interests from his father, a publisher whose clients had included Leigh Hunt, Charles Lamb, Shelley, and Keats. T. W. A. Buckley (1825–1856; *DNB*) was a largely self-taught scholar, who not only wrote a variety of books and contributed to periodicals but also edited works by writers such as Chaucer and Milton and translated others by classical authors including Homer, Sophocles, Aristotle, Horace, and Virgil.

George Augustus Sala and his contribution to this Christmas production deserve special mention. Sala (1828–1895; *DNB*) was a prolific writer who ultimately achieved international, although short-lived, recognition for his books and articles. He and Dickens quarrelled temporarily over a series of sketches which Sala had been sent to Russia to write in 1856, but in 1851, the year in which Sala began to write for *Household Words,* Dickens thought very highly of him as a promising young author.[18] Sala possessed the ability to imitate some of Dickens' own stylistic devices to a remarkable degree—an ability which occasionally led nineteenth-century readers, as well as a few of their twentieth-century successors, into mistaking his work for that of his more talented "conductor." His contribution on this occasion, "What Christmas is in the Company of John Doe," recently received unexpected publicity when it was reprinted in abridged form by the *New York Times* and attributed to Dickens.[19]

A ROUND OF STORIES BY THE CHRISTMAS FIRE (1852)

The Poor Relation's Story	Charles Dickens
The Child's Story	Charles Dickens
Somebody's Story	[William Moy] Thomas*
The Old Nurse's Story	Mrs. [Elizabeth] Gaskell*
The Host's Story	E[dmund] Ollier*
The Grandfather's Story	[Rev. James] White*
The Charwoman's Story	[Edmund Saul] Dixon*[20]
The Deaf Playmate's Story	[Harriet] Martineau*
The Guest's Story	[Samuel] Sidney*
The Mother's Story	[Eliza] Griffiths*

Like the compositions for the two previous Christmases, this holiday creation consisted of a series of separate pieces by divers hands. After Dickens' own stories, perhaps the most skillful portion of this Christmas number is that by Mrs. Gaskell (1810–1865; *DNB*). The latter author, who published *Mary Barton* in 1848, was already an established novelist when she began to write for *Household Words.* Although Dickens valued her literary ability, she gradually began to resent his efforts to interfere with her work (for example, she rejected his proposed ending to "The Old Nurse's Story").[21] She continued to contribute to *Household Words* and afterwards *All the Year Round,* but she eventually began to send what she considered to be her best work to *The Cornhill*—a monthly magazine (where she could avoid the problem of weekly serialization over which she and Dickens frequently collided); initially edited by Thackeray, *The Cornhill* paid unusually high prices and numbered G. H. Lewes, George Eliot, Ruskin, and Thackeray himself among its contributors.[22]

The remaining authors included earlier Christmas figures as well as new ones. Harriet Martineau, who was deaf from childhood, added "The Deaf Playmate's Story." Among the new members of the holiday company was William Moy Thomas (1828–1910; *DNB*), an active journalist who wrote for *Household Words* from 1851 to 1858 and also contributed to a variety of other periodicals; he served on the staff of *The Daily News* from 1868 to 1901. Other contributors were the Reverend James White (1803–1862; *DNB*), a close friend of Dickens and a dramatist, who lived on the Isle of Wight, and the Reverend Edmund Saul Dixon (1809–1893), rector of Intwood with Keswick, in Norfolk, from 6 June 1842 until his death. This last individual was the author of writings on horticultural and ornithological topics as well as a variety of other subjects.[23]

ANOTHER ROUND OF STORIES BY THE CHRISTMAS FIRE (1853)

The Schoolboy's Story	Charles Dickens
The Old Lady's Story	[Eliza] Lynn*
Over the Way's Story	[George Augustus] Sala*
The Angel's Story	[Mary] Berwick*
The Squire's Story	Mrs. [Elizabeth] Gaskell*
Uncle George's Story	[Edmund Saul] Dixon and W[illiam] H[enry] W[ills]*
The Colonel's Story	[Samuel] Sidney*
The Scholar's Story	Mrs. [Elizabeth] Gaskell*[24]
Nobody's Story	Charles Dickens

As its title indicates, this Christmas number consisted of "another round" of disparate stories connected only by the pretence of being narrated before a Christmas fire. Foremost among the new authors on this holiday occasion was the novelist Eliza Lynn (1822–1898; *DNB*) who later married William James Linton and adopted the name of Mrs. Lynn Linton; she occupies a significant niche in Dickens' biography as the person from whom he bought Gad's Hill Place. Another new Christmas contributor was Adelaide Anne Procter (1825–1864; *DNB*) who temporarily submitted her work to *Household Words* under the assumed name of "Mary Berwick" in order to conceal the fact that she was the daughter of Bryan Waller Procter, the poet "Barry Cornwall," one of Dickens' friends (see Dickens' introduction to the 1866 edition of Miss Procter's *Legends and Lyrics*).

THE SEVEN POOR TRAVELLERS (1854)

The First	Charles Dickens
The Second	George Augustus Sala†*
The Third	Adelaide [Anne] Procter*
The Fourth	Wilkie Collins†*
The Fifth	George Augustus Sala†*
The Sixth	Eliza Lynn†*
The Seventh	Adelaide Anne Procter†*
The Road	Charles Dickens

The Seven Poor Travellers marks an important change in the format of the Christmas numbers. Here, as in most of its successors, the composition consists of a framework, customarily by Dickens, which provides an excuse for interpolated pieces by the other contributors. The novelist Wilkie Collins (1824–1889; *DNB*), whose name is the only new one in this collection of holiday writers, soon grew to be not only one of Dickens' closest friends but the most important of his Christmas collaborators. As the ensuing tables of contents indicate, Collins was the only writer besides himself whom Dickens permitted to work on the opening and closing sections of these productions, and in two cases *(The Perils of Certain English Prisoners* and *No Thoroughfare)* Dickens abandoned the idea of framework and attached stories in prose and verse in favor of a more unified number written with Collins alone.

THE HOLLY-TREE INN (1855)

The Guest	Charles Dickens
The Ostler	Wilkie Collins†*
The Boots	Charles Dickens
The Landlord	William Howitt†*
The Barmaid	Adelaide Anne Procter†*
The Poor Pensioner	Harriet Parr ("Holme Lee")†*
The Bill	Charles Dickens

The two new Christmas contributors who appeared in *The Holly-Tree Inn* were active figures on the fringes of nineteenth-century literature. One of them, Harriet Parr (1828–1900; *DNB*), had published the first of what was to be a long succession of novels in 1854 under the name of "Holme Lee." The second, William Howitt (1792–1879; *DNB*) industriously wrote and edited an enormous number of literary works, many of them in conjunction with his wife Mary. He contributed to *Household Words* from its inauguration and in 1852 travelled to Australia with R. H. Horne—an experience which undoubtedly explains the Australian interests of "The Landlord." Beginning in 1859, he became engaged in a public controversy with Dickens about the subject of spiritualism (see *The Haunted House*).

Appendix A

THE WRECK OF THE GOLDEN MARY. BEING THE CAPTAIN'S
ACCOUNT OF THE LOSS OF THE SHIP, AND THE MATE'S
ACCOUNT OF THE GREAT DELIVERANCE OF HER PEOPLE IN
AN OPEN BOAT AT SEA (1856)

The Wreck	Charles Dickens
The Beguilement in the Boats	
—the armourer's story	Percy Fitzgerald†*
—poor Dick's story	Harriet Parr ("Holme Lee")†*
—the supercargo's story	Percy Fitzgerald†*
—the old seaman's story	Adelaide Anne Procter†*
—the Scotch boy's story	Rev. James White†*
The Deliverance	Wilkie Collins†*

The truncated version of *The Wreck of the Golden Mary* which customarily appears in editions of Dickens' "Christmas Stories"—apparently ending with two boatloads of survivors helplessly floating on the open sea—graphically illustrates the importance of a reader's familiarity with the construction
of the Christmas numbers. In this case, Dickens allowed Collins to handle the
conclusion, and, as Stone has observed, Collins also wrote most of John Steadiman's (The Mate's) section of "The Wreck."[25] The poem at the end of "poor
Dick's story" may not be by Dickens although it appears in his collected
works under the title of "A Child's Hymn."[26] The only new Christmas contributor among the authors whose tales were interpolated into "The Beguilement in the Boats" was Percy Fitzgerald (1834–1925), a young man from Ire-
land whom Dickens befriended and helped to launch on what was to be a
long and prolific literary career.[27]

THE PERILS OF CERTAIN ENGLISH PRISONERS, AND THEIR
TREASURE IN WOMEN, CHILDREN, SILVER, AND JEWELS (1857)

The Island of Silver-Store	Charles Dickens
The Prison in the Woods	Wilkie Collins*
The Rafts on the River	Charles Dickens

The Perils of Certain English Prisoners, which Dickens described as
"the whole No. one story,"[28] represents a temporary divergence from what
had by 1857 come to be established as the customary holiday format. Here,
Dickens worked solely in conjunction with Collins, and the work as a whole
reflects Collins' usual concern with an exciting and suspenseful plot.[29]

A HOUSE TO LET (1858)

Over the Way	Charles Dickens and Wilkie Collins†
The Manchester Marriage	Mrs. [Elizabeth] Gaskell†*
Going into Society	Charles Dickens
Three Evenings in the House	Adelaide Anne Procter†*
Trottle's Report	Wilkie Collins†*
Let At Last	Charles Dickens and Wilkie Collins†*

With this number, Dickens returned to the familiar form and a familiar group of contributors. However, Collins' influence on the production is marked, and the four middle chapters are not so easily detached from their setting as some of the earlier interpolated pieces—a fact which explains the seemingly strange appearance of "Going into Society," the only section of *A House to Let* usually reprinted in Dickens' collected works.

ALL THE YEAR ROUND

THE HAUNTED HOUSE (1859)

The Mortals in the House	Charles Dickens
The Ghost in the Clock Room	Hesba Stretton‡
The Ghost in the Double Room	G[eorge] A[ugustus] Sala‡
The Ghost in the Picture Room	Adelaide [Anne] Procter‡
The Ghost in the Cupboard Room	Wilkie Collins‡
The Ghost in Master B.'s Room	Charles Dickens
The Ghost in the Garden Room	Mrs. [Elizabeth] Gaskell‡
The Ghost in the Corner Room	Charles Dickens‡

As Harry Stone has recently demonstrated, an important impetus behind this Christmas number was Dickens' private and public controversy with William Howitt, a believer in spiritualism, over the issue of ghostly visitation.[30] *The Haunted House* debunked credulous acceptance of supernatural phenomena and infuriated Howitt.

The hauntings in this case prove to be their narrators' recollections, and the only new figure among the authors is that of Hesba Stretton (1832–1911; *DNB*), whose original name was the somewhat more ordinary one of Sarah Smith. In 1867, she achieved fame with a book called *Jessica's First Prayer* and went on to produce a large number of similar works.

A MESSAGE FROM THE SEA (1860)

The Village	Charles Dickens
The Money	Charles Dickens and Wilkie Collins‡
The Club-Night	Charles Dickens, Charles Collins, Harriet Parr ("Holme Lee"), H[enry] F[othergill] Chorley, and Amelia B. Edwards‡
The Seafaring Man	Wilkie Collins‡
The Restitution	Charles Dickens and Wilkie Collins‡

There is conflicting evidence concerning the contributors to this Christmas number. The 1868 and 1907 editions of the Christmas numbers from *All the Year Round* give the attributions which I have listed. *The New Cambridge Bibliography of English Literature* likewise attributes "The Village" and part of "The Club-Night" to Dickens as well as "The Money" and "The Restitution" to both Dickens and Wilkie Collins.[31] However, Frederic G. Kitton, who consulted the now missing marked office set of *All the Year Round,* indicates that "The Money" and "The Restitution" are by Dickens alone and that, even though Dickens wrote "nearly all" of "The Village," Wilkie Collins also "was responsible for a share of Chapter I"; rather ambiguously, he contends that chapters 3 and 4 "contain insertions by him [Dickens]," although he states that "Wilkie Collins was responsible for . . . the whole of Chapter IV."[32] "The Club-Night," according to Kitton, contains passages by Dickens and Wilkie Collins as well as a poem by R. (presumably Robert) Buchanan.[33]

Not all of this conflict can be resolved, and the extent of Buchanan's possible contribution remains unclear. On the subject of Dickens' share in this Christmas number, however, a recent article by Stone provides some important clarification. According to Stone, chapters 1, 2, and 5 ("The Village," "The Money," and "The Restitution"), which are attributed to Dickens in editions of his collected works, "are probably not entirely by Dickens"; Stone further suggests that although Wilkie Collins may have been the primary author of chapter 4 ("The Seafaring Man") Dickens apparently "also had a hand."[34] In the case of chapter 3 ("The Club-Night"), Stone argues that Dickens rewrote and expanded Wilkie Collins' first draft of its introduction and "probably" added sections connecting and concluding the interpolated stories by other contributors.[35]

Of these contributors, the first was Charles Collins (1828–1873; *DNB*), a painter as well as a writer, the younger brother of Wilkie Collins, and the husband of Dickens' daughter Kate, whom he married in July, 1860. Among the other participants in "The Club-Night" were Henry Fothergill Chorley (1808–1872; *DNB*), a musical and literary critic for the *Athenaeum,* and Amelia B. Edwards (1831–1892; *DNB*), a journalist and novelist who travelled up the Nile in 1873–74 and subsequently became an enthusiastic Egyptologist.

TOM TIDDLER'S GROUND (1861)

Picking up Soot and Cinders	Charles Dickens
Picking up Evening Shadows	Charles Collins‡
Picking up Terrible Company	Amelia B. Edwards‡
Picking up Waifs at Sea	Wilkie Collins‡
Picking up a Pocket-Book	John Harwood‡
Picking up Miss Kimmeens	Charles Dickens
Picking up the Tinker	Charles Dickens

Here, the only name new to the Christmas numbers is that of John Harwood—probably John Berwick Harwood, an elusive novelist whom the redoubtable cataloguer Michael Sadleir dates as 1828–?late 1880s and describes as "one of the minor mysteries of mid-nineteenth-century authorship."[36]

SOMEBODY'S LUGGAGE (1862)

His Leaving it till called for	Charles Dickens
His Boots	Charles Dickens
His Umbrella	John Oxenford‡
His Black Bag	Charles Collins‡
His Writing-Desk	Charles Collins‡
His Dressing-Case	Arthur Locker‡
His Brown-Paper Parcel	Charles Dickens
His Portmanteau }	Authoress of "The Valley of a
His Hat-Box }	Hundred Fires"‡
His Wonderful End	Charles Dickens

The pieces in *Somebody's Luggage* included contributions by three new Christmas writers. The first, John Oxenford (1812–1877; *DNB*), was a dramatist, translator, and theatrical critic for the *Times;* Kitton attributes part of "His Umbrella" to Dickens[37]—not an unlikely possibility in view of Dickens' willingness to touch up his contributors' manuscripts—but the 1868 and 1907 editions of the Christmas numbers from *All the Year Round* simply give the piece to Oxenford as indicated above. The second new author on this occasion was Arthur Locker (1828–1893; *DNB*), who turned to literature after recovering from a seizure of gold fever which led him, temporarily, to emigrate to Australia; he industriously contributed to magazines and newspapers after coming back to England in 1861 and in 1870 became editor of the *Graphic.* The last, Julia Cecilia Stretton (1812–1878), was the author of several novels including *The Valley of a Hundred Fires* (1860).[38]

MRS. LIRRIPER'S LODGINGS (1863)

How Mrs. Lirriper carried on the Business	Charles Dickens
How the First Floor went to Crowley Castle	Mrs. [Elizabeth] Gaskell‡
How the Side-Room was attended by a Doctor	Andrew Halliday‡
How the Second Floor kept a Dog	Edmund Yates‡
How the Third Floor knew the Potteries	Amelia B. Edwards‡
How the Best Attic was under a Cloud	Charles Collins‡
How the Parlours added a few words	Charles Dickens

Mrs. Lirriper's Lodgings contained only two unfamiliar Christmas contributors. The proprietor of "the Side-Room" was Andrew Halliday (1830–1877; *DNB*), a playwright and journalist. The holder of "the Second Floor" was Edmund Yates (1831–1894; *DNB*), a long-time employee of the Post Office as well as a novelist and journalist; in 1858, Dickens took Yates' side in a quarrel with Thackeray—an action resulting in a serious estrangement between Dickens and Thackeray which ended only shortly before the latter's death.

MRS. LIRRIPER'S LEGACY (1864)

Mrs. Lirriper Relates how She Went on, and Went Over	Charles Dickens
A Past Lodger Relates a Wild Legend of a Doctor	Charles Collins‡
Another Past Lodger Relates His Experience as a Poor Relation	Rosa Mulholland‡
Another Past Lodger Relates What Lot He Drew at Glumper House	Henry Spicer‡
Another Past Lodger Relates His Own Ghost Story	Amelia B. Edwards‡
Another Past Lodger Relates Certain Passages to Her Husband	Hesba Stretton‡
Mrs. Lirriper Relates how Jemmy Topped Up	Charles Dickens

The sequel to *Mrs. Lirriper's Lodgings* contained two more new Christmas writers. One of these was a young Irishwoman, Rosa Mulholland (1841–1921), who married Sir John T. Gilbert, an Irish historian, in 1891.[39] The other, Henry Spicer (?–1891) was a dramatist who apparently first came to public attention in the 1840s.[40]

DOCTOR MARIGOLD'S PRESCRIPTIONS (1865)

To Be Taken Immediately	Charles Dickens
Not To Be Taken at Bed-Time	Rosa Mulholland‡
To Be Taken at the Dinner-Table	Charles Collins‡
Not To Be Taken for Granted	Hesba Stretton‡
To Be Taken in Water	Walter Thornbury‡
To Be Taken with a Grain of Salt	Charles Dickens
To Be Taken and Tried	Mrs. Gascoyne‡
To Be Taken for Life	Charles Dickens

Walter Thornbury and Mrs. Gascoyne, who each produced one of Doctor Marigold's "prescriptions," are the only remaining contributors to the Christmas numbers not previously mentioned. Thornbury (1828–1876; *DNB*) wrote novels, contributed to periodicals—often on topographical subjects—and travelled extensively. Mrs. Gascoyne is a more elusive figure. She is probably

Caroline Leigh (née Smith) Gascoigne (1813–1883), an obscure novelist who married General Ernest Frederick Gascoigne in 1834.[41]

One of the other "prescriptions" in this number needs special comment. Information about the authorship of "To Be Taken with a Grain of Salt" is contradictory. On the one hand, there is convincing evidence that Dickens wrote it without collaboration with anyone else. It appears in Dickens' collected works, and the 1868 and 1907 editions of the Christmas numbers from *All the Year Round* list him as sole author as shown in the table above. The edition by Charles Dickens the Younger also attributes it to Dickens alone.[42] In an apparent reference to this ghost story in *Doctor Marigold's Prescriptions* as his own work, Dickens wrote to Miss Mary Boyle:

> I am charmed to learn that you have had a freeze out of my ghost story. It rather did give me a shiver up the back in the writing. Dr. Marigold has just now accomplished his two hundred thousand.[43]

On the other hand, without identifying himself as author, Dickens remarked in a letter to Percy Fitzgerald, "I recommend to your perusal a certain ghost story, headed 'To be taken with a grain of salt,' "[44] and a footnote to this letter in the Nonesuch edition as well as in an earlier edition of Dickens' letters by Georgina Hogarth and Mamie Dickens attributes the story to Charles Collins.[45]

An early reader of *The Dickensian* noticed this discrepancy and wrote to its editor, B. W. Matz, asking if the story were by Dickens or Collins or if it might be a composite piece written by both. Matz declared categorically that Dickens was the author of "To be Taken with a Grain of Salt." However, Matz stated that he based his conclusions "on the authority of the editorial book kept in the office of *Household Words*"[46]—a remark which raises more problems than it solves, for the Office Book of *Household Words* contains no information about contributions to *All the Year Round* and Matz apparently did not have an Office Book or a marked office set of *All the Year Round* at the time of answering this question. Matz's basis for this statement may have been Kitton's *Minor Writings of Charles Dickens.* Kitton identified Dickens' contributions to *All the Year Round* on the basis of an office set identifying the anonymous authors (which, as mentioned earlier, has since disappeared), and Matz used Kitton's authority for the pieces that he included in his edition of *Miscellaneous Papers* for the National edition of Dickens' works (1906–1908).[47] Unfortunately, Kitton's remark about the authorship of this particular story is ambiguous. According to Kitton, Dickens' contributions to *Doctor Marigold's Prescriptions* include " 'To be Taken with a Grain of Salt' (i.e., the portion describing the trial for murder)."[48] Since almost all of the story is related to the trial, the crucial question of whether the piece was written by Dickens alone or in collaboration is unresolved.

Thus, despite Matz's attempt to settle the issue, confusion still remains. The story is reprinted as "The Trial for Murder" in an anthology called *Great Tales of Terror and the Supernatural,* and a headnote in this anthology states, without giving the source of its information, that the piece "was probably originally written by Collins and subsequently revised by

Dickens."[49] In view of these conflicting claims, one cannot rule out the possibility that Charles Collins had a share in this story, although there is strong evidence that a large portion, if not all of it, was written by Dickens alone.

MUGBY JUNCTION (1866)

Barbox Brothers	Charles Dickens
Barbox Brothers and Co.	Charles Dickens
Main Line. The Boy at Mugby	Charles Dickens
No. 1 Branch Line. The Signalman	Charles Dickens
No. 2 Branch Line. The Engine-Driver	Andrew Halliday
No. 3 Branch Line. The Compensation House	Charles Collins
No. 4 Branch Line. The Travelling Post-Office	Hesba Stretton
No. 5 Branch Line. The Engineer	Amelia B. Edwards

NO THOROUGHFARE (1867)

The Overture	Charles Dickens
Act I	Charles Dickens and Wilkie Collins
The Curtain Rises Enter the Housekeeper The Housekeeper Speaks New Characters on the Scene Exit Wilding	
Act II Vendale Makes Love Vendale Makes Mischief	Wilkie Collins
Act III In the Valley On the Mountain	Charles Dickens
Act IV	Charles Dickens and Wilkie Collins
The Clock-Lock Obenreizer's Victory The Curtain Falls	

After *Doctor Marigold's Prescriptions,* Dickens' interest in what had become the traditional Christmas number apparently declined. In *Mugby Junction,* as its table of contents indicates, he added the stories by other writers as a kind of inevitable supplement at the end of his own contributions. With *No Thoroughfare,* the holiday production for the following year, he dropped his usual format and leaned heavily on the help of Wilkie Collins. In 1868, he jettisoned the Christmas number altogether. Publicly, he declared to his readers that he was unwillingly giving up this seasonal creation because it "has now been so extensively, and regularly, and often imitated, that it is in very great danger of becoming tiresome."[50] Privately, he explained, "My reason for abandoning the Christmas number was, that I became weary of having my own writing swamped by that of other people."[51]

Viewed as a group, these "other people" represent a remarkably heterogeneous assortment. From the perspective of the latter half of the twentieth century, one can say that although Dickens attracted a few literary luminaries to his Christmas company—notably Mrs. Gaskell and Wilkie Collins—he relied primarily on lesser lights, and the resulting discrepancies in talent form one of the most serious problems of the Christmas numbers. Nevertheless, the total contents of these annual productions must not be forgotten. They provide the only context in which the strengths as well as the weaknesses of Dickens' own contributions can genuinely be assessed.

APPENDIX B

Chronological Frame

In the following table, as an aid to the reader, the short stories by Dickens examined in this study are listed in the order of their publication. For information concerning the tales analyzed from *Sketches by Boz,* I am indebted to Duane DeVries' remarks about "The Publishing History of *Sketches by Boz,*" in *Dickens's Apprentice Years: The Making of a Novelist* (Hassocks, England: Harvester Press; New York: Barnes & Noble, 1976), pp. 147–57.

1836   8 February, *Sketches by Boz,* First Series
　　　 —"The Black Veil"

　　　 8 February, *Sketches by Boz,* First Series
　　　 —"The Great Winglebury Duel"

　　　 April, *Library of Fiction*
　　　 —"The Tuggses at Ramsgate" (included in 1837–39 edition in
　　　　 monthly parts of *Sketches by Boz*)

　　　 May, in second monthly number of *Pickwick Papers*
　　　 —"The Stroller's Tale"

　　　 June, in third monthly number of *Pickwick Papers*
　　　 —"The Convict's Return"

　　　 July, in fourth monthly number of *Pickwick Papers*
　　　 —"A Madman's Manuscript"

　　　 August, in fifth monthly number of *Pickwick Papers*
　　　 —"The Bagman's Story"

　　　 September, in sixth monthly number of *Pickwick Papers*
　　　 —"The Parish Clerk: A Tale of True Love"

　　　 November, in eighth monthly number of *Pickwick Papers*
　　　 —"The Old Man's Tale about the Queer Client"

　　　 17 December, *Sketches by Boz,* Second Series
　　　 —"The Drunkard's Death"

1837   January, in tenth monthly number of *Pickwick Papers*
　　　 —"The Story of the Goblins who stole a Sexton"

January, *Bentley's Miscellany*
—"Public Life of Mr. Tulrumble Once Mayor of Mudfog"

April, in thirteenth monthly number of *Pickwick Papers*
—"The True Legend of Prince Bladud"

September, in seventeenth monthly number of *Pickwick Papers*
—"[T]he Story of the Bagman's Uncle"

1838　May, in second monthly number of *Nicholas Nickleby*
—"The Five Sisters of York"
—"The Baron of Grogzwig"

1840　(4 April, inauguration of *Master Humphrey's Clock*)

11 April, in second weekly number of *Master Humphrey's Clock*
—"First Night of the Giant Chronicles"

18 April, in third weekly number of *Master Humphrey's Clock*
—"A Confession Found in a Prison in the Time of Charles the Second"

2–9 May, in fifth and sixth weekly numbers of *Master Humphrey's Clock*
—"Mr. Pickwick's Tale"

1843　*A Christmas Carol*

1844　*The Chimes*

1845　*The Cricket on the Hearth*

1846　*The Battle of Life*

1848　*The Haunted Man*

1852　in *A Round of Stories by the Christmas Fire* (Christmas number, *Household Words*)
—"The Poor Relation's Story"
—"The Child's Story"

1853　in *Another Round of Stories by the Christmas Fire* (Christmas number, *Household Words*)
—"The Schoolboy's Story"
—"Nobody's Story"

1854　in *The Seven Poor Travellers* (Christmas number, *Household Words*)
—framework ("The First" and "The Road")

1855　in *The Holly-Tree Inn* (Christmas number, *Household Words*)
—framework ("The Guest" and "The Bill")
—"The Boots"

1856　June, in seventh monthly number of *Little Dorrit*
—story by Little Dorrit about the tiny woman and the shadow

in *The Wreck of the Golden Mary. Being the Captain's Account of the Loss of the Ship, and the Mate's Account of the Great Deliverance of Her People in an Open Boat at Sea* (Christmas number, *Household Words*)
—incomplete story by Dickens in "The Wreck"

1857   March, in sixteenth monthly number of *Little Dorrit*
       —"The History of a Self Tormentor"

       24 October, *Household Words,* in fourth weekly installment of *The
       Lazy Tour of Two Idle Apprentices*
       —"The Bride's Chamber"

       *The Perils of Certain English Prisoners, and Their Treasure in
       Women, Children, Silver, and Jewels* (Christmas number,
       Household Words), three-part story consisting of "The Island of
       Silver-Store" by Dickens, "The Prison in the Woods" by Wilkie
       Collins, and "The Rafts on the River" by Dickens

1858   in *A House to Let* (Christmas number, *Household Words*)
       —framework ("Over the Way" and "Let at Last") in collaboration
       with Wilkie Collins
       —"Going into Society"

1859   in *The Haunted House* (Christmas number, *All the Year Round*)
       —framework ("The Mortals in the House" and "The Ghost in the
       Corner Room")
       —"The Ghost in Master B.'s Room"

1860   8 September, *Household Words,* in "Nurse's Stories"
       —description of Captain Murderer and other embryonic stories

       in *A Message from the Sea* (Christmas number, *All the Year Round*)
       —framework ("The Village," "The Money," the opening section of
       "The Club-Night," "The Seafaring Man," and "The Restitution")
       in collaboration with Wilkie Collins. See Appendix A, pp. 147–48,
       for a discussion of the somewhat contradictory evidence
       concerning Dickens' and Collins' respective contributions.

1861   in *Tom Tiddler's Ground* (Christmas number, *All the Year Round*)
       —framework ("Picking up Soot and Cinders" and "Picking up the
       Tinker")
       —"Picking up Miss Kimmeens"

1862   in *Somebody's Luggage* (Christmas number, *All the Year Round*)
       —framework ("His Leaving it till called for" and "His Wonderful
       End")
       —"His Boots"
       —"His Brown-Paper Parcel"

1863   in *Mrs. Lirriper's Lodgings* (Christmas number, *All the Year Round*)
       —framework ("How Mrs. Lirriper carried on the Business" and
       "How the Parlours added a few words")

1864   in *Mrs. Lirriper's Legacy* (Christmas number, *All the Year Round*)
       —framework ("Mrs. Lirriper Relates how She Went on, and Went
       Over" and "Mrs. Lirriper Relates how Jemmy Topped Up")

1865   in *Doctor Marigold's Prescriptions* (Christmas number, *All the Year
       Round*)
       —framework ("To Be Taken Immediately" and "To Be Taken for
       Life")

1866 in *Mugby Junction* (Christmas number, *All the Year Round*)
—initial story ("Barbox Brothers" and "Barbox Brothers and Co.")
—"Main Line. The Boy at Mugby"
—No. 1 Branch Line. The Signalman"

1867 *No Thoroughfare* (Christmas number, *All the Year Round*), five-part story ("overture" plus four "acts") in collaboration with Wilkie Collins. See Appendix A, p. 152, for a description of Dickens' and Collins' respective contributions.

1868 January, February, March, *Atlantic Monthly* (subsequently 1, 15, 29 February, *All the Year Round*)
—"George Silverman's Explanation"

January, March, April, May, *Our Young Folks* (subsequently 25 January, 8 February, 14 March, 4 April, *All the Year Round*)
—"Holiday Romance"

NOTES

CHAPTER 1

Imaginative License

1. Significant exceptions to this widespread neglect are the outstanding studies of various aspects of Dickens' short writing by Duane DeVries (*Dickens's Apprentice Years: The Making of a Novelist*— a discussion of *Sketches by Boz* [Hassocks, England: Harvester Press; New York: Barnes & Noble, 1976]); Robert L. Patten (e.g., his treatment of the place of the interpolated tales in *Pickwick Papers* as in his introductory comments about these tales in his edition of this novel [Harmondsworth, England: Penguin, 1972]); Michael Slater (e.g., the general critical introduction to his edition of the *Christmas Books*, 2 vols. [Harmondsworth, England: Penguin, 1971]); and Harry Stone (e.g., his edition of *Charles Dickens' Uncollected Writings from "Household Words" 1850–1859*, 2 vols. [Bloomington: Indiana University Press, 1968] as well as his comments on various short pieces in *Dickens and the Invisible World: Fairy Tales, Fantasy, and Novel-Making* [Bloomington: Indiana University Press, 1979]). Nevertheless, as Philip Collins suggests in his "Presidential Message to The Dickens Society," the tendency even of most Dickens critics to overlook writings such as those collected as *Christmas Stories* remains to be corrected (*Dickens Studies Newsletter* 7 [1976]: 7). As Collins emphasizes in *Victorian Fiction: A Second Guide to Research*, ed. George H. Ford (New York: Modern Language Association of America, 1978)—quoting and reiterating Ada Nisbet's comment in *Victorian Fiction: A Guide to Research*, ed. Lionel Stevenson (Cambridge: Harvard University Press, 1964)— "But still 'the short stories in general have been neglected by critics' " (Collins, p. 109; Nisbet, p. 100*n*).

2. Sylvère Monod, *Dickens the Novelist* (Norman: University of Oklahoma Press, 1968), p. xiii. My own recent edition of Dickens' *Selected Short Fiction* (Harmondsworth, England: Penguin, 1976) has remedied some of this common oversight of Dickens' short writing, but the kind of detailed critical study that Monod suggests has not previously been written.

3. Percy Fitzgerald, *Memories of Charles Dickens with an Account of "Household Words" and "All the Year Round" and of the Contributors Thereto* (London: Simpkin, Marshall, Hamilton, Kent, 1913), p. 113.

4. George Orwell, "Charles Dickens," *The Collected Essays, Journalism and Letters of George Orwell*, ed. Sonia Orwell and Ian Angus, 4 vols. (London: Secker and Warburg, 1968), I, 450.

5. Aspects of this subject have occasionally been treated in articles such as that by Robert Hamilton, "The Creative Eye: Dickens as Essayist," *Dickensian* 64 (1968): 36–42,

and I have touched upon it briefly in the introduction to my edition of *Selected Short Fiction*, which contains a section devoted to Dickens' "Impressionistic Sketches" including "A Flight" and "The Calais Night-Mail" as well as other pieces. More recently, Gordon Spence has provocatively but still somewhat briefly dealt with this topic in *Charles Dickens as a Familiar Essayist* (Salzburg: Institut für Englische Sprache und Literatur, Universität Salzburg, 1977 [Romantic Reassessment 71]).

6. For example, in the proposal for *Master Humphrey's Clock*, which he sent to John Forster in 1839, Dickens explained that he intended "to vary the form of the papers by throwing them into sketches, essays, tales, adventures, letters from imaginary correspondents and so forth" (*PL*, I, 563–64, [14 July 1839]). The distinction between story-like material and sketch-like material here is vague, in keeping with the often vague distinction between fiction and nonfiction in Dickens' acknowledged eighteenth-century models for *Master Humphrey's Clock*, *"The Tatler, The Spectator,* and Goldsmith's *Bee"* (ibid., p. 563); indeed Steele felt it necessary to note in the *Tatler* (no. 172) his "libertine manner of writing by way of essay." By the time of his editorship of *Household Words* in the 1850s, Dickens' concept of the short story and the essay or sketch as distinctive varieties of short writing, implicit in his remarks about *Master Humphrey's Clock*, seems to have become more specific. Thus, a few weeks before the appearance of the first issue of *Household Words*, he wrote to Mary Howitt, emphasizing his hope that she and William Howitt would become contributors to the new periodical and explaining that "the kind of papers of which I stand most in need, are *short stories*, with such a general purpose in them as we all three have in all we do" (quoted from a previously unpublished letter included by Carl Ray Woodring in *Victorian Samplers: William and Mary Howitt* [Lawrence, Kans.: University of Kansas Press, 1952], p. 152). As editor of *Household Words,* in an even more revealing although less enthusiastic vein, Dickens rejected the material forwarded to him by an anonymous female contributor on the grounds that "the writing is very agreeable and ladylike; but there is no novelty of observation or charm of expression, or plain form of purpose, or compactness of treatment, to separate it from hundreds upon hundreds of similar contributions that are for ever coming here. . . . The Bittern is an essay on the ordinary essayical model, which tells the reader nothing previously unknown, and which could only be made acceptable for the sake of what it does tell, by the information being communicated in a picturesque and special way. Exactly the same objection applies with at least equal force to the essay called The Victories of Love. The Village Home and The Brother and Sister are children's stories, and quite out of the road of a publication addressing so large an audience as this of ours does—in which the constant endeavour is, to adapt every paper to the reception of a number of classes and various orders of mind at once." (*NL*, II, 401–2, to Charles Mayne Young, 21 July 1852).

7. For example, see James' objections to Thackeray's *The Newcomes,* Dumas' *Les Trois Mousquetaires,* and Tolstoy's *War and Peace,* "what do such large loose baggy monsters, with their queer elements of the accidental and the arbitrary, artistically mean?" (preface to *The Tragic Muse,* in *The Art of the Novel: Critical Prefaces by Henry James,* introduction by Richard P. Blackmur [New York: Scribners, 1934], p. 84); and Percy Lubbock's study, *The Craft of Fiction* (1921; reprint ed., New York: Viking, 1957).

For a useful corrective of the kind of critical approach illustrated by Lubbock's valuable but overly rigid treatment of the novel, see Bradford A. Booth, "Form and Technique in the Novel," *The Reinterpretation of Victorian Literature,* ed. Joseph E. Baker (1950; reprint ed., New York: Russell and Russell, 1962), pp. 67–96. Booth observes that it does seem more appropriate to talk about "the advance . . . of the short story" (p. 94) than about "the 'advance' of the novel" (p. 67). Indeed, in the hands of writers like Katherine Mansfield and Ernest Hemingway, the short story does appear to have benefited from the historical trend in which, in Booth's words, "The old overstuffed plots, with their melodramatic incidents and anemic conclusions, were swept away by the inexorable logic of Poe's position in theory, strengthened by the success of that theory in practice" (p. 94). Nonetheless, while the development in the direction of the so-called modern short story may, on the whole, be an artistically satisfactory one, it seems critically dangerous, as historians of the short story have often done, to dismiss Dickens for failing to perceive this eventual trend or to confine himself within limits of which he was happily oblivious and wiser simply to examine the significance of his short stories in their own terms.

8. H. E. Bates, *The Modern Short Story* (London: Thomas Nelson and Sons, 1941), p. 14.

9. T. O. Beachcroft, *The English Short Story,* 2 vols. (London: Longmans, Green & Co., 1964), I, 13.

10. Wendell V. Harris, "Vision and Form: The English Novel and the Emergence of the Short Story," *Victorian Newsletter* 47 (1975): 11. However, Harris also notes that "Dickens, [Mrs.] Gaskell, [Wilkie] Collins, and [George] Eliot . . . all produced stories and tales which strike the contemporary reader as too formless to be regarded as first-class short stories, but which one would not willingly lose and for which one might very well be content to give up a number of recognizedly successful twentieth-century stories" (*British Short Fiction in the Nineteenth Century: A Literary and Bibliographic Guide* [Detroit: Wayne State University Press, 1979], p. 60).

11. *NL,* II, 385, to R. H. Horne, 6 April 1852.

12. *NL,* II, 422, to Rev. James White, 19 October 1852.

13. For example, see Dickens' repetition of Forster's astonished praise of the character of Doctor Marigold in *Doctor Marigold's Prescriptions,* the Christmas number of *All the Year Round* for 1865, conceived by Dickens (*NL,* III, 438, to John Forster, [September] 1865) as a relief from the writing of *Our Mutual Friend:* "He has perfectly astonished Forster, who writes: 'Neither good, gooder, nor goodest, but super-excellent; all through there is such a relish of you at your best, as I could not have believed in, after a long story' " (*NL,* III, 442, to William Charles Kent, 6 November 1865). Also, see Master Humphrey's allusion to *Barnaby Rudge* as "a long story" (*MHC,* p. 109) and Dickens' letter to W. H. Wills quoted in note 14.

14. Unlike his novels, most of Dickens' short stories were not serialized. However, a few of the pieces that fall within the confines of this study—notably "George Silverman's Explanation" and "Holiday Romance"—appeared in a limited number of installments. As editor of *Household Words,* Dickens explicitly restricted the maximum number of installments of a desirable short story to four. As he explained his objections to Wilkie Collins' novel *The Dead Secret* in a letter to W. H. Wills, "Now, as to a long story itself, I doubt its value to us. And I feel perfectly convinced that it is not one quarter so useful to us as detached papers, or short stories in four parts. But I am quite content to try the experiment" (*NL,* II, 801, 18 September 1856). Less charitably, Dickens rejected *Gilbert Massenger* by Harriet Parr ("Holme Lee") on the ground that "experience shows me that a story in four portions is best suited to the peculiar requirements of such a journal" (*NL,* II, 684, to Miss Harriet Parr, 14 August 1855).

15. Jack Lindsay, *Charles Dickens: A Biographical and Critical Study* (London: Andrew Dakers, 1950), p. 242.

16. John Forster, *The Life of Charles Dickens,* ed. J. W. T. Ley (London: Cecil Palmer, 1928), p. 727.

17. Ibid.

18. Ibid., pp. 727–28.

19. As P[hilip] Collins notes, "Dickens . . . inherited the Romantic aesthetic, in which 'Fancy' and 'Imagination' were so important. He did not, however, habitually

differentiate between the two terms, as Wordsworth and Coleridge had done" (" 'Keep *Household Words* Imaginative!,' " *Dickensian* 52 [1956]: 120*n*).

20. Barbara Hardy, *Tellers and Listeners: The Narrative Imagination* (London: Athlone Press, 1975), p. 165.

21. Ibid., p. 169.

CHAPTER 2

Imaginative Overindulgence

1. Quoted in Fred[eric] G. Kitton, *Dickensiana: A Bibliography of the Literature Relating to Charles Dickens and His Writings* (1886; reprint ed., New York: Haskell House Publishers, 1971), p. 226.

2. Angus Wilson, *The World of Charles Dickens* (1970; reprint ed., New York: Viking, 1972), p. 27.

3. F. B. Perkins, *Charles Dickens: A Sketch of His Life and Works* (1870; reprint ed., Folcroft, Pa.: Folcroft Library Editions, 1973), p. 61. Dickens asserted in his 1848 preface to *The Old Curiosity Shop* that *Master Humphrey's Clock* "was intended to consist, for the most part, of detached papers, but was to include one continuous story, to be resumed, from time to time, with such indefinite intervals between each period of resumption as might best accord with the exigencies and capabilities of the proposed Miscellany" (*OCS*, p. xi). However, the agreement that Dickens signed with Chapman and Hall for *Master Humphrey's Clock* on 31 March 1840 contained no reference to a "continuous story" (*PL*, II, 464–71).

4. *PL*, II, 40 to John Forster, [?8 March 1840]. For a discussion of the manner in which Dickens transformed this "little child-story" into *The Old Curiosity Shop*, see Robert L. Patten, " 'The Story-Weaver at His Loom': Dickens and the Beginning of *The Old Curiosity Shop*," *Dickens the Craftsman: Strategies of Presentation*, ed. Robert B. Partlow, Jr. (Carbondale: Southern Illinois University Press, 1970), pp. 44–64, 191–93, 205.

5. For example, see Trevor Blount, *Charles Dickens: The Early Novels* (London: Longmans, Green & Co., 1968), p. 21; Sylvère Monod, *Dickens the Novelist* (Norman: University of Oklahoma Press, 1968), pp. 168–70; and Angus Wilson, p. 27.

6. G. K. Chesterton, *Appreciations and Criticisms of the Works of Charles Dickens* (London: J. M. Dent and Sons, 1911), p. 237.

7. Duane DeVries, *Dickens's Apprentice Years: The Making of a Novelist* (Hassocks, England: Harvester Press; New York: Barnes & Noble, 1976), pp. 4–8, 24–26.

8. George Gissing, *Charles Dickens: A Critical Study* (London: Blackie & Son, 1898), p. 27.

9. K[athleen] T[illotson], "Writers and Readers in 1851," *Mid-Victorian Studies*, by Geoffrey and Kathleen Tillotson (London: Athlone Press, 1965), p. 309.

10. *"A Christmas Carol" and "The Chimes,"* introduction by Walter Allen (New York: Harper & Row, 1965), p. xv.

11. *NL*, II, 654, to John Forster, 14 April 1855.

12. *PL*, I, 563–64, to John Forster, [14 July 1839].

13. Malcolm Andrews, "Introducing Master Humphrey," *Dickensian* 67 (1971): 71.

14. *PL*, I, 564, to John Forster, [14 July 1839].

15. Ibid. In *The Development of the American Short Story: An Historical Survey* (New York: Harper & Brothers, 1923), Fred Lewis Pattee describes *The Alhambra* as "an Arabesque, as redolent of the Orient as the tales of Scheherezade" (p. 17).

16. DeVries, pp. 1–2, 51, 109, et passim.

17. Gissing, p. 30.

18. Jane W. Stedman, "Good Spirits: Dickens's Childhood Reading," *Dickensian* 61 (1965): 150–54.

19. Harry Stone, "Fire, Hand, and Gate: Dickens' *Great Expectations,*" *Kenyon Review* 24 (1962): 667; see also idem, *Dickens and the Invisible World: Fairy Tales, Fantasy, and Novel-Making* (Bloomington: Indiana University Press, 1979), p. xi.

20. For a detailed discussion of such motifs, see Stone, *Dickens and the Invisible World.*

21. For example, see R. D. McMaster, "Dickens and the Horrific," *Dalhousie Review* 38 (1958): 18–28.

22. Sigmund Freud, "The 'Uncanny'," *Collected Papers,* authorized trans. under the supervision of Joan Riviere, 5 vols. (New York: Basic Books, 1959), IV, 404.

23. Ibid. For a discussion of the way in which the element of the uncanny operates in *Bleak House,* in connection with the dual perspective of that novel, see Robert Newsom, *Dickens on the Romantic Side of Familiar Things: "Bleak House" and the Novel Tradition* (New York: Columbia University Press, 1977), chap. 3.

24. *NL,* II, 360, to Mrs. Gaskell, 25 November 1851.

25. John Forster, *The Life of Charles Dickens,* ed. J. W. T. Ley (London: Cecil Palmer, 1928), p. 840.

26. DeVries, pp. 31, 43, 43*n,* and 93.

27. Ibid., p. 31 and n. 3. These eight early tales are "Mr. Minns and His Cousin" (first published as "A Dinner at Poplar Walk"), "Mrs. Joseph Porter" (first published as "Mrs. Joseph Porter, 'Over the Way' "), "Horatio Sparkins," "The Bloomsbury Christening," "The Boarding House," "The Steam Excursion," "Passage in the Life of Mr. Watkins Tottle," and "Sentiment"(first published as "Original Papers").

28. Ibid., pp. 56–58, 107.

29. Ibid., pp. 97, 107–9. These five tales are "Miss Evans and the Eagle," "The Dancing Academy," "Making a Night of It," "The Misplaced Attachment of Mr. John Dounce" (first published as "Love and Oysters"), and "The Mistaken Milliner. A Tale of Ambition" (first published as "The Vocal Dress-Maker").

In his capacity as editor of *Household Words*, later in his career, Dickens frequently warned contributors about the hazards of inexperience, and in one letter, he emphasized the danger of a false pose of cynicism:

> These Notes are destroyed by too much smartness. . . . Airiness and good spirits are always delightful, and are inseparable from notes of a cheerful trip; but they should sympathise with many things as well as see them in a lively way. It is but a word or a touch that expresses this humanity, but without that little embellishment of good nature there is no such thing as humour. In this little MS. everything is too much patronised and condescended to, whereas the slightest touch of feeling for the rustic who is of the earth earthy, or of sisterhood with the homely servant who has made her face shine in her desire to please, would make a difference that the writer can scarcely imagine without trying it. The only relief in the twenty-one slips is the little bit about the chimes. It *is* a relief, simply because it is an indication of some kind of sentiment. You don't want any sentiment laboriously made out in such a thing. You don't want any maudlin show of it. But you do want a pervading suggestion that it is there. It makes all the difference between being playful and being cruel. Again I must say, above all things—especially to young people writing: For the love of God don't condescend! Don't assume the attitude of saying, "See how clever I am, and what fun everybody else is!" Take any shape but that.
>
> (*NL,* II, 851–52, to Frank Stone, 1 June 1857)

In the eight tales from Dec. 1833 to Feb. 1835, Dickens himself often seems to have stumbled into this pitfall of inexperienced "smartness." For example, "The Bloomsbury

Christening" portrays a dismal personage named Nicodemus Dumps, who hates children and ruins his godson's christening party with a gloomy description of disasters that may happen to the parents and the boy; the child's mother goes into hysterics, but most of the guests are favorably impressed with the speech, "for people like sentiment, after all" (*SB*, p. 482). However, in the tales published in autumn 1835 and eventually grouped by Dickens under the heading of "Characters," this note of "smartness," while still present, is not so jarringly apparent.

30. DeVries, pp. 111, 132, 137. For a valuable discussion of Dickens' revisions in successive editions of the pieces collected in *Sketches by Boz,* see John Butt and Kathleen Tillotson, *Dickens at Work* (London: Methuen & Co., 1957), chap. 2.

31. For a comparison of Dickens' treatment of the black veil in this story with the manner in which this motif is treated by Ann Radcliffe in *The Mysteries of Udolpho* and Nathaniel Hawthorne in "The Minister's Black Veil," see M. L. Allen, "The Black Veil: Three Versions of a Symbol," *English Studies* 47 (1966): 286–89. In "The Bloomsbury Christening," the narrator observes in passing, as part of a description of a rainy day, that "cabs whisked about, with the 'fare' as carefully boxed up behind two glazed calico curtains as any mysterious picture in any one of Mrs. Radcliffe's castles" (*SB*, p. 471).

32. Harvey Peter Sucksmith, "The Secret of Immediacy: Dickens' Debt to the Tale of Terror in *Blackwood's,*" *Nineteenth-Century Fiction* 26 (1971): 146.

33. Ibid., pp. 149–50.

34. DeVries, p. 125.

35. For example, in addition to DeVries as well as Butt and Tillotson, see J. Hillis Miller, "The Fiction of Realism: *Sketches by Boz, Oliver Twist,* and Cruikshank's Illustrations," *Dickens Centennial Essays,* ed. Ada Nisbet and Blake Nevius (Berkeley and Los Angeles: University of California Press, 1971), pp. 85–153.

36. DeVries, pp. 31–32, 55. As DeVries notes, both "The Great Winglebury Duel" and, evidently, "The Black Veil" were written in late 1835—in October and November, respectively—although these stories were not published until 1836 (ibid., pp. 111*n* and 121*n*).

37. Edmund Wilson, "Dickens: The Two Scrooges," *The Wound and the Bow* (1941; reprint ed., New York: Oxford University Press, 1965), p. 10.

38. Edgar Johnson, *Charles Dickens: His Tragedy and Triumph,* 2 vols. (New York: Simon and Schuster, 1952), I, 165.

39. Butt and Tillotson, p. 73.

40. Edmund Wilson, pp. 10–12.

41. Johnson, I, 163. Also see Steven Marcus, *Dickens: From Pickwick to Dombey* (1965; reprint ed., New York: Simon and Schuster, 1968), pp. 41–44.

42. *PL,* I, 145–46, to Robert Seymour, [14 April 1836].

43. Heinz Reinhold, " 'The Stroller's Tale' in *Pickwick,*" *Dickensian* 64 (1968): 141–51.

44. Robert Patten, "The Unpropitious Muse: *Pickwick*'s 'Interpolated' Tales," *Dickens Studies Newsletter* 1, i (1970): 10.

45. For example, see Patten's comments about the tales in the introduction to his edition of *Pickwick Papers* (Harmondsworth, England: Penguin, 1972), pp. 25–26, as well as in his articles on "The Interpolated Tales in *Pickwick Papers,*" *Dickens Studies* 1 (1965): 86–89, and "The Art of *Pickwick*'s Interpolated Tales," *ELH* 34 (1967): 349–66. In addition, see William Axton's discussion of the tales in "Unity and Coherence in *The Pickwick Papers,*" *Studies in English Literature* 5 (1965): 674–76 and *Circle of Fire: Dickens' Vision & Style & the Popular Victorian Theater* (Lexington: University of Kentucky Press, 1966), pp. 75–79.

46. Garrett Stewart, *Dickens and the Trials of Imagination* (Cambridge: Harvard University Press, 1974), p. 32. In *"Master Humphrey's Clock:* Dickens' 'Lost' Book," Carol

de Saint Victor also observes in passing that the stories introduced into *Pickwick Papers* "are, in brief, about some aspect of the life of the imagination" (*Texas Studies in Literature and Language* 10 [1969]: 572).

47. Stewart uses this phrase in the title for part 1 of *Dickens and the Trials of Imagination.*

48. Stewart, p. 33.

49. Ibid., p. 42. Robert E. Lougy also calls attention to the difference between "The Parish Clerk" and the other tales in *Pickwick Papers;* he argues perceptively that "The Parish Clerk" offers "a fictional parallel" (p. 101) to Pickwick's experience in the previous episode, when the latter attempted to stop a supposed elopement between Jingle and an heiress at a boarding school, and marks a turning point in Dickens' characterization of Pickwick ("Pickwick and 'The Parish Clerk,'" *Nineteenth-Century Fiction* 25 [1970]: 100–104). However, since the novel attributes "The Parish Clerk" indirectly to Sam Weller and presents Pickwick as simply its editor as I discuss in my text, Lougy's contention that "this tale is written by Pickwick himself" (pp. 100–101) seems debatable.

50. These pieces are "Public Life of Mr. Tulrumble Once Mayor of Mudfog," "The Pantomine of Life," "Some Particulars concerning a Lion," "Full Report of the First Meeting of the Mudfog Association for the Advancement of Everything," and "Full Report of the Second Meeting of the Mudfog Association for the Advancement of Everything" (appearing respectively in the January, March, May, and October 1837 and September 1838 issues of *Bentley's Miscellany*). Dickens apparently completed "Public Life of Mr. Tulrumble" in early December 1836, although the story was not published until January 1837, in the first issue of *Bentley's Miscellany* (see *PL,* I, 206, to George Cruikshank, [5 December 1836] and 206, n. 1).

William J. Carlton has presented evidence indicating that the piece entitled "Mr. Robert Bolton"—published in the August 1838 issue of *Bentley's Miscellany* and usually attributed to Dickens—may, in fact, have been written by John H. Leigh Hunt (the son of Leigh Hunt) and extensively revised by Dickens ("Who Wrote 'Mr. Robert Bolton'?," *Dickensian* 54 (1958): 178–81).

51. Angus Wilson, p. 110.

52. For example, Dickens wrote to W. Harrison Ainsworth at the end of January 1838, in connection with a projected collaborative collection of stories dealing with past and present London to be entitled *The Lions of London,* "I should have written to you before, but my month's work has been dreadful—Grimaldi, the anonymous book for Chapman and Hall, Oliver and the Miscellany. They are all done, thank God, and I start on my pilgrimage to the cheap schools of Yorkshire (a mighty secret of course) next Monday Morning" (*PL,* I, 359, [25 January 1838]). The project with Ainsworth was eventually dropped, although Dickens' later idea of having Gog and Magog narrate "a series of papers . . . containing stories and descriptions of London as it was many years ago, as it is now, and as it will be many years hence" in his proposal for *Master Humphrey's Clock* may be, at least in part, an incorporation of this earlier plan.

Dickens subsequently wrote another volume for Chapman and Hall similar to *Sketches of Young Gentlemen,* entitled *Sketches of Young Couples* and occasioned by Queen Victoria's marriage (1840).

53. *PL,* I, 227, to Richard Bentley, [24 January 1837], and 227, n. 3.

54. *PL,* I, 395–96, to John Forster, [?15 April 1838], and 396, n. 1. For a recent discussion of the function of these tales within the setting in which they are told and their use of the topic of memory, see Ruth Glancy, "The Significance of the *Nickleby* Stories," *Dickensian* 75 (1979): 12–15.

55. *PL,* I, 562, to John Forster, [14 July 1839]. As the Pilgrim editors note, *Master Humphrey's Clock* was "advertised as 'A New Work on an entirely new plan' in the Aug *Nickleby*" (ibid., p. 562, n. 2).

56. Forster, p. 139.

57. For example, see Andrews, pp. 70–71; Marcus, p. 130; and Monod, p. 167.

58. *PL*, I, 567, to Daniel Maclise, [?24 July 1839].

59. Andrews, pp. 75–76.

60. *PL*, II, 267, to Washington Irving, 21 April 1841. Dickens continued in the same letter, alluding to scenes which the Pilgrim editors attribute to *The Sketch-Book of Geoffrey Crayon, Gent.* (1820), *Voyages and Discoveries of the Companions of Columbus* (1831), *A Chronicle of the Conquest of Granada* (1829), and *A History of New York, . . .* By Diedrich Knickerbocker (1809),

> I should love to go with you—as I have gone, God knows how often—into Little Britain, and Eastcheap, and Green Arbour Court, and Westminster Abbey. I should like to travel with you, outside the last of the coaches, down to Bracebridge Hall. It would make my heart glad to compare notes with you about that shabby gentleman in the oilcloth hat and red-nose who sat in the nine-cornered back parlor at the Masons' Arms—and about Robert Preston—and the tallow-chandler's widow whose sitting room is second nature to me—and about all those delightful places and people that I used to walk about and dream of in the daytime when a very small and not over-particularly-taken-care-of boy. I have a good deal to say too about that dashing Alonzo De Ojeda that you can't help being fonder of than you ought to be—and much to hear concerning Moorish Legend, and poor unhappy Boabdil. Diedrich Knickerbocker I have worn to death in my pocket—and yet I should shew you his mutilated carcass—with a joy past all expression.
>
> I have been so accustomed to associate you with my pleasantest and happiest thoughts, and with my leisure hours, that I rush at once into full confidence with you, and fall—as it were naturally, and by the very laws of gravity—into your open arms. (*PL*, II, 267–68, 21 April 1841)

61. For example, see the assertions by Ernest Boll in "Charles Dickens and Washington Irving," *Modern Language Quarterly* 5 (1944): 453–67, corrected and qualified by Christof Wegelin who contends that "what influence Irving may have had on Dickens seems limited to a few genres, such as the *Sketches by Boz* and the set tales inserted into *Pickwick,* possibly also to some of the short pieces written for periodicals" (p. 90), "Dickens and Irving: The Problem of Influence," *Modern Language Quarterly* 7 (1946): 83–91. Also see, more recently, Katherine Carolan, "The Dingley Dell Christmas," *Dickens Studies Newsletter* 4 (1973): 41–48; idem, "The Dingley Dell Christmas Continued: 'Rip Van Winkle' and the Tale of Gabriel Grub," *Dickens Studies Newsletter* 5 (1974): 104–6. However, the Pilgrim editors conclude cautiously that "well as CD knew Irving's work . . . its influence on his writing was of little account, though some contemporary English (but not American) reviewers claimed to have found evidence of it in *Sketches* and *Pickwick*" (*PL*, II, 268, n. 8).

62. David Sonstroem, "Fettered Fancy in *Hard Times,*" PMLA 84 (1969): 520.

63. Andrews, p. 85.

64. In view of this emphasis in the initial *Clock* material on demonstrating what is suitable to Master Humphrey's circle, Stewart's remarks in *Dickens and the Trials of Imagination* about the artistic inappropriateness of the reincarnation of Pickwick and Sam Weller, conjoined with Pickwick's liking for the company of Jack Bamber and his emulation of Bamber's taste in literature, need qualification. Indubitably, the difference in tone between this abortive *Clock* machinery and the primary narrative of the earlier novel is jarring. In Stewart's words, "How can we imagine *Pickwick's* Pickwick as a gothic author?" (p. 45). However, *Master Humphrey's* Pickwick is not *"Pickwick's* Pickwick" but rather a Pickwick "retired into private life" (*MHC,* p. 86) and thus, in Dickens' thinking at this point, appropriate company for the other retired and retiring individuals in Master Humphrey's group.

Notes

65. *PL,* III, 385, to Edgar Allan Poe, 27 November 1842. For an exhaustive discussion of Dickens' somewhat distant attitude toward Poe and Poe's attitude toward Dickens, see Gerald G. Grubb, "The Personal and Literary Relationships of Dickens and Poe," *Nineteenth-Century Fiction* 5 (1950): 1–22, 101–20, 209–21.

66. *NL,* III, 51, to Wilkie Collins, 6 September 1858.

CHAPTER 3

Storybooks in a Workaday World

1. For example, see Kathleen Tillotson's discussion of the difference between *Dombey and Son* (1846–1848) and the novels that preceded it in *Novels of the Eighteen-Forties* (Oxford: Clarendon Press, 1954) as well as her discussion of "The Middle Years: From the *Carol* to *Copperfield,"* *Dickens Memorial Lectures* (London: The Dickens Fellowship, 1970)—supplement to *Dickensian* (September 1970).

2. John Forster, *The Life of Charles Dickens,* ed. J. W. T. Ley (London: Cecil Palmer, 1928), p. 317.

3. For example, see John Butt, "Dickens's Christmas Books," *Pope, Dickens, and Others* (Edinburgh: Edinburgh University Press, 1969), pp. 127–48; Michael Slater, "The Christmas Books," *Dickensian* 65 (1969): 17–24, as well as Slater's general critical introduction to his edition of *The Christmas Books,* 2 vols. (Harmondsworth, England: Penguin, 1971); Harry Stone, *Dickens and the Invisible World: Fairy Tales, Fantasy, and Novel-Making* (Bloomington: Indiana University Press, 1979), pp. 119–45; and Tillotson, "The Middle Years."

4. James A. H. Murray et al., eds., *The Oxford English Dictionary* (Oxford: Clarendon Press, 1888–1933), s.v. Story sb[1].

5. Earle Davis, *The Flint and the Flame: The Artistry of Charles Dickens* (Columbia: University of Missouri Press, 1963), pp. 148–49.

6. *NL,* II, 231, to Miss Coutts, 6 September 1850. Dickens himself had agreed with Tegg in August 1836 to author a "child's book, to be called *Solomon Bell the Raree Showman . . .* by Christmas next." However, Dickens never wrote this book, and Tegg eventually published a volume with a similar title by a different person in 1839 (*PL,* I, 163, to Thomas Tegg, 11 August 1836, and 163, n. 2).

7. The full title of this Christmas Book is *A Christmas Carol, in Prose: Being a Ghost Story of Christmas.*

Dickens' comments about the *Carol* and the subsequent Christmas Books frequently emphasize their diminutive nature. For example, see his remark to C. C. Felton (2 January 1844) about "this little book, the Carol" as well as his statement to Lady Holland (10 June 1844) about the next Christmas Book, "a small successor to the little Carol" (*PL,* IV, 3, 145). Also, see his enthusiastic description of *The Chimes*—"my little Christmas Book"—to W. C. Macready: "God forgive me,—but I think there are good things in the little Story!" (*PL,* IV, 232, 28 November 1844). On a more harried note, see the confession to Forster about *The Battle of Life:* "It would be such a great relief to me to get that small story out of the way" (*PL,* IV, 600 [9 and 10 August 1846]).

Similarly, Dickens' explanation of his reasons for deciding to take *"sledge-hammer"* action when the *Carol* was pirated alludes to the difference in size between the *Carol* and "a long story" (*PL,* IV, 16, to Thomas Mitton, 7 January 1844).

8. Humphry House, *The Dickens World,* 2d ed. (1942; reprint ed., London: Oxford University Press, 1960), p. 52.

9. For an analysis of Scrooge as "a personification of economic man" (p. 485) and

the social implications of this personification, see Edgar Johnson, *Charles Dickens: His Tragedy and Triumph,* 2 vols. (New York: Simon & Schuster, 1952), 484–89. For analyses that, respectively, stress festive, religious, and fairy-tale aspects of *A Christmas Carol,* see Philip Collins, " '*Carol* Philosophy, Cheerful Views,' " *Études Anglaises* 23 (1970):158–67; Robert L. Patten, "Dickens Time and Again," *Dickens Studies Annual,* ed. Robert B. Partlow, Jr., II (Carbondale: Southern Illinois University Press, 1972), 163–96, 362–66; and Stone, *Dickens and the Invisible World,* pp. 120–26.

10. Sigmund Freud, "Humour," *Collected Papers,* authorized trans. under the supervision of Joan Riviere, 5 vols. (New York: Basic Books, 1959), V, 217.

11. Slater, "The Christmas Books," p. 20.

12. *The Christmas Books,* ed. Slater, I, xi–xii. See also Slater, "The Christmas Books," p. 20.

13. *The Speeches of Charles Dickens,* ed. K. J. Fielding (Oxford: Clarendon Press, 1960), p. 246, see also pp. 169 and 259. In keeping with contemporary custom, Dickens' speeches were often reported in the third person (ibid., p. xvii).

14. For example, see Stone, *Dickens and the Invisible World,* p. 119.

15. Butt, "Dickens's Christmas Books," pp. 133–35.

16. Harry Stone, "Dickens' Artistry and *The Haunted Man,*" *South Atlantic Quarterly* 61 (1962): 495, reprinted with slightly different wording in Stone, *Dickens and the Invisible World,* p. 119. See also Robert L. Patten's discussion of " 'A Surprising Transformation': Dickens and the Hearth," *Nature and the Victorian Imagination,* ed. U. C. Knoepflmacher and G. B. Tennyson (Berkeley and Los Angeles: University of California Press, 1977), 153–70.

17. From the 1868 preface to the "Charles Dickens" edition of *The Christmas Books.* The 1852 preface to the Cheap edition of *The Christmas Books* (reprinted *CB,* p. xv) made the same statement with the omission of the word "chief" (*The Christmas Books,* ed. Slater, I, xxix).

18. As Slater has noted, this newspaper description is based on a contemporary case that had aroused a public protest:

> Dickens is here alluding to the case of Mary Furley, tried and sentenced for infanticide on 16 April 1844. In her evidence, reported in *The Times* on 17 April, she said that she had quitted the Whitechapel workhouse because of the brutal ill-treatment suffered there by her young child; she had tried to support herself and the baby by sewing shirts but, since the most she was able to earn that way was 5¼*d.* a day, she had borrowed a few shillings to buy ribbons to make up dress-caps for sale. This money was stolen from her and she then frantically resolved to drown herself and the child rather than return to the workhouse. When they were pulled out of the Thames the child was dead. Sentencing her to death, the judge remarked, "Your act, which would have been at any time cruel, is rendered more so by the fact of the crime being committed by you—the mother of the child." After a public outcry, in which Dickens joined (see his "Threatening Letter to Thomas Hood from an Ancient Gentleman", (*Hood's Magazine,* May 1844), her sentence was commuted to seven years' transportation. (*The Christmas Books,* ed. Slater, I, 264, n. 18.)

See also Michael Slater, "Dickens's Tract for the Times," *Dickens 1970,* ed. Michael Slater (New York: Stein and Day, 1970), pp. 102–4.

19. Slater, "The Christmas Books," p. 17. See also idem, "Dickens's Tract for the Times," 99–123, as well as Slater's discussion of and notes on *The Chimes* in his edition of *The Christmas Books.*

20. *PL,* IV, 200, to John Forster, [8 October 1844].

21. Slater, "The Christmas Books," p. 19. See also Michael Slater, "Dickens (and Forster) at Work on *The Chimes,*" *Dickens Studies* 2 (1966): 109 and 109, n. 4.

22. J. Hillis Miller, introduction to *Bleak House,* ed. Norman Page (Harmondsworth, England: Penguin, 1971), p. 11. For a discussion of the manner in which the motif of interpretation pervades one of Dickens' last novels and reflects the gradual, corrective disillusionment of its central character, see Max Byrd, " 'Reading' in *Great Expectations,"* *PMLA* 91 (1976): 259–65.

23. *The Christmas Books,* ed. Slater, I, xvii.

24. Ibid.

25. *PL,* IV, 623, to John Forster [?20 September 1846].

26. *PL,* IV, 625, to John Forster, [26 September 1846].

27. *The Christmas Books,* ed. Slater, II, 124.

28. Katherine Carolan, "The Battle of Life, A Love Story," *Dickensian* 69 (1973): 106.

29. House, pp. 109–10.

30. *PL,* V, 517, to Miss Burdett Coutts, 29 March 1849.

31. Cf. the 1807 sonnet by William Wordsworth that begins, "The world is too much with us; late and soon, / Getting and spending, we lay waste our powers."

In a similar although somewhat more ironic sounding of the note which Dickens strikes at the end of "Frauds on the Fairies," the narrator of *Hard Times* observes in chapter 8 that, to Gradgrind's chagrin, Goldsmith is a more popular writer among patrons of the Coketown library than Cocker (the author of a book on mathematics).

32. Oliver Goldsmith, *The Vicar of Wakefield and Other Writings,* ed. Frederick W. Hilles (New York: Random, 1955), p. 317.

33. Carolan, p. 106.

34. Goldsmith, p. 408.

35. Steven Marcus, *Dickens: From Pickwick to Dombey* (1965; reprint ed., New York: Simon & Schuster, 1968), p. 289. Marcus does not discuss the connections that I have noted between *The Vicar of Wakefield* and *The Battle of Life.* While Marcus attributes the artistic failure of this Christmas Book to Dickens' failure to deal effectively with his current autobiographical impulses, he analyzes the autobiographical aspects of the *Battle* primarily in terms of the link between Doctor Jeddler's daughters—called Grace and Marion—and Georgina and Mary Hogarth (ibid., pp. 289–92).

36. The precise date of this fragment is uncertain. Slater observes that Dickens "had written, probably in 1847, some chapters of an autobiography in which he revealed to Forster the scars that the debtors' prison and the blacking factory of his boyhood had left upon his memory" ("The Christmas Books," p. 24). Albert D. Hutter places it sometime between 1847 and 1849, when Dickens' "eldest child, Charles Culliford [born 6 January 1837], was somewhere between ten and twelve, that is, between the ages when David went to work at Murdstone and Grinby and when Charles actually went to work at Warren's" ("Reconstructive Autobiography: The Experience at Warren's Blacking," *Dickens Studies Annual,* ed. Robert B. Partlow, Jr., VI [Carbondale: Southern Illinois University Press, 1977], p. 10). However, Hutter comments that "there is some confusion over the exact date of the autobiographical fragment: Forster suggests 1847 in one place, several months before Dickens conceived the idea of *David Copperfield* in another (which would put it late in 1848 or early 1849), and several years before writing *Copperfield* in yet another reference. Edgar Johnson, noting these discrepancies, suggests somewhere between September 1845 and May 1846" (ibid., p. 187, n. 21).

On the basis of a recent reexamination of the available evidence, Nina Burgis has concluded that the cleanly written autobiographical fragment, which Forster records as having seen in January 1849, was the result of drafts produced over several years and that its composition was facilitated by letters and conversations between Dickens and Forster in 1847 and 1848 (Charles Dickens, *David Copperfield,* ed. Nina Burgis [Oxford: Clarendon Press, 1981], p. xx). Drawing upon Burgis' findings, the Pilgrim editors remark: "It seems likely that the illness and death of his sister Fanny in 1848 took his mind back to further childhood memories; and that he wrote at least the major part of the autobiographical fragment in the autumn or winter of that year" (*PL*, V, xii).

37. Forster, p. 508.

38. Stone, "Dickens' Artistry and *The Haunted Man*," p. 504.

39. Forster, p. 508.

40. Jack Lindsay, *Charles Dickens: A Biographical and Critical Study* (London: Andrew Dakers, 1950), p. 29.

41. [James Ridley], *The Tales of the Genii; or, The Delightful Lessons of Horam the Son of Asmar,* trans. from the Persian by Sir Charles Morell [pseud.], new ed., collated and edited by Philo-juvenis [pseud.] (London: Henry G. Bohn, 1857), p. 24.

42. Ibid., p. 65.

43. Ibid., p. 66.

44. As Davis has noted (pp. 102, 142), Dickens had previously incorporated this story of Valentine and Orson for satiric effect in his depiction of the relationship between Sir John Chester and Hugh in *Barnaby Rudge* (1841).

45. Philip Collins, "Dickens on Ghosts: An Uncollected Article," *Dickensian* 59 (1963): 9. As Collins notes, Dickens' remark about "the Kilmarnock weaver's prayer for grace to see themselves as others see them" is an allusion to Robert Burns' "To a Louse" (ibid., p. 9*n*).

46. Hans Christian Andersen, *The Fairy Tale of My Life: An Autobiography* (New York: Paddington Press, 1975, reprint of 1871 Eng. trans. of *Mit Livs Eventyr,* including 1855 and 1868 texts), p. 301.

47. Hans Christian Andersen, *A Christmas Greeting to My English Friends* (London: Richard Bentley, 1847), pp. iii–iv. As Elias Bredsdorff notes in *Hans Andersen and Charles Dickens: A Friendship and Its Dissolution* (Copenhagen: Rosenkilde & Bagger, 1956), "Andersen's Danish draft of this dedication . . . says 'five short stories' " (p. 29*n*). (Ejnar Munksgaard gives this remark as simply "five little tales"—*Hans Christian Andersen's Visits to Charles Dickens as Described in His Letters Published with Six of Dickens' Letters in Facsimile* [Copenhagen: Levin & Munksgaard; Ejnar Munksgaard, 1937], p. 25.) However, as Bredsdorff explains, in addition to the five unpublished stories that Andersen originally proposed, Bentley had included two others, previously published in Denmark, which had been sent to him for *Bentley's Miscellany.*

48. *PL*, V, 243, to Hans Christian Andersen, [?late January 1848]. The Pilgrim editors note that the story that Dickens describes as reading and rereading is "now known in England as 'The Tin Soldier' " (ibid., p. 243, n. 2).

49. Quoted in Bredsdorff, p. 96. Unfortunately, this second visit undermined the friendship that the earlier visit had begun. Andersen apparently failed to perceive the strains in the Dickens marriage which was to terminate in separation in the following year —he wrote in the same letter to Henriette Wulff that "Mrs. Dickens is so mild, so motherly, so exactly like Agnes in 'David Copperfield' "—and he greatly outstayed his welcome at Gadshill. Dickens exerted himself to be a good host, but after Andersen's departure, he wrote on a card that he attached to a mirror in the room his guest had vacated: "Hans Andersen slept in this room for five weeks—which seemed to the family AGES!" (quoted in Bredsdorff, p. 115). For a discussion of additional factors that apparently contributed to the dissolution of Dickens' friendship with Andersen, see ibid., pp. 116–17, 131–33.

50. *NL*, III, 661, to W. H. Wills, 31 July 1868.

51. Slater, "The Christmas Books," p. 18.

52. Forster, p. 512.

Notes

CHAPTER 4

The Chord of the Christmas Season

1. John Forster, *The Life of Charles Dickens,* ed. J. W. T. Ley (London: Cecil Palmer, 1928), p. 466. This comment occurs in the context of Dickens' discussion of his reluctant postponement of *The Haunted Man* from 1847 to 1848.

2. Harry Stone's edition of *Charles Dickens' Uncollected Writings from "Household Words" 1850–1859,* 2 vols. (Bloomington: Indiana University Press, 1968) contains a valuable survey of the development of Dickens' Christmas numbers (II, 523) and reprints previously uncollected portions of several of the Christmas numbers of *Household Words,* including *The Holly-Tree Inn.* Stone notes that the modifications permitting Dickens' portions of *The Holly-Tree Inn,* as well as those of some of the other Christmas numbers, to be detached from their original format were made by Dickens for the Diamond edition of his works, published in the United States in 1867 (II, 542). However, it remains difficult for modern readers to understand all aspects of Dickens' contributions to the Christmas numbers apart from the original contexts. For example, the opening chapter of the *Household Words* version of *The Holly-Tree Inn* ends with a decision by the bashful narrator of the framework of this Christmas number that he will become acquainted not just with the Boots but with several of the people at the inn; this large-scale decision underscores the sense of fellow feeling that Dickens associated with Christmas. The original format of *The Holly-Tree Inn* also makes clear that Dickens intended "The Boots," which begins on page eighteen, to stand at the midpoint of this thirty-six page Christmas number.

3. For example, the narrator of Dickens' opening chapter of *The Haunted House,* the Christmas number of *All the Year Round* for 1859, describes Twelfth Night as "the last night of holy Christmas" (*CS,* p. 239.)

Twelfth Night also had particular festive significance for the Dickens family since the birthday of Dickens' oldest child—Charles Culliford Boz Dickens—occurred on January 6th.

4. *NL,* II, 431–32, to Rev. James White, 22 November 1852. Dickens had previously solicited one of the contributions to this *Round of Stories by the Christmas Fire* from White with the declaration *"I don't care about their referring to Christmas at all"* (*NL,* II, 422, 19 October 1852).

5. *NL,* II, 714, to Wilkie Collins, 12 December 1855.

6. See Harry Stone, *Dickens and the Invisible World: Fairy Tales, Fantasy, and Novel-Making* (Bloomington: Indiana University Press, 1979), p. 119, and *NL,* II, 714, to Wilkie Collins, 12 December 1855.

7. On a comparable note, in Lewis Carroll's *Through the Looking-Glass* (first published in December 1871), the White Queen offers Alice a job whose recompense, in part, resembles Boots' observation. As the Queen explains, "The rule is, jam to-morrow and jam yesterday—but never jam *to-day.*"

8. From "H. W." (16 April 1853), with Henry Morley, reprinted in *Uncollected Writings,* ed. Stone, II, 468. The passage quoted in my text is from a section of this composite article which Stone believes is "probably" by Dickens (ibid., p. 467).

9. *NL,* III, 630, to Charles Fechter, 8 March 1868.

10. *NL,* III, 659–60, to W. H. Wills, 26 July 1868.

11. K. J. Fielding, review of *Charles Dickens' Uncollected Writings from "Household Words" 1850–1859,* ed. Harry Stone, *Victorian Studies* 13 (1969): 217.

For a recent discussion of the connection between the frameworks and inset tales of Dickens' Christmas numbers, see Ruth F. Glancy, "Dickens and Christmas: His Framed-Tale Themes," *Nineteenth-Century Fiction* 35 (1980): 53–72. Glancy's emphasis on "the relationship between teller and tale" (ibid., p. 67) is perceptive. Her contention that the stories in the Christmas numbers offered occasions "for autobiographical storytelling, the relating of tales derived from the memory of the teller" (ibid., p. 55) supports my own, more general argument that in many of his contributions to the Christmas numbers, Dickens was concerned with depicting what he viewed as the world of the imagination, often a distinctive character's interior, mental world as revealed through first-person monologue. However, Glancy's focus on the autobiographical and remembering aspects of the Christmas numbers seems too narrow. As I indicate in chapters 4 and 5, Dickens attempted to fictionalize whatever impulses from his own life might surface in his "Christmas Stories," and in addition to that of memory, he dealt with a variety of subjects in his writings for the Christmas numbers.

12. Garrett Stewart, *Dickens and the Trials of Imagination* (Cambridge: Harvard University Press, 1974), pp. xxi, 160ff.

13. Harry Stone reprints this section, "The Ghost in the Corner Room," in "The Unknown Dickens: With a Sampling of Uncollected Writings," *Dickens Studies Annual,* ed. Robert B. Partlow, Jr., I (Carbondale: Southern Illinois University Press, 1970), 20–21.

14. Ibid., p. 21.

15. Ibid., pp. 8–12, 14.

16. *The Haunted House,* extra Christmas number of *All the Year Round* for 1859, p. 27. This passage appears in the Oxford Illustrated edition of *Christmas Stories* (p. 242), although "ever" (in "ever in his Buoyant Boyhood") is erroneously printed there as "even."

17. *The Haunted House,* extra Christmas number of *All the Year Round* for 1859, p. 27. This passage appears in the Oxford Illustrated edition of *Christmas Stories* (p. 243) with slight changes in punctuation.

18. *NL,* III, 310, to Wilkie Collins, 14 October 1862.

19. Forster, p. 726. This story, from chapter 2 of *The Lazy Tour of Two Idle Apprentices* (a collective description of a trip taken by Dickens and Collins to the north of England), was included with a slightly altered ending in Collins' *The Queen of Hearts* (1859).

20. *NL,* II, 814, to Miss Coutts, 4 December 1856.

21. *NL,* II, 834, to Rev. James White, 8 February 1857.

22. *Uncollected Writings,* ed. Stone, II, 564.

23. Ibid., pp. 564–65.

24. Ibid., p. 564.

25. *The Wreck of the Golden Mary,* extra Christmas number of *Household Words* for 1856, p. 30.

26. Ibid., p. 34.

27. Ibid., pp. 34–35.

28. T. S. Eliot has called attention to this distinction between Dickens and Collins: "Dickens excelled in character; in the creation of characters of greater intensity than human beings. Collins was not usually strong in the creation of character; but he was a master of plot and situation, of those elements of drama which are most essential to melodrama" ("Wilkie Collins and Dickens," *Selected Essays,* new ed. [New York: Harcourt, Brace & Co., 1950], pp. 410–11).

29. *Uncollected Writings,* ed. Stone, II, 564, 569.

30. William Oddie, "Dickens and the Indian Mutiny," *Dickensian* 68 (1972): 14.

31. Ibid., p. 6.

32. *Uncollected Writings,* ed. Stone, II, 595, 597, 598, 610.

33. Earle Davis, *The Flint and the Flame: The Artistry of Charles Dickens* (Columbia: University of Missouri Press, 1963), p. 196.

CHAPTER 5

Public Entertainment

1. John Forster, *The Life of Charles Dickens,* ed. J. W. T. Ley (London: Cecil Palmer, 1928), p. 726.

2. Charles Dickens, *Selected Short Fiction,* ed. Deborah A. Thomas (Harmondsworth, England: Penguin, 1976), p. 262.

3. *NL,* III, 304, to Wilkie Collins, 20 September 1862.

4. I have discussed the way in which Dickens' characterization of Mrs. Lirriper evolves from that of Flora Finching and earlier versions of this kind of comic female figure in Dickens' fiction in "Dickens' Mrs. Lirriper and the Evolution of a Feminine Stereotype," *Dickens Studies Annual,* ed. Robert B. Partlow, Jr., VI (Carbondale: Southern Illinois University Press, 1977), pp. 154–66, 196–98. See also Harry Stone, "Dickens and Interior Monologue," *Philological Quarterly* 38 (1959): 55–59.

5. *Selected Short Fiction,* ed. Thomas, pp. 345–46. This passage, with minor typographic modifications, appears in the Oxford Illustrated edition of *Christmas Stories,* p. 438, but "imitation" is printed there as "imagination."

6. In the first volume edition of *Master Humphrey's Clock* (1840–41); reprinted in *The Old Curiosity Shop,* ed. Angus Easson (Harmondsworth, England: Penguin, 1972), p. 39.

7. Forster, p. 646.

8. Charles Dickens, *The Public Readings,* ed. Philip Collins (Oxford: Clarendon Press, 1975), p. xxii.

9. Forster, p. 689. This comment to Forster, as well as Dickens' earlier statement about "that particular relation (personally affectionate and like no other man's)," is quoted and discussed by Collins, *Public Readings,* p. xxii and note.

10. Forster, p. 647.

11. Despite the amusingly colloquial idiom in which it is narrated and its comic assortment of circus characters, the contemplative nature of "Going into Society" (with the dying dwarf's repetition of his favorite concluding comment that "the little man will now walk three times round the Cairawan, and retire behind the curtain" [*CS,* pp. 213–14, 217, 220]) differentiates this piece from the later ones, written between 1862 and 1866, which deal more ebulliently with the idea of public entertainment—a distinction that Dickens seems to have sensed. In the summer of 1861, as Philip Collins has noted, Dickens prepared a reading from this piece entitled *Mr. Chops the Dwarf,* although this particular reading evidently was not performed until Dickens decided to use it for a few of his farewell appearances (*Public Readings,* p. 295). As Collins observes, "one can only surmise why he read it so little." One reason may have simply been, as Collins suggests, that Dickens had other items in his repertoire which he believed that his audience would prefer. However, another reason may have been Dickens' possible awareness that *Mr. Chops* was not sufficiently distanced from his own disappointments for comfortable performance.

12. See Philip Collins, "The Popularity of Dickens," *Dickensian* 70 (1974): 6, 16, et passim. In the introduction to his edition of *The Public Readings,* Collins quotes one contemporary critic, writing in 1869, who described Dickens as "the greatest reader of the greatest writer of the age" (p. liv).

13. Wilson raises the suggestion that the scene in which Marigold's child dies in his arms while he entertains a group of people with his cheap-jack talk may reflect the death of Dickens' child by Ellen Ternan ("Dickens: The Two Scrooges," *The Wound and the Bow* [1941; reprint ed., New York: Oxford University Press, 1965], p. 60). Wilson

subsequently observes in his foreword to Ada Nisbet's examination of the then available facts that there is no convincing evidence that Dickens and Ellen Ternan actually had a child (*Dickens & Ellen Ternan* [Berkeley and Los Angeles: University of California Press, 1952], p. x). More recently, David Parker and Michael Slater have presented material which suggests that the question of Dickens' possible child by Ellen Ternan is still open to discussion ("The Gladys Storey Papers," *Dickensian* 76 [1980]:3–16). However, see also Katharine M. Longley, Letter to the Editor, *Dickensian* 76 (1980):17–19.

14. These "Christmas Stories" between 1862 and 1866 which display the idea of public entertainment seem in large part examples of "fictional self-consciousness" in the sense that Robert Alter has used the term to describe "a novel that systematically flaunts its own condition of artifice and that by so doing probes into the problematic relationship between real-seeming artifice and reality" (*Partial Magic: The Novel as a Self-Conscious Genre* [Berkeley and Los Angeles: University of California Press, 1975], p. x).

15. *Selected Short Fiction,* ed. Thomas, p. 262.

16. Ibid. Most of this passage, with slight changes in punctuation, appears in the Oxford Illustrated edition of *Christmas Stories,* p. 330, but the sentence that reads "The writings are consequently called, here, by the names of the articles of Luggage to which they was found attached" is omitted.

17. *Selected Short Fiction,* ed. Thomas, p. 280. This passage, with minor typographic modifications, appears in the Oxford Illustrated edition of *Christmas Stories,* p. 365, although "give" (in "Sol give him warning") is erroneously corrected there to "gave."

18. The Berg Collection of the New York Public Library contains the texts of portions of *The Seven Poor Travellers, The Holly-Tree Inn, Somebody's Luggage, Mrs. Lirriper's Lodgings, Mrs. Lirriper's Legacy, Doctor Marigold's Prescriptions,* and *Mugby Junction*—showing Dickens' handwritten changes, evidently made for the inclusion of these extracts in the Diamond edition of *The Uncommercial Traveller, and Additional Christmas Stories* (Boston: Ticknor & Fields, 1867). My remarks about Dickens' 1867 modifications are based on an examination of these texts as well as on Harry Stone's analysis—with particular reference to *The Holly-Tree Inn*—of Dickens' changes on this occasion (*Charles Dickens' Uncollected Writings from "Household Words" 1850–1859,* 2 vols. [Bloomington: Indiana University Press, 1968], II, 542–44).

19. For example, Marigold's allusion to *All the Year Round* appears in brackets in the Oxford Illustrated edition of *Christmas Stories,* where this work is entitled simply "Doctor Marigold."

20. J[ohan] Huizinga, *Homo Ludens: A Study of the Play-Element in Culture,* trans. anon. (Boston: Beacon Press, 1955), p. 119. (The first edition of *Homo Ludens* was published in 1938.)

21. I am indebted here to Harry Stone's discussion of Dickens' experimentation with interior monologue in *Mrs. Lirriper's Lodgings* and *Mrs. Lirriper's Legacy* ("Dickens and Interior Monologue," pp. 56–58, 65).

22. *NL,* III, 493, to Thomas Beard, 15 December 1866.

23. See Robert Langbaum's analysis of this kind of "split between sympathy and judgment" as the distinguishing feature of the dramatic monologue (*The Poetry of Experience* [1957; reprint ed., New York: Norton, 1963], p. 105).

24. See the discussion of the authorship of this piece in Appendix A, pp. 151–52.

25. In keeping with Dickens' plans, Wilkie Collins subsequently adapted *No Thoroughfare* for the stage. In this context, Dickens' interest in producing what he described in a semi-serious letter to Collins as the "long and heavy pages" (*NL,* III, 535, 2 July 1867) of this Christmas number seems to have been largely determined by the

pragmatic considerations suggested in his 1867 letter to James T. Fields (*NL,* III, 564): he needed to meet his Christmas deadline before sailing for America, and he wished to leave the holiday number in a form in which it could be readily dramatized after his departure.

CHAPTER 6

Murder and Self-Effacement

1. Harry Stone, who discusses this story as part of the background of *Great Expectations,* has likewise adopted this title (*Dickens and the Invisible World: Fairy Tales, Fantasy, and Novel-Making* [Bloomington: Indiana University Press, 1979], p. 288).

2. Citations in my text from *The Lazy Tour of Two Idle Apprentices* are to the Oxford Illustrated edition of *Christmas Stories.* All passages cited appear in chapter 4 of *The Lazy Tour,* a section of the first book edition of this work (London: Chapman & Hall, 1890) which Nuel Pharr Davis has attributed to Dickens (*The Life of Wilkie Collins* [Urbana: University of Illinois Press, 1956], p. 326, n. 24).

3. In 1937, the *Dickensian* reported an American law case centering on the application of "A Madman's Manuscript" to real life: "A young wife obtained annulment of her marriage on the ground that her husband had forced her, within two days of their marriage, to sit with him in a darkened room and read 'A Madman's Manuscript.' 'It'll frizzle anybody's hair,' said the lady's lawyer to the Judge" (*Dickensian* 33 [1937]: 227–28). Had the unfortunate wife been forced to endure a reading of "The Bride's Chamber," she would undoubtedly have been even more alarmed.

4. John Forster, *The Life of Charles Dickens,* ed. J. W. T. Ley (London: Cecil Palmer, 1928), p. 38.

5. As Dickens described his state in his letter to Collins proposing the excursion depicted in the *Lazy Tour,* "We want something for Household Words, and I want to escape from myself. For when I *do* start up and stare myself seedily in the face, as happens to be my case at present, my blankness is inconceivable—indescribable—my misery amazing" (*NL,* II, 873, 29 August 1857).

6. Stone, *Dickens and the Invisible World,* pp. 291–92.

7. Barbara Hardy, *Tellers and Listeners: The Narrative Imagination* (London: Athlone Press, 1975), pp. 170–71.

8. Ibid., p. 170. Dickens' reason for not titling the story about the Bride's chamber in *The Lazy Tour* and allowing some of its details to mingle with those of the framing narrative, as well as his decision in the previous year to allow Little Dorrit's tale about the tiny woman to emerge naturally from the events of its enclosing novel, may have been an effort at "making the introduced story so fit into surroundings impossible of separation from the main story, as to make the blood of the book circulate through both"—a goal which, as he explained to Forster, he had attempted but evidently failed to achieve in "The History of a Self Tormentor" in *Little Dorrit* (*NL,* II, 776, to John Forster, dated in *NL* as [1856]).

9. Robert Louis Brannan, ed., *Under the Management of Mr. Charles Dickens: His Production of "The Frozen Deep"* (Ithaca: Cornell University Press, 1966), pp. 2–5.

10. *NL,* III, 14, to Wilkie Collins, 21 March 1858.

11. *NL,* II, 797, to John Forster, 15 August 1856.

12. Brannan, pp. 10–12, 84–88.

13. C. B. Phipps to Charles Dickens, 5 July 1857, Pierpont Morgan Library M.A. 81, quoted in Brannan, pp. 67–68.

14. Brannan, p. 88. See also George H. Ford's remark about the connection be-

tween Wardour and Sydney Carton in "Dickens's Notebook and 'Edwin Drood,'" *Nineteenth-Century Fiction* 6 (1952):275 as well as his comment about the renunciatory similarities of Wardour, Carton, and Eugene Wrayburn in *Dickens and His Readers: Aspects of Novel-Criticism since 1836* (1955; reprint ed., New York: Norton, 1965), p. 67 and note.

15. *NL*, II, 881, to Georgina Hogarth, 9 September 1857.

16. "The Late Mr. Douglas Jerrold," *The Times,* 13 July 1857, p. 12. Brannan quotes from this review (pp. 81–82) which he attributes to John Oxenford, a theatrical critic for *The Times* who contributed occasionally to *Household Words* and, later, to *All the Year Round.*

17. Citations in my text from *The Frozen Deep* are to Brannan's edition of *Under the Management of Mr. Charles Dickens.* Brannan observes that Dickens wrote the prologue and spoke it during the July and August performances (ibid., p. 98n).

18. Brannan, pp. 43–45.

19. *NL*, II, 890, to Miss Coutts, 4 October 1857.

20. Fred Kaplan, *Dickens and Mesmerism: The Hidden Springs of Fiction* (Princeton: Princeton University Press, 1975), p. 237.

21. Ibid., pp. 204–7. Kaplan analyzes the relationships between "operators and subjects" (ibid., p. 195) in Dickens' fiction against the background of Dickens' interest in mesmerism and argues that ". . . forces of will and energy in concentrated and unmistakably mesmeric forms in the Dickens world are often instruments of control, rarely mitigated by other impulses, rarely turned to beneficent and self-sacrificing ends" (ibid., p. 200). In "The Bride's Chamber," the old man's power over both the Bride and Mr. Goodchild, the "idle apprentice" who hears the story, offers an additional illustration of the mesmeric nature of the "forces of will and energy" which Kaplan perceives in Dickens' fiction. Thus, the man kills the Bride by sitting in a chair in front of her and repeating the word *die:*

> He sat before her in the gloomy Bride's Chamber, day after day, night after night, looking the word at her when he did not utter it. As often as her large unmeaning eyes were raised from the hands in which she rocked her head, to the stern figure, sitting with crossed arms and knitted forehead, in the chair, they read in it, "Die!" When she dropped asleep in exhaustion, she was called back to shuddering consciousness, by the whisper, "Die!" When she fell upon her old entreaty to be pardoned, she was answered, "Die!" When she had out-watched and out-suffered the long night, and the rising sun flamed into the sombre room, she heard it hailed with, "Another day and not dead?—Die!" (*CS,* p. 732.)

As a phantom narrator, the man appears to mesmerize Mr. Goodchild into listening to his tale: "Mr. Goodchild believed that he saw threads of fire stretch from the old man's eyes to his own, and there attach themselves" (p. 728). When the clock strikes two and the old man turns into "two old men," the "films of fire" (p. 737) are also duplicated, although Mr. Goodchild finally escapes from this influence in his terror at discovering that his companion has fallen asleep and that he is the phantom's solitary listener: "he struggled so hard to get free from the four fiery threads, that he snapped them, after he had pulled them out to a great width" (p. 741).

22. Forster, p. 808.

23. *NL*, II, 888, to W. H. Wills, 2 October 1857.

24. "Frauds on the Fairies," *Household Words,* 1 October 1853.

25. Kate Millett, *Sexual Politics* (1970; reprint ed., New York: Avon Books, 1971). Millett defines *politics* as "power-structured relationships, arrangements whereby one group of persons is controlled by another" (ibid., p. 23).

26. For an excellent discussion of Dickens' performance of the murder of Nancy,

see Philip Collins' introduction to the text of *Sikes and Nancy* in his edition of Charles Dickens, *The Public Readings* (Oxford: Clarendon Press, 1975), pp. 465–71. Collins observes about the *Sikes and Nancy* reading that Dickens' "desire to repeat it became a fierce obsession" (p. 470), although he does not explore the possible motives behind this obsession. (See also Philip Collins, *Dickens and Crime*, 2d ed. [1964; reprint ed., Bloomington: Indiana University Press, 1968], pp. 265–72).

27. George Saintsbury, "Dickens," *Cambridge History of English Literature*, ed. A. W. Ward and A. R. Waller, 15 vols. (Cambridge: The University Press, 1907–27), XIII, 334.

28. *The Works of Charles Dickens*, 36 vols. (London: Chapman & Hall, 1897–1908), XXV, xiii.

29. Edmund Wilson, "Dickens: The Two Scrooges," *The Wound and the Bow* (1941; reprint ed., New York: Oxford University Press, 1965), pp. 3–85; J. Hillis Miller, *Charles Dickens: The World of His Novels* (Cambridge: Harvard University Press, 1958); Taylor Stoehr, *Dickens: The Dreamer's Stance* (Ithaca: Cornell University Press, 1965); Sylvère Monod, *Dickens the Novelist* (Norman: University of Oklahoma Press, 1968), pp. 382, 472; K. J. Fielding, *Charles Dickens: A Critical Introduction*, 2d ed. (Boston: Houghton Mifflin Co., 1965), p. 202. Jack Lindsay gives some attention to this work as an indication of Dickens' feelings about his sister Fanny (*Charles Dickens: A Biographical and Critical Study* [London: Andrew Dakers, 1950], pp. 33–34, 169–70); however, Lindsay's remarks do not deal with the complex portrayal of a carefully created personality which the work contains.

30. Harry Stone, "Dickens's Tragic Universe: 'George Silverman's Explanation,' " *Studies in Philology* 55 (1958): 95.

31. Barry D. Bart, " 'George Silverman's Explanation,' " *Dickensian* 60 (1964): 50.

32. Dudley Flamm, "The Prosecutor Within: Dickens's Final Explanation," *Dickensian* 66 (1970): 23.

33. Q. D. Leavis, "How we must read *Great Expectations*," in *Dickens the Novelist*, by F. R. Leavis and Q. D. Leavis, 3d ed. (London: Chatto & Windus, 1973), p. 283.

34. Flamm observes that Dickens uses the form of a first-person confession not only in "George Silverman's Explanation" but in "A Madman's Manuscript" in *Pickwick Papers* and "The History of a Self Tormentor" in *Little Dorrit* (p. 21).

35. Stone describes Silverman as a "saintly" (p. 90) person who suffers from "a flawed society" (p. 95). Bart attributes Silverman's troubles to the fact that the world fails to understand "his selflessness" (p. 50) and "his humility" (ibid). Flamm perceptively calls attention to the discrepancy between a reader's vision and that of Silverman; however, Flamm also contends that this discrepancy lies in the fact that while a reader is aware of "the truth that George Silverman was victim and those around him the oppressors, he himself is not in full command of this knowledge" (p. 22). Leavis thoughtfully stresses the manner in which Silverman has been influenced by his childhood experiences and argues that " . . . George's intentionally noble behaviour, originally right in the case of the fever-infection and Sylvia because spontaneously evolved, is wrong in the later contexts, not noble but inappropriate, merely compulsive and therefore self-defeating" (p. 286). Nevertheless, as my own analysis of this work suggests, the extent to which even Silverman's behavior toward Sylvia is "right" seems debatable.

36. Lionel Trilling, *"Little Dorrit,"* introduction to *Little Dorrit* (London: Oxford University Press, 1953), reprinted in *The Dickens Critics*, ed. George H. Ford and Lauriat Lane, Jr. (Ithaca, New York: Cornell University Press, 1961), p. 287.

37. Robert Langbaum, *The Poetry of Experience* (1957; reprint ed., New York: Norton, 1963), p. 85. As my discussion indicates, I disagree with Flamm's contention that Miss Wade's "days of self-torment are over" (p. 21).

38. *UT & RP.* The second section of "Holiday Romance" still possesses a surprising degree of popularity. George H. Ford notes that over three thousand copies of it, under the title of the "Magic Fishbone," were apparently sold in the United States in 1968 ("Dickens in the 1960s," *Dickensian* 66 [1970]: 170).

39. *NL,* III, 535, to John Forster, 2 July 1867; III, 539, to James T. Fields, 25 July 1867. See also the letter of 21 July 1867 to Percy Fitzgerald cited below.

40. Flamm, p. 21.

41. Forster, p. 745.

42. *NL,* III, 538, to Percy Fitzgerald, 21 July 1867.

43. Edgar Johnson, *Charles Dickens: His Tragedy and Triumph,* 2 vols. (New York: Simon & Schuster 1952), II, 1071.

44. M. K. Bradby, "An Explanation of *George Silverman's Explanation,*" *Dickensian* 36 (1940): 17. Despite a few perceptive comments, much of Bradby's discussion seems vague or insufficiently substantiated.

45. *NL,* III, 533, to W. H. Wills, 28 June 1867.

46. Flamm and Bart perceptively explore connections between "George Silverman's Explanation" and *The Mystery of Edwin Drood,* but they neglect an important implication raised by these connections: the implication that Silverman's motives may not be so straightforward as he believes them to be.

47. Philip Collins, "Dickens's Reading," *Dickensian* 60 (1964): 149.

48. Ibid., p. 150.

49. Ford, *Dickens and His Readers,* p. 67 and note.

CHAPTER 7

Unrestrained Invention

1. John Forster, *The Life of Charles Dickens,* ed. J. W. T. Ley (London: Cecil Palmer, 1928), p. 721. Forster phrases Bulwer-Lytton's objection in the following terms: "Five years before he [Dickens] died, a great and generous brother-artist, Lord Lytton, amid much ungrudging praise of a work he was then publishing, asked him to consider, as to one part of it, if the modesties of art were not a little overpassed" (ibid.).

2. *Selected Short Fiction,* ed. Thomas, p. 370. (The word "The"—in "The Refreshment Room"—should begin with a capital letter, as in *All the Year Round.*) This passage appears in the Oxford Illustrated edition of *Christmas Stories,* p. 515, with only lowercase letters in the phrases "The Boy," "Boy at what is called," and "Me" (in "That's Me"). However, as I have indicated, Dickens used capital letters in these places in *All the Year Round.*

3. As Philip Collins observes, ". . . Emlyn Williams has lately had some success" with a public reading of "The Signalman," although, as Collins also notes, Williams' rendition of this story "is much more succinct than" the reading version of "The Signalman" that Dickens prepared but did not perform (*The Public Readings,* ed. Collins [Oxford: Clarendon Press, 1975], p. 453).

4. Henry Seidel Canby, *The Short Story in English* (New York: Henry Holt and Company, 1909), p. 270.

APPENDIX A

Contributors to the Christmas Numbers of *Household Words* and

All the Year Round, 1850–1867

1. The *New York Times'* recent attribution to Dickens of a story by Sala from the Christmas number for 1851 demonstrates that this danger is still a very real one (*New York Times,* 25 December 1971, p. 17; see my Letter to the Editor, *New York Times,* 11 February 1972, p. 34).

2. The Office Book is located in the Princeton University Library. It had not been published at the time I conducted my original research into the contributors to Dickens' Christmas numbers, although it was then being edited by Anne Lohrli who subsequently published it under the title of *"Household Words": A Weekly Journal 1850–1859, Conducted by Charles Dickens. Table of Contents, List of Contributors and Their Contributions Based on the "Household Words" Office Book in the Morris L. Parrish Collection of Victorian Novelists, Princeton University Library* (Toronto: University of Toronto Press, 1973).

3. Philip Collins, "Dickens's Weeklies," *Victorian Periodicals Newsletter,* No. 1 (January 1968), pp. 18–19. Collins has engaged in the monumental task of identifying as many of the *AYR* contributors as possible on the basis of information contained in sources such as letters, biographies, and the collected works of individuals who were known to write for Dickens' magazines (p. 19; see also Collins, "The *All the Year Round* Letter Book," *Victorian Periodicals Newsletter,* No. 10 [November 1970], p. 27). For a recent compilation of information concerning the authorship of items in *All the Year Round*—incorporating material supplied by Collins as well as that provided by the initial version of the *AYR* part of this Appendix in the *Dickensian* 70 (1974): 21-29—see Ella Ann Oppenlander, *Dickens' "All the Year Round": Descriptive Index and Contributors List,* Diss. University of Texas at Austin, 1978 (Ann Arbor, Mich.: University Microfilms International, 1978).

4. My remarks about these editions, which I have seen only briefly, are based on information in letters from Michael Slater, 13 February 1970, and from the late Leslie C. Staples, 7 March 1970. The copy of the 1868 edition owned by Staples, from which my material about this collection of Christmas numbers is taken, bears no date and may be an 1870 reprint.

5. The abbreviation *DNB* in parentheses indicates authors about whom additional information can be found in the *Dictionary of National Biography: From the Earliest Times to 1900,* ed. Leslie Stephen and Sidney Lee, 22 vols. (1885–1901; reprint ed., London: Oxford University Press, 1967–68); *Supplement January 1901–December 1911,* ed. Sidney Lee (1912; reprint ed., London: Oxford University Press, 1966). Part two of Lohrli's edition of the Office Book provides extensive biographical information about the authors who contributed to *Household Words.*

6. My remarks are based not only on Lohrli's painstaking 1973 edition of the Office Book but also on my own earlier research. The *Household Words* Office Book was essentially a business record. Its entries are handwritten, and not all of them are easily legible or completely accurate. In many cases, it identifies contributors simply by last name; occasionally, it specifies last name and one or more initials. Thus, although the authors to whom we refer are identical, in some instances the more detailed versions of these authors' names given in my tables differ slightly from those supplied by Lohrli. The titles that I have listed in my tables—generally following the titles and section titles as they appeared in the individual Christmas numbers—occasionally differ in small details from those used by Lohrli.

7. *Charles Dickens' Uncollected Writings from "Household Words" 1850–1859,* ed. Harry Stone, 2 vols. (Bloomington: Indiana University Press, 1968), I, 48.

8. For example, see *Uncollected Writings,* ed. Stone, II, 524.

9. In recent articles, Stone has carefully identified Dickens' previously uncollected contributions to *The Haunted House* and *A Message from the Sea* (two of the nine Christmas numbers from *All the Year Round*), and he has directed attention to the vitally important and long overlooked attributions contained in the 1868 edition of the Christmas numbers from *All the Year Round* ("The Unknown Dickens: With a Sampling of Uncollected Writings," *Dickens Studies Annual,* ed. Robert B. Partlow, Jr., I [Carbondale: Southern Illinois University Press, 1970], 1–22, 275–76; idem, "Dickens Rediscovered: Some Lost Writings Retrieved," *Dickens Centennial Essays,* ed. Ada Nisbet and Blake Nevius (Berkeley and Los Angeles: University of California Press, 1971), 205–26. My own tables of contents, which are designed primarily to put basic information about the Christmas numbers at a reader's fingertips, are reinforced by Stone's discoveries.

10. I wish here to emphasize my thanks to those who have generously supplied helpful information, particularly to Dr. Michael Slater and the late Mr. Leslie C. Staples.

11. Lohrli notes that the "K" (for "Knight") is not clearly legible (p. 71). The 1906 Chapman and Hall edition of the Christmas numbers from *Household Words* erroneously lists this contributor as K. H. Hunt (I have seen this edition only briefly, and my comments are based on material in a letter from Staples, 5 July 1970).

12. See Lohrli, p. 71. Lohrli observes (p. 427) that Siddons often used the pseudonym "J. H. Stocqueler"—under which he is listed in the *DNB* and other biographical reference works—and Lohrli quotes (pp. 427–28) from a letter by Siddons' son in order to provide the following explanation:

> In answer to an inquiry from the Library of Congress, Siddons's son, Frederick Lincoln Siddons (1864–1931), associate justice of the Supreme Court of the District of Columbia, wrote to the librarian, Feb. 19, 1917: ". . . my father's full name was Joachim Heyward Siddons, and as I remember the date of his birth, it was July 21, 1801. I think in his earlier life he frequently used as a pseudonym an anglicized form of his mother's name, and in that form as you have it 'J. H. Stocqueler'; but he did not always use the pseudonym in writing. . . ."

The *Household Words* Office Book identifies the author of "Christmas in India" as J. Stoqueler, an approximate spelling of this pseudonym.

Siddons apparently knew Dickens when the latter was a child in Chatham and, after Dickens' death, published a somewhat inaccurate account of their friendship (John Archer Carter, Jr., "Memories of 'Charley Wag'," *Dickensian* 62 [1966]: 147–51). Carter and Lohrli, on the basis of Siddons' *Memoirs,* give 1843 as the date of his last departure from India rather than 1841 as in the *DNB,* although Carter refers to Stocqueler as this writer's actual name and mentions Siddons as his pseudonym.

A letter from Dickens, written shortly before the inauguration of *The Daily News* (first published 21 January 1846), establishes his correspondence with "Stocqueler" within a few years of this Christmas number as well as his awareness of the latter's interest in matters relating to India—*PL,* IV, 446, to J. H. Stocqueler, [?1–4 December 1845]; the biographical note here again uses Stocqueler as this individual's name and refers to Siddons as a pseudonym (ibid., p. 446, n. 1). See also ibid., p. 504, to [J. H. Stocqueler], 24 February 1846.

13. *Uncollected Writings,* ed. Stone, I, 183–84; II, 655; Lohrli, pp. 349–50.

14. *Uncollected Writings,* ed. Stone, II, 652–53.

15. Ibid., I, 183; Lohrli, p. 350.

16. J. W. T. Ley, *The Dickens Circle: A Narrative of the Novelist's Friendships* (London: Chapman & Hall, 1919), pp. 324–26; R. K. Webb, *Harriet Martineau: A Radical Victorian* (London: Heinemann, 1960), p. 312.

17. For an illuminating discussion of Dickens' disagreement with Miss Martineau and the differing views on the subject of political economy which lay behind their dispute, see K. J. Fielding and Anne Smith, *"Hard Times* and the Factory Controversy: Dickens vs. Harriet Martineau," *Dickens Centennial Essays,* ed. Ada Nisbet and Blake Nevius, pp. 22–45.

18. *NL,* II, 337, to W. H. Wills, 13 August 1851.

19. See above, p. 178, note 1.

20. Lohrli, p. 103. The Office Book lists this contributor, as well as the person who collaborated with W. H. Wills in "Uncle George's Story" for the 1853 Christmas number, simply as Dixon. The 1906 edition of the Christmas numbers from *Household Words* further identifies this author as W. Hepworth Dixon, an identification that I followed in the initial version of this Appendix as it was published in the *Dickensian* (69 [1973]: 163–72; 70 [1974]:21–29). However, although R. C. Lehmann describes W. Hepworth Dixon in *Charles Dickens as Editor* as "a fairly regular contributor to the paper" ([1912; reprint ed., New York: Kraus, 1971], p. 101*n*), Lohrli offers persuasive evidence (pp. 256–61) that the Dixon mentioned in the *Household Words* Office Book was, in fact, Edmund Saul Dixon.

21. See the letters of 6 and 9 November as well as 1 and 17 December 1852 to Mrs. Gaskell, *NL,* II, 428–29, 433–35.

22. A. B. Hopkins, *Elizabeth Gaskell: Her Life and Work* (London: John Lehmann, 1952), pp. 155–56.

23. Frederic Boase, *Modern English Biography,* 6 vols. (1892–1921; reprint ed., London: Frank Cass & Co., 1965), V, Supplement II, 113; Lohrli, pp. 256–61.

24. Mrs. Gaskell apparently wrote only the introduction to "The Scholar's Story"; the remainder is a translation of a Breton ballad by her husband William Gaskell (Hopkins, p. 336). See also George Watson, ed., *The New Cambridge Bibliography of English Literature,* III (Cambridge: Cambridge University Press, 1969), 874, s.v. Gaskell. Also see Lohrli, pp. 118, 280, 282–83.

25. *Uncollected Writings,* ed. Stone, II, 564. See also Lohrli, p. 161.

26. F[rederic] G. Kitton and, more recently, Stone attribute it to Dickens on the basis of a letter to the Rev. R. H. Davies (*The Poems and Verses of Charles Dickens,* ed. F. G. Kitton [New York: Harper & Brothers, 1903], pp. 203–4; *Uncollected Writings,* ed. Stone, II, 564). However, Dickens' comment in this letter is ambiguous in its context in Forster's *Life,* and there is persuasive evidence that the poem is the work of Harriet Parr —see John Forster, *The Life of Charles Dickens,* ed. J. W. T. Ley (London: Cecil Palmer, 1928), p. 820, and *New Cambridge Bibliography of English Literature,* III, 817, s.v. Dickens, as well as B. W. M[atz] and J. T. Page in *Dickensian* 12 (1916): 128–30, 192–93. See also Lohrli, pp. 161, 395–96.

27. John S. Crone, *A Concise Dictionary of Irish Biography* (New York: Longmans Green & Co., 1928), p. 69.

28. *NL,* II, 894, to Benjamin Webster, 24 November 1857.

29. See T. S. Eliot's distinction between Dickens and Collins ("Wilkie Collins and Dickens," *Selected Essays,* new ed. [New York: Harcourt, Brace & Co., 1950], pp. 410–11). For a discussion of the events that prompted this Christmas number, see William Oddie, "Dickens and the Indian Mutiny," *Dickensian* 68 (1972): 3–15.

30. Stone, "The Unknown Dickens," pp. 8–12.

31. *New Cambridge Bibliography of English Literature,* III, 813, s.v. Dickens.

32. Frederic G. Kitton, *The Minor Writings of Charles Dickens: A Bibliography and Sketch* (London: Elliot Stock, 1900), p. 163.

33. Ibid. and p. 163*n*.

34. Stone, "Dickens Rediscovered," p. 209.

35. Ibid., p. 211.

36. Michael Sadleir, *XIX Century Fiction: A Bibliographical Record Based on His Own Collection,* 2 vols. (London: Constable, 1951), I, 171.

37. Kitton, *Minor Writings,* p. 166.

38. Boase, *Modern English Biography,* VI, Supplement III, 640–41.

39. Crone, pp. 76–77.

40. Boase, III, 688.

41. Joseph Thomas, *Universal Pronouncing Dictionary of Biography and Mythology,* 5th ed. (Philadelphia: J. B. Lippincott, 1930), p. 1080; *Burke's Genealogical and Heraldic History of the Landed Gentry,* ed. Peter Townend, 18th ed., 3 vols. (London: Burke's Peerage, 1965–72), I, 301. The attribution of chapters 1 and 7 of this Christmas number to Dickens in the *New Cambridge Bibliography of English Literature* is apparently a misprint for chapters 1 and 8 (III, 813, s.v. Dickens).

42. *Charles Dickens's Stories from the Christmas Numbers of "Household Words" and "All the Year Round" 1852–1867* (New York: Macmillan, 1896), p. xxi.

43. *NL,* III, 453, 6 January 1866.

44. Ibid., p. 447, 30 November 1865.

45. *The Letters of Charles Dickens* (London: Macmillan, 1893), p. 593n.

46. [B. W. Matz], in *Dickensian* 2 (1906): 280.

47. See Kitton, *Minor Writings,* p. vii, and *Miscellaneous Papers,* reprinted in the Gadshill edition, 36 vols. (London: Chapman & Hall, 1897–1908), XXXV, xii.

48. Kitton, *Minor Writings,* p. 169.

49. *Great Tales of Terror and the Supernatural,* ed. Herbert A. Wise and Phyllis Fraser (New York: Random House, 1944), p. 356.

50. Notice announcing the new series of *All the Year Round, AYR,* 28 November 1868.

51. *NL,* III, 676–77, to James T. Fields, 30 October 1868.

Selected Bibliography

The following works have been especially useful in contributing to my thinking about Dickens' short stories. For reasons of economy, all other works employed in this study—including letters, reviews, memoirs, and many editions of Dickens' writings—are cited only in the introductory explanation of abbreviations or in the footnotes.

ALLEN, M. L. "The Black Veil: Three Versions of a Symbol." *English Studies* 47 (1966): 286–89.

ALLEN, WALTER. Introduction to *"A Christmas Carol" and "The Chimes,"* by Charles Dickens. New York: Harper & Row, 1965.

ANDREWS, MALCOLM. "Introducing Master Humphrey." *Dickensian* 67 (1971): 70–86.

AXTON, WILLIAM. "Unity and Coherence in *The Pickwick Papers.*" *Studies in English Literature* 5 (1965): 663–76.

————. *Circle of Fire: Dickens' Vision & Style & the Popular Victorian Theater.* Lexington: University of Kentucky Press, 1966.

BART, BARRY D. " 'George Silverman's Explanation.' " *Dickensian* 60 (1964): 48–51.

BLOUNT, TREVOR. *Charles Dickens: The Early Novels.* London: Longmans Green & Co., 1968.

BOLL, ERNEST. "Charles Dickens and Washington Irving." *Modern Language Quarterly* 5 (1944): 453–67.

BRADBY, M. K. "An Explanation of *George Silverman's Explanation.*" *Dickensian* 36 (1940): 13–18.

BRANNAN, ROBERT LOUIS, ed. *Under the Management of Mr. Charles Dickens: His Production of "The Frozen Deep."* Ithaca: Cornell University Press, 1966.

BREDSDORFF, ELIAS. *Hans Andersen and Charles Dickens: A Friendship and Its Dissolution.* Copenhagen: Rosenkilde & Bagger, 1956.

BUTT, JOHN. "Dickens's Christmas Books." *Pope, Dickens, and Others.* Edinburgh: Edinburgh University Press, 1969.

————, and Tillotson, Kathleen. *Dickens at Work.* London: Methuen and Co., 1957.

CAROLAN, KATHERINE. "The Battle of Life, A Love Story." *Dickensian* 69 (1973): 105–10.

————. "The Dingley Dell Christmas." *Dickens Studies Newsletter* 4 (1973): 41–48.

————. "The Dingley Dell Christmas Continued: 'Rip Van Winkle' and the Tale of Gabriel Grub." *Dickens Studies Newsletter* 5 (1974): 104–6.

CHESTERTON, G. K. *Appreciations and Criticisms of the Works of Charles Dickens.* London: J. M. Dent and Sons, 1911.

COLLINS, P[HILIP] A[RTHUR] W[ILLIAM]. " 'Keep *Household Words* Imaginative!' " *Dickensian* 52 (1956): 117–23.

————. "Queen Mab's Chariot Among the Steam Engines: Dickens and 'Fancy.' " *English Studies* 42 (1961): 78–90.

————. "Dickens on Ghosts: An Uncollected Article." *Dickensian* 59 (1963): 5–14.

————. "Dickens's Reading." *Dickensian* 60 (1964): 136–51.

————. *Dickens and Crime.* 2d ed. 1964. Reprint. Bloomington: Indiana University Press, 1968.

————. " '*Carol* Philosophy, Cheerful Views.' " *Études Anglaises* 23 (1970): 158–67.

————. "The Popularity of Dickens." *Dickensian* 70 (1974): 5–20.

————. "Presidential Message to The Dickens Society." *Dickens Studies Newsletter* 7 (1976): 3–8.

————, ed. *Dickens: The Critical Heritage.* New York: Barnes & Noble, 1971.

————, ed. *The Public Readings.* By Charles Dickens. Oxford: Clarendon Press, 1975.

DAVIS, EARLE. *The Flint and the Flame: The Artistry of Charles Dickens.* Columbia: University of Missouri Press, 1963.

DEVRIES, DUANE. *Dickens's Apprentice Years: The Making of a Novelist.* Hassocks, England: Harvester Press; New York: Barnes & Noble, 1976.

EASSON, ANGUS, ed. *The Old Curiosity Shop.* By Charles Dickens. Introduction by Malcolm Andrews. Harmondsworth, England: Penguin, 1972.

ELIOT, T. S. "Wilkie Collins and Dickens." *Selected Essays.* New ed. New York: Harcourt, Brace & Co., 1950.

FIELDING, K. J. *Charles Dickens: A Critical Introduction.* 2d ed. Boston: Houghton Mifflin Co., 1965.

FLAMM, DUDLEY. "The Prosecutor Within: Dickens's Final Explanation." *Dickensian* 66 (1970): 16–23.

FORD, GEORGE H. *Dickens and His Readers: Aspects of Novel-Criticism since 1836.* 1955. Reprint. New York: Norton, 1965.

FORSTER, JOHN. *The Life of Charles Dickens.* Edited by J. W. T. Ley. London: Cecil Palmer, 1928.

GISSING, GEORGE. *Charles Dickens: A Critical Study.* London: Blackie & Son, 1898.

GLANCY, RUTH. "The Significance of the *Nickleby* Stories." *Dickensian* 75 (1979): 12–15.

————. "Dickens and Christmas: His Framed-Tale Themes." *Nineteenth-Century Fiction* 35 (1980): 53–72.

GRUBB, GERALD G. "The Personal and Literary Relationships of Dickens and Poe." *Nineteenth-Century Fiction* 5 (1950): 1–22, 101–20, 209–21.

HARDY, BARBARA. *Tellers and Listeners: The Narrative Imagination.* London: Athlone Press, 1975.

HARRIS, WENDELL V. "Vision and Form: The English Novel and Emergence of the Short Story." *Victorian Newsletter* 47 (1975): 8–12.

_____. *British Short Fiction in the Nineteenth Century: A Literary and Bibliographic Guide.* Detroit: Wayne State University Press, 1979.

HOUSE, HUMPHRY. *The Dickens World.* 2d ed. 1942. Reprint. London: Oxford University Press, 1960.

HUTTER, ALBERT D. "Reconstructive Autobiography: The Experience at Warren's Blacking." In *Dickens Studies Annual,* vol. 6, edited by Robert B. Partlow, Jr. Carbondale: Southern Illinois University Press, 1977.

JOHNSON, EDGAR. *Charles Dickens: His Tragedy and Triumph.* 2 vols. New York: Simon & Schuster, 1952.

KAPLAN, FRED. *Dickens and Mesmerism: The Hidden Springs of Fiction.* Princeton: Princeton University Press, 1975.

KITTON, FREDERIC G. *The Minor Writings of Charles Dickens: A Bibliography and Sketch.* London: Elliot Stock, 1900.

LANGBAUM, ROBERT. *The Poetry of Experience: The Dramatic Monologue in Modern Literary Tradition.* 1957. Reprint. New York: Norton, 1963.

LEAVIS, F. R. AND Q. D. *Dickens the Novelist.* 3d ed. London: Chatto & Windus, 1973.

LINDSAY, JACK. *Charles Dickens: A Biographical and Critical Study.* London: Andrew Dakers, 1950.

LOHRLI, ANNE, comp. *"Household Words": A Weekly Journal 1850–1859, Conducted by Charles Dickens. Table of Contents, List of Contributors and Their Contributions Based on the "Household Words" Office Book in the Morris L. Parrish Collection of Victorian Novelists, Princeton University Library.* Toronto: University of Toronto Press, 1973.

LOUGY, ROBERT E. "Pickwick and 'The Parish Clerk.' " *Nineteenth-Century Fiction* 25 (1970): 100–104.

MCMASTER, R. D. "Dickens and the Horrific." *Dalhousie Review* 38 (1958): 18–28.

MARCUS, STEVEN. *Dickens: From Pickwick to Dombey.* 1965. Reprint. New York: Simon & Schuster, 1968.

MILLER, J. HILLIS. *Charles Dickens: The World of His Novels.* Cambridge: Harvard University Press, 1958.

_____. "The Fiction of Realism: *Sketches by Boz, Oliver Twist,* and Cruikshank's Illustrations." In *Dickens Centennial Essays,* edited by Ada Nisbet and Blake Nevius. Berkeley and Los Angeles: University of California Press, 1971.

MONOD, SYLVÉRE. *Dickens the Novelist.* Norman: University of Oklahoma Press, 1968.

MUNKSGAARD, EJNAR. *Hans Christian Andersen's Visits to Charles Dickens as Described in His Letters Published with Six of Dickens' Letters in Facsimile.* Copenhagen: Levin & Munksgaard; Ejnar Munksgaard, 1937.

NEWSOM, ROBERT. *Dickens on the Romantic Side of Familiar Things: "Bleak House" and the Novel Tradition.* New York: Columbia University Press, 1977.

ODDIE, WILLIAM. "Dickens and the Indian Mutiny." *Dickensian* 68 (1972): 3–15.

PATTEN, ROBERT L. "The Interpolated Tales in *Pickwick Papers.*" *Dickens Studies* 1 (1965): 86–89.

――――. "The Art of *Pickwick*'s Interpolated Tales." *ELH* 34 (1967): 349–66.

――――. "The Unpropitious Muse: *Pickwick*'s 'Interpolated' Tales." *Dickens Studies Newsletter* 1, i (1970): 7–10.

――――. " 'The Story-Weaver at His Loom': Dickens and the Beginning of *The Old Curiosity Shop.*" In *Dickens the Craftsman: Strategies of Presentation,* edited by Robert B. Partlow, Jr. Carbondale: Southern Illinois University Press, 1970.

――――. "Dickens Time and Again." In *Dickens Studies Annual,* vol. 2, edited by Robert B. Partlow, Jr. Carbondale: Southern Illinois University Press, 1972.

――――. " 'A Surprising Transformation': Dickens and the Hearth." In *Nature and the Victorian Imagination,* edited by U. C. Knoepflmacher and G. B. Tennyson. Berkeley and Los Angeles: University of California Press, 1977.

――――, ed. *The Posthumous Papers of the Pickwick Club.* By Charles Dickens. Harmondsworth, England: Penguin, 1972.

REINHOLD, HEINZ. " 'The Stroller's Tale' in *Pickwick.*" *Dickensian* 64 (1968): 141–51.

SAINT VICTOR, CAROL DE. *"Master Humphrey's Clock:* Dickens' 'Lost' Book." *Texas Studies in Literature and Language* 10 (1969): 569–84.

SLATER, MICHAEL. "Dickens (and Forster) at Work on *The Chimes.*" *Dickens Studies* 2 (1966): 106–40.

――――. "The Christmas Books." *Dickensian* 65 (1969): 17–24.

――――. "Dickens's Tract for the Times." In *Dickens 1970,* edited by Michael Slater. New York: Stein and Day, 1970.

――――, ed. *The Christmas Books.* By Charles Dickens. 2 vols. Harmondsworth, England: Penguin, 1971.

SONSTROEM, DAVID. "Fettered Fancy in *Hard Times.*" *PMLA* 84 (1969): 520–29.

STEDMAN, JANE W. "Good Spirits: Dickens's Childhood Reading." *Dickensian* 61 (1965): 150–54.

STEWART, GARRETT. *Dickens and the Trials of Imagination.* Cambridge: Harvard University Press, 1974.

STOEHR, TAYLOR. *Dickens: The Dreamer's Stance.* Ithaca: Cornell University Press, 1965.

STONE, HARRY. "Dickens's Tragic Universe: 'George Silverman's Explanation.' " *Studies in Philology* 55 (1958): 86–97.

――――. "Dickens and Interior Monologue." *Philological Quarterly* 38 (1959): 52–65.

――――. "Dickens' Artistry and *The Haunted Man.*" *South Atlantic Quarterly* 61 (1962): 492–505.

————. "Fire, Hand, and Gate: Dickens' *Great Expectations.*" *Kenyon Review* 24 (1962): 662–91.

————. "The Unknown Dickens: With a Sampling of Uncollected Writings." In *Dickens Studies Annual,* vol. 1, edited by Robert B. Partlow, Jr. Carbondale: Southern Illinois University Press, 1970.

————. "Dickens Rediscovered: Some Lost Writings Retrived." In *Dickens Centennial Essays,* edited by Ada Nisbet and Blake Nevius. Berkeley and Los Angeles: University of California Press, 1971.

————. *Dickens and the Invisible World: Fairy Tales, Fantasy, and Novel-Making.* Bloomington: Indiana University Press, 1979.

————, ed. *Charles Dickens' Uncollected Writings from "Household Words" 1850–1859.* 2 vols. Bloomington: Indiana University Press, 1968.

SUCKSMITH, HARVEY PETER. "The Secret of Immediacy: Dickens' Debt to the Tale of Terror in *Blackwood's.*" *Nineteenth-Century Fiction* 26 (1971): 145–57.

THOMAS, DEBORAH A. "Contributors to the Christmas Numbers of *Household Words* and *All the Year Round,* 1850–1867." *Dickensian* 69 (1973): 163–72; 70 (1974): 21–29.

————. "The Equivocal Explanation of Dickens' George Silverman." In *Dickens Studies Annual,* vol. 3, edited by Robert B. Partlow, Jr. Carbondale: Southern Illinois University Press, 1974.

————. "The Chord of the Christmas Season: Playing House at the Holly-Tree Inn." *Dickens Studies Newsletter* 6 (1975): 103–8.

————. "Dickens' Mrs. Lirriper and the Evolution of a Feminine Stereotype." In *Dickens Studies Annual,* vol. 6, edited by Robert B. Partlow, Jr. Carbondale: Southern Illinois University Press, 1977.

————, ed. *Selected Short Fiction.* By Charles Dickens. Harmondsworth, England: Penguin, 1976.

TILLOTSON, KATHLEEN. *Novels of the Eighteen-Forties.* Oxford: Clarendon Press, 1954.

————. "Writers and Readers in 1851." *Mid-Victorian Studies,* by Geoffrey and Kathleen Tillotson. London: Athlone Press, 1965.

————. "The Middle Years: From the *Carol* to *Copperfield.*" *Dickens Memorial Lectures, 1970.* London: The Dickens Fellowship, 1970. (Supplement to September 1970 *Dickensian*).

WEGELIN, CHRISTOF. "Dickens and Irving: The Problem of Influence." *Modern Language Quarterly* 7 (1946): 83–91.

WILSON, ANGUS. *The World of Charles Dickens.* 1970. Reprint. New York: Viking, 1972.

WILSON, EDMUND. "Dickens: The Two Scrooges." *The Wound and the Bow: Seven Studies in Literature.* 1941. Reprint. New York: Oxford University Press, 1965.

ZABEL, MORTON DAUWEN, ed. *Charles Dickens' Best Stories.* Garden City, New York: Hanover House, 1959.

Index

DATE DUE